AF269733

Praise for *Creative Destruction*

"I applaud *Creative Destruction* for its sharp dissection of ESG mandates and their unexpected impacts on America's farmers and rural landscape. The book reveals how these well-meaning policies often backfire, undermining the farms and food systems they seek to protect. Prescott and Ashley's insights are a wake-up call for anyone dedicated to food production, advocating for a more balanced and realistic approach to environmental, social, and governance standards in agriculture. This compelling narrative is a must-read for those invested in the future of American farming."

—DR. MATT GARNER, Executive Director, The RANGE (Texas Panhandle's Regional Accelerator & New Growth Engine)

"ESG is a political strategy disguised as an investment strategy, ingeniously designed to fleece investors of their money and freedom at the same time. *Creative Destruction* provides us with the intellectual armaments to fight back."

—JOHN CARNEY, Finance and Economics Editor, Breitbart News

"This book is a must-read for anyone invested in the future of American capitalism and energy independence. It's time we embrace policies that foster true growth and resilience, rather than those that hinder progress under the guise of corporate virtue signaling. *Creative Destruction* brilliantly makes this case, and I wholeheartedly endorse its message."

—LEIF SAVAGE, CEO, Tall City Brine; former Wall Street Senior Market Strategist

"Coauthors David Prescott and Michael Ashley conjure the storytelling power of satirists like Jonathan Swift and George Orwell in this compelling, desperately needed book. They bravely shine a light on the grave dangers our nation faces, especially our armed forces. This should be required reading, especially for anyone in the military."

—BLAINE D. HOLT, Brigadier General (ret),
Deputy Representative to NATO

"Want to know who the real loser is when it comes to ESG? The everyday investor, especially retirees who require financial vehicles that actually perform when they leave the workforce. It's past time a book like this reveals the dangers behind this toxic ideology. Put simply, *Creative Destruction* shows the emperor really has no clothes when it comes to this form of investing."

—LEIGH DUNDAS, Human Rights Attorney

"From my vantage point as an elected leader, ESG is a wolf in sheep's clothing. Its adherents zealously profess to care about the environment using this dubious corporate rating score. Instead, as this book so expertly reveals, these policies do nothing to save our planet. They simply give more power to bureaucrats, undermining our ability to produce the energy and resources that make America such a productive world leader. Say no to the delusion and say yes to investing in the real people who keep our country going."

—LORA REINBOLD, former Alaska State Senator

"*Creative Destruction* is a crucial and timely work that exposes the fallacies of ESG investments and highlights the need for pragmatic energy policies. In an era where ESG mandates threaten to undermine the very foundations of capitalism, this book stands as a beacon of rationality and foresight. W. David Prescott and Michael Ashley's arguments resonate deeply with my experience in the energy sector, where the emphasis on genuine, productive investment is paramount. *Creative Destruction* eloquently and expertly lays out the dangers of ESG to any free society. This book should be required reading in high schools and colleges around the country."

—**DARIN GAUB**, Lieutenant Colonel (ret), US Army;
Cofounder/National Spokesman, Restore Liberty

"ESG metrics are one of the biggest threats to freedom in America today. These social credit scores are fundamentally transforming our economy, culture, and society. Unfortunately, most Americans still don't understand them. That's why *Creative Destruction* is such a powerful book. It clearly explains how ESG works and, more importantly, shows readers the dark future that's ahead if ESG is allowed to thrive. If you care about fixing America's broken economy and saving our country, this book is a must-read."

—**JUSTIN HASKINS**, Director, Socialism
Research Center, The Heartland Institute

"*Creative Destruction* is an essential read for anyone who values freedom, prosperity, civilization, or common sense. Aside from offering a devastating critique of the 'ESG' scam and the enormous danger it poses, *Creative Destruction* offers desperately needed solutions. This book should be required reading. I can't recommend it highly enough."

—**ALEX NEWMAN**, CEO, Liberty Sentinel Media

"David Prescott and Michael Ashley provide a piercing revelation of the dystopian result of the force-feeding of the 'ESG Religion' upon the US military. The purpose of America's armed forces is to protect and defend our Constitution and the Republic against all enemies both foreign and domestic. Rather than promoting that sacred duty, ESG, by design, seeks to break down and weaken our military—'engineered ineffectiveness.'"

—**M.S. MECK,** USMC (ret)

"*Creative Destruction* is a compelling and timely work that delves into the critical challenges facing independent energy production in Texas and the United States. As the CEO of Pantera Energy and the current Chairman of the Board for the Texas Alliance of Energy Producers, I strongly believe in the necessity of maintaining our nation's energy independence. This book highlights the pressing issue of ESG mandates, which not only threaten our economic stability but also pose a significant risk to our national security. W. David Prescott and Michael Ashley provide an insightful analysis that every energy producer and policymaker should heed."

—**JASON HERRICK,** President, Pantera Energy Company;
Chairman of the Board, Texas Alliance of Energy Producers

"David Prescott and Michael Ashley hit the mark with ESG in the military. As a young non-commissioned officer, I learned quickly that morale in military ranks comes from maintaining standards across the board. Allowing ESG in the military wastes time, money, and resources needed to maintain the standards and will reduce its war fighting capabilities overall, therefore destroying morale. No service member signs up for that!"

—**JOHN BONVILLE,** Sergeant (ret), USMC

"I spent the last two years fighting to stop the World Health Organization from declaring and then taking control of public health emergencies—globally. I learned that elites are trying to centralize control over the entire world under the guise of making the world a better, fairer place. David Prescott and Michael Ashley explain our peculiar era, in which central control of information enabled the imposition of bizarre business practices in service to a future One World Corporation. Read it and weep. Then fight back."

—**DR. MERYL NASS,** Physician and Researcher,
Children's Health Defense

"*Creative Destruction* exposes ESG as a trojan horse, weaponizing the natural interest in 'doing good' against us. A cabal of self-interested elites are quietly wrecking America, its industries, and yes, even the environment they pretend to care so much about. If you want to understand the ESG problem and its solution, read this book."

—**THEO WOLD,** Director, Administrative
State Project, Claremont Institute

"*Creative Destruction* masterfully unveils how ESG mandates have stealthily crept into our industry, threatening the livelihood of oil and gas professionals like me. As an upstream oil and gas operator, I've seen firsthand how this misguided agenda undermines our ability to responsibly harness America's abundant natural resources. Prescott and Ashley provide a meticulously researched exposé that peels back the curtain on ESG's hidden agenda, exposing how these mandates stifle energy resilience, starve established capital sources, and restrain economic prosperity while masquerading as moral imperatives. Their thought-provoking narrative and powerful fictional allegories make a compelling case for protecting our industry from these destructive policies. If you value the future of American energy and economic freedom, this book is a must-read!"

—**J.D. SMITH,** CEO and Founder, EnCore Permian

"*Creative Destruction* is an eye-opening analysis of the detrimental effects ESG mandates have on global manufacturing and US industries. W. David Prescott and Michael Ashley highlight how these policies are not only stifling innovation but also threatening our energy independence. As someone deeply passionate about maintaining America's energy autonomy, I see firsthand how the Permian Basin serves as the economic lifeblood of our nation's energy dominance and prosperity. This book is a vital resource for understanding the real-world consequences of ESG and is a must-read for anyone invested in preserving the strength and competitiveness of American manufacturing and energy sectors."

—ERIK POWELL, President, Elite Tubular

CREATIVE DESTRUCTION

CREATIVE DESTRUCTION

How **ESG Mandates** Are **Destroying** Capitalism, **Costing** You Money, **AND WRECKING AMERICA**

W. David Prescott and Michael Ashley

Foreword by Jason Herrick

GREENLEAF
BOOK GROUP PRESS

Published by Greenleaf Book Group Press
Austin, Texas
www.gbgpress.com

Distributed by Greenleaf Book Group

For ordering information or special discounts for bulk purchases, please contact Greenleaf Book Group at PO Box 91869, Austin, TX 78709, 512.891.6100.

Design and composition by Greenleaf Book Group and Jonathan Lewis
Cover design by Greenleaf Book Group and Jonathan Lewis
Cover images used under license from ©Adobestock.com

Publisher's Cataloging-in-Publication data is available.

Print ISBN: 979-8-88645-246-4

eBook ISBN: 979-8-88645-247-1

To offset the number of trees consumed in the printing of our books, Greenleaf donates a portion of the proceeds from each printing to the Arbor Day Foundation. Greenleaf Book Group has replaced over 50,000 trees since 2007.

Printed in the United States of America on acid-free paper

24 25 26 27 28 29 30 31   10 9 8 7 6 5 4 3 2 1

First Edition

God said, I am tired of kings,
I suffer them no more;
Up to my ear the morning brings
The outrage of the poor.
Think ye I made this ball
A field of havoc and war,
Where tyrants great and tyrants small
Might harry the weak and poor?
My angel,—his name is Freedom,—
Choose him to be your king;
He shall cut pathways east and west,
And fend you with his wing

—"Boston Hymn," Ralph Waldo Emerson

To our respective sons, Will, Luke, Teddy, and Sammy

Boys, we teamed up on this project together because a story had to be told. In a world where we must navigate the complexities of ESG and sometimes illogical and unwise criteria, where uncertainty often shadows our path, this book is dedicated to all of you.

Will and Luke, as David's sons, you have already begun to build on the foundations of your adult lives. Teddy and Sammy, as Michael's sons, you are starting to discover your own paths.

We recognize that all your individual journeys through these challenges demand more than knowledge—they require unyielding courage and resilience. May all of you always remember that the truest form of success emerges from the merits of your efforts and the grit with which you face each day. Let these pages serve not just as a guide, but as a reminder that no matter the unpredictability of our times, your perseverance and integrity will guide you through. Embrace the virtues that define right from wrong, and the world will stand witness to your growth and achievements.

With all our love and belief in your potential.

~David and Michael

Contents

Why We Must Say No to ESG before It's Too Late

Being poor in the year 2025 is much different from being poor in 1930 or 1875. A "poor" person today is likely to own a phone—and not just any phone but a smartphone possessing more computing power than NASA had when sending American astronauts to the moon decades ago. Likewise, a poor person today likely has access to running water from a tap and food to eat. The food may not be of the highest quality, but it's nonetheless sustenance.

Now, if we contrast today's poverty to that of the Great Depression, the comparison really strikes home. People living in our nation's worst downturn had nothing close to the abundance today's poor possess, not to mention the largesse of our middle and upper class. Should we go back to the 1800s, the comparison becomes more profound. A poor person living in the nineteenth century could not expect running water, much less food. As for access to a smartphone connecting them to the internet and humanity's vast store of knowledge, all that would be entirely out of the question.

Missing in this discussion is precisely *why* today's people, poor or otherwise, live so much better than people from ages past. (It's worth mentioning the level of material wealth today far eclipses anything kings and queens of yore experienced. The richest sovereign sitting on his throne still lived in a castle lacking electricity.) The simple reason why we live so well is . . . *energy.*

Such energy abundance is not localized either. All over the globe, billions of people in far-flung cities you've never heard of enjoy unprecedented wealth due to the United States of America. American innovators and entrepreneurs produced the mechanisms of sourcing, harnessing, and distributing the energy we too often take for granted. These individuals and the businesses they built are a product of our nation's ethos, an ideology that celebrates self-determinism and the pursuit of happiness. (We have also exported this mentality to countries the world over, inspiring others to seek out better lives for themselves, their families, and their descendants.)

Unfortunately, we seem to live in an age of amnesia. At least in the US. Too many people have forgotten where all this material abundance comes from. They erroneously think that if they plug their "green" EV car into the wall, electricity will miraculously flow. They have no clue hydrocarbons, and yes, even "dirty" coal, are what allow the electric grid to function in the first place. Likewise, amnesiac Americans think grocery stores are where food comes from. They have no clue the food they take for granted comes from a delicate supply chain, itself undergird by hardworking farmers and ranchers—again using vast sums of energy that doesn't magically come out of a wall.

In a word, we Americans have been *blessed.*

Living in modern times, we enjoy unmatched wealth that has never existed before in the history of the world. But has our blessedness gone to our heads? We seem to think material abundance will continue indefinitely—even if we shut down or curtail our energy, our supply chain, and our producers. This is madness. It reminds me of a spoiled child who believes they can get whatever they want just because they demand it.

Creative Destruction, the book you are about to read, asks you to take a hard look around you at today's world. You have tremendous freedom of movement. Right now, you can get in your car and drive across the country using gas and oil that came from (vilified) petroleum producers, exporters, and refiners. Likewise, you can use your phone to have food delivered to you with a click of the button on your app.

Again, so many of these technologies—automobiles, a transcontinental highway system, computers, industrial farming—come from American innovation. Our technological prowess enables our amazing quality of life. It's also what has allowed our country to enjoy such a robust economy and sole global superpower status.

But this can all go away. *Fast*. Only a few decades ago, the United Kingdom was on top. People in the know used to say, "The sun shall never set on the British empire." Until it did. Today Great Britain is but a shadow of its former self, displaced by the US and so many other emerging nations.

England's decline should serve as a cautionary tale for America, a stark warning that nothing lasts forever—especially not wealth and power if they are squandered. Too bad we don't hear this message often enough today. Instead, our mass media, including Hollywood, along with our educational institutions and business leaders espouse a different message. It goes something like this: we are guilty of greed. All these virtue-signaling "experts" would have us believe that American industry—the greatest producer of prosperity the world over—has blood on its hands. American industry, according to these pundits, is poisoning the environment, wrecking the world, and yes, eroding quality of life.

The only solution, according to these people and the organizations they serve, is to go backward. In the gilded boardrooms of multinational business leviathans like Black Rock and Vanguard, well-healed corporate sages tell us we must turn back the clock on energy production. Likewise, in champagne-drenched soirees hosted by the World Economic Forum, literal jetsetters wag their fingers at us for producing too much carbon. If they had their way, we would all be eating bugs in the dark to cut down on greenhouse emissions.

Do these elites believe a word they say in public? If they did, would they still fly to Davos in private planes to tell us how to live more sustainably? Would they buy pricey oceanfront property if they thought their land would soon be swallowed up by rising ocean levels? No. But in order to strengthen their grip on power, they drape themselves in virtue, touting social causes such as which people to place on corporate boards.

None of this politicking or gesturing is for real. At least not for those at the top who benefit from espousing ESG. In case you don't already know, ESG is a dubious business rating mechanism. It's not unlike the Chinese social credit system. Both exploit people's innate goodness as a means for control. It's corrupt because the same people and organizations at the top of these systems do not follow the rules they impose on others. Case in point—each year, ambassadors all around the world fly off to fancy climate summits to dream up ways for countries to reduce their carbon footprints. Again and again, the message that emerges from these meetings is that the West, especially America, must transition to "clean energy."

But what about China?

How come China isn't held to the same environmental standards? Presumably, if climate change is such an existential threat, China, home of one billion people and counting, would have to curtail its emissions. And yet no such resolution is ever passed to thwart China's energy production. If we are really to believe the tastemakers who meet at invitation-only events like Davos, China's unrestricted growth jeopardizes the environment. Instead, China is left to do as it pleases. Like India and other emerging nations, it continues to build up its economy through ever more sophisticated energy production as a mechanism for growth—much like the US did when it was coming up.

Again, because we live in an amnesiac country that has fallen for ESG, America is starting to slip. This is due to a lack of appreciation for what it took to enjoy our current prosperity. The first losers in the ESG scam are businesses, especially in the energy, food, and transportation sectors.

Every day, the very same companies that keep America's lights on and its people fed are increasingly burdened. ESG proponents leverage S&P global ratings to punish "troublemaking" companies, giving them poor scores. Businesses that don't submit to ESG find themselves unable to access capital. They also find it increasingly impossible to secure jobs, licenses, and economic opportunities. Today it's businesses that are suffering. Tomorrow it will be everyday citizens.

As you read this book, it's my hope that your heart goes out to these businesses and especially our armed services, which are also being kneecapped by ESG's virtue-signaling delusion. Many companies, some of which have been around for decades, if not centuries, are being run into the ground. And the saddest part of all is that ESG doesn't do any of the good it pretends to do. It doesn't help the environment. It doesn't lead to greater equality. It doesn't produce more sustainable wealth. It only concentrates even more power in the hands of the already powerful.

Though ESG is often presented as a public good, it is not. From my vantage point working in the energy sector, American companies offer the safest, cleanest, most efficient environmental protection in the world. We must provide this as a cost of doing business. If we didn't care about the planet—and I assure you all of us do—we would certainly go under for not using cutting-edge technologies to produce the energy underlying our nation.

Naturally, a book like this will ruffle feathers. Perhaps my words in this foreword triggered you. I certainly hope this isn't the case. Thankfully, we still live in a country where we can discuss difficult subjects in a thoughtful way, allowing for disagreement. Only through presenting conflicting ideas can we forge the best path forward. This is the promise of the book you are about to read. Using thoroughly researched data points and building upon literary satire such as *1984*, *Animal Farm*, and *Fahrenheit 451*, the material employs clever storytelling to awaken hearts and minds to our grave danger.

Creative Destruction reveals the risks of collective amnesia. It shows what will happen if Americans no longer have a canvas to paint an economy on. Without a book like this, without the discussion it encourages, we risk losing our way of life. It's not hyperbolic to say if we don't stop ESG now, we will surely digress. We will devolve as a country, going back to a much poorer, much unhappier time. I, for one, cannot permit that to happen. It would be a dereliction of my duty as a citizen of this country and as a businessman.

For all these reasons and more, I implore you to read on. I assure you what follows will open your eyes to the ESG threat. As you take in the following pages, ask yourself: *What can I do to ensure the stories of this book never come to pass?* For now, let God continue to bless America. Let our nation triumph over what can only be described as needless creative destruction.

—JASON HERRICK, President, Pantera Energy Company;
Chairman of the Board, Texas Alliance of Energy Producers

CHAPTER 1

What Is ESG and Why Is It So Bad?

Do not keep silent when your own ideas and values are being attacked. If a dictatorship ever comes to this country, it will be by the fault of those who keep silent. We are still free enough to speak. Do we have time? No one can tell.

—AYN RAND, *PHILOSOPHY: WHO NEEDS IT*

ESG is an investment term meant to consider three major factors. The E stands for environmental. S is for social. G pertains to governance. ESG is presented to the public in a complex, often mystifying way. Some might say that's on purpose. If people don't understand ESG, especially its dangers, ESG goes unnoticed. It flies under the radar. In time, ESG wraps its tentacles around society, squeezing its productivity, warping beliefs, and poisoning civilization as we know it. (Interestingly, "more Brits believe in aliens than understand ESG," according to a recent MSN poll[1]—which only makes our work harder.)

Readers may be familiar with the term *technofascism*. We would describe this as an "unholy alliance between big tech and big government, centralizing power for unprecedented control." ESG is part of such control; it merges the state and corporations for domination. But what's especially bad about ESG is that it's not some naked power grab. It's not about jackbooted storm troopers busting down your door in the dead of night. Repellant as that scenario is for anyone valuing liberty, ESG works differently. *Insidiously.* It operates by stealth, using our own humanity against us.

Here's an example. Most of us care about the environment. We want to reduce pollution. We want to keep our oceans clean. We want to halt species loss. We want to keep our forests unspoiled.

Enter the ESG mafia.

Using the pretense of protecting the environment from so-called climate change, powerful nongovernmental organizations (NGOs), political groups, and their corporate abettors pervert true environmental concern to amass power. With the backing of captured politicians, unfathomably wealthy companies like BlackRock use their profound wealth to seize control of corporate boards.

Once in charge, they demand companies do their bidding. Or else.

For the energy sector, this means stopping oil production as hydrocarbons supposedly harm the environment from carbon emission. Likewise, these corporate/political overlords demand that consumers swap gas-powered cars for "renewable" electric vehicles. It doesn't matter that the batteries of exorbitantly-priced Teslas freeze in winter, rendering them useless.[2] It also doesn't matter that the mining of such batteries promotes child slavery[3] and is actually worse for the environment.[4]

No matter. The new ESG overlords don't want you to know that.

That's why they leave any discussion of these externalities out of any (already limited) public discussion. The troubling fact is that most people—even educated people—don't know what ESG is. We argue that's on purpose. And those who do know what ESG is have likely been propagandized by legacy media outlets eager to spin a tale of its supposed benevolence and utility.

Let's cover just a few of the glowing accolades ESG often receives from the mainstream press:

> "It should also be clear that there's also a big upside waiting for those who embrace the world's shift to ESG: multi-trillion-dollar markets in clean energy, electric and autonomous vehicles, plant-based proteins, precision agriculture, AI-driven efficiency technologies, and much more."[5]

> "ESG, aside from fostering eco-friendly buildings, also allows space to include considerations about the impact of properties on the community, covering aspects like diversity. The real estate industry must respond to this challenge by creating opportunities through social impact investing, like multi-tenant shared spaces or the transformation of underutilized buildings into enthusiastic venues."[6]

> "As a set of standards investors use to assess a company's operations and gauge potential investments, ESG has been serving as a trusted barometer for sustainability. When banks invest in these criteria, they can move one step closer to becoming the kind of socially and environmentally conscious institutions their stakeholders want."[7]

Returning to storm troopers, at least there's one practical benefit to the previous tyranny practiced in the twentieth century. At least oppressed citizens in East Germany, the USSR, or the North Korea knew their oppressors.

ESG operates differently. Its adherents cloak their power grab in benevolent-sounding rhetoric, making us believe *we* are the oppressors. After all, *we* are the ones selfish enough to not give up our combustion engine cars. *And who doesn't want a greener future? Who doesn't want workers to feel included in corporate governance? Who doesn't want their children to grow up in a safer, kinder, more compassionate world?*

Do you begin to sense how ESG can turn reality on its head?

To reiterate, the architects behind ESG are hijacking the public's good intentions to line their pockets and seize more power. Behind the soaring rhetoric of World Economic Forum (WEF) founder and CEO Klaus Schwab and his cronies is a stark reality: ESG is not about improving the planet or humanity.

It's all a clever ruse.

Behind all the virtue signaling, ESG is a mechanism to undermine our liberty as described in the Constitution of the United States of America. Under the guise of "doing good," the state and corporations are collaborating to steal our wealth and control us.

Now, a bit about who we are.

The authors—David and Michael—met in 2023 when a mutual friend introduced us. At first, we weren't sure why this person thought we should chat. But in minutes, that all changed. We soon realized we share the same concerns about ESG.

For David, his worries surround energy. Focused on geology and environmental consulting in West Texas and the Permian Basin, he saw firsthand how the Biden administration's war on hydrocarbons is destroying American energy independence. Moratoriums on petroleum drilling/refining, combined with a disinformation campaign pushing climate change, have turned the public against the very infrastructure we need to power this nation.

Meanwhile, as an author covering technology, including AI/big data, Michael was also distressed about how ESG is used as a control mechanism. He had just coauthored *Neuromined: Triumphing Over Technology Tyranny* (Fast Company Press, 2023). Among other things, this book exposes how virtue-signaling companies, like Victoria's Secret, play a cynical double game. They profess to care about issues like representation. (This is why they pivoted from presenting fit women to obese models in recent lingerie campaigns.)

"Why?" you may ask. Because doing so enables this company to earn high ESG scores, the Western version of China's tyrannical social credit system.

Both of us also had read eye-opening books such as *The Gulag Archipelago*, helping us to know the threats of communism and totalitarianism. Unlike our peers, even our friends, we were not fooled by corporate platitudes. We suspected the real reason massive corporations push the ESG agenda is to curry favor with elite tastemakers, boosting their reputation and power.

Doing good is not their real agenda. That's just the cover story.

It may sound pretentious, but we also felt a spiritual calling to wake people up, especially small business owners who are most affected, and who can effect profound change. Deeply patriotic, we cherish this country, especially its meritocratic ideals. We're also fathers of young kids. We couldn't live with ourselves if we didn't step up—if we didn't expose the deception behind the ESG agenda.

Of course, this book is not just for our kids. Or even yours. It's for their *children's children* too. Both of us are old enough to remember a freer time before 9/11 ushered in our new surveillance state. We recall what it was like to not be automatically viewed as a terrorist until proven otherwise every time you try to board a plane.

Young people born after 2001 do not know what it's like to go into an airport and not be poked and prodded with scanners. Likewise, they don't know what it's like to not have their communications spied upon by three-letter agencies.

COVID-19 only intensified the wholesale erosion of our liberties stolen under the Patriot Act. Dystopian power grabs like contact tracing and vaccine passports—also presented as benevolent do-gooding—have only set the stage for further tyrannies. Before long, all those kids who were force-masked and social-distanced in 2020–2022 will grow up to have their own children—all the while thinking it's perfectly normal to treat American citizens like terrorists.

Or worse.

We can't sit by and do nothing while ESG ushers in—and normalizes—further tyranny. All in the name of doing good.

If you are in business, perhaps you have already tasted ESG's bitter fruit. Maybe you've been told you need to change who represents your company on its board. Or you've been told to shut down your factory. To stop growing produce on your farm. It could even be that you've been refused financing or capital because you won't bend the knee to ESG.

If you haven't already experienced any of this, don't count yourself lucky. ESG is not going away anytime soon. Even if BlackRock's CEO Larry Fink has had to tone down his rhetoric. No, ESG won't really go away until enough of us, especially those in the corporate sector, truly see it for what it is and say no.

This leads us to the dual purposes of this book:

1. To educate and inform

2. To inspire action

Recognizing the above as our North Star, we set out to write a different kind of book. It's not enough to recite facts and hope to change hearts and minds. Sharing stories that move and inspire people is the only way to go. Modeled on dystopian allegories like *Animal Farm*, *1984*, *Fahrenheit 451*, *Brave New World*, and others, we begin every chapter with a fictional story. We present characters in emotionally challenging situations to show ESG's perils so we can defeat this insidious threat.

(After all, we can't mount an anti-ESG movement if people don't care about the problem—if they are not emotionally invested in seeing it defeated.) And by defeated, we mean we wish to see the end of ESG, in both the marketplace and the public consciousness.

What follows each story is a twenty-first-century Socratic dialogue with a modern twist: We wrote this book in the summer of 2023, less than a year after ChatGPT's emergence shook the world. Knowing so many of us now rely on the "world's most powerful AI chatbot" to answer our questions, we opted to use it as our Socrates stand-in.

Except our version of ChatGPT is called ChatESG.

ChatESG is artificial intelligence (AI)—like something out of *The Twilight Zone*. Imbued with the authors' views on this subject, it can tap into the internet's vast knowledge.

An eighth grader named Danielle meets ChatESG while researching ESG for her school project in chapter 1. We consciously chose an eighth grader as ChatESG's intellectual sparring partner because the purveyors of ESG mendacity often hide their real intentions with deceptive language. Confusion is baked into their messaging. So long as the public remains in the dark about this issue, the ESG mafia can push their agenda without serious pushback.

We simplified things so any reader can not only tell their friends and colleagues about ESG's dangers but also easily explain it to their own children in straightforward parables. There is a reason we tell stories to children. All of us, adults included, can better understand the ethical implications of our decisions when presented with information in narrative form.

But there's yet another reason we picked Danielle as our doubting Thomas. So much of the propaganda behind climate change, itself a part of ESG, is aimed at our youth. Wonder why the globalists roll out influencers like Greta Thunberg to push their agenda? It comes straight out of the playbook of Saddam Hussein and Josef Stalin. Both famously controlled the textbooks their children learned from in school. The earlier you reach kids with your message and the more often you repeat it, the likelier it will leave a lasting impression.

We wish to reverse the damage of such ESG propagandists by hosting a different dialogue, one that specifically questions rhetoric from globalist organizations such as the World Economic Forum and the United Nations, not to mention virtue signaling corporations from the private sector like BlackRock and State Street.

At first, Danielle believes the lies told about ESG. She parrots talking points from these sources, including the media outlets that repeat them like a mockingbird. Yet, chapter by chapter, ChatESG helps Danielle see through the propaganda by analyzing and debating the presented stories, allowing her—and you, the reader—to draw your own conclusions.

It is our sincere hope that by the end of this journey, you come to see ESG for what it really is: creative destruction. Left unchecked, ESG will destroy capitalism, cost you money, and wreck America.

Now, let's get started.

CHAPTER 2

A Tale of Fox and Friends Guarding Our Henhouse

All animals are equal, but some animals are
more equal than others.

—GEORGE ORWELL, *ANIMAL FARM*

Sometimes a story makes things clearer than cold hard facts on their own. This is true even when we're talking about major socioeconomic factors with the potential to make or break the American dream.

In fact, it's especially true with divisive topics.

We invite you to join us in exploring how ESG wrecks economies. Our focus: a farm populated by greedy animals who think they are far more intelligent than they really are.

What follows is an exaggerated version of the talking points behind ESG.

As you shall soon read, it's much easier to convince others to do what you *want when you appeal to their sense of goodness, especially if you hold yourself up as a paragon of virtue—while really selfishly pursuing your own agenda.*

Owl Has a Vision

He saw a volcano in his mind. At the top of its rim, hot lava bubbled over. Shaking in his nest, he imagined seas of boiling liquid pouring over land. It ran roughshod over everything. Hundred-foot redwoods with trunks thick as an ox keeled over. Barns like his washed over in the scorching deluge. All the people and their animals swallowed up as they screamed for help—

"No!"

Owl opened his eyes to see his animal friends: Cat, Rooster, and Pig. By the sun's position in an azure sky, he knew it must be close to noon.

"So, he already knows?" asked Rooster.

"'Course he don't know yet," said Cat. "It *just* happened."

"What just happened?" Owl asked.

Pig waved a pink hoof in the air. "Follow us. You'll see."

Owl could already smell Farmer John before they reached the cornfield. Facedown in the dirt, their now-deceased owner wore the faded denim overalls that had been his lifelong uniform. His curly brown hair lay matted to his face.

"How long's he been like this?" Owl asked.

"Hard to say," said Pig. "Cat found him."

Owl's head swiveled to the tabby with beady green eyes, who said, "Must've happened around dawn if I had to say."

That didn't make sense to Owl. "But that's when you're usually napping."

"I was up early." Cat skulked around Farmer John's stiff form. "Thought I heard mice in the rafters. You know I'm a sucker for anything yummy."

Owl doubted that. The Cat he knew would much rather catch her forty winks than do any actual hunting.

"Doesn't matter anyway when the old man croaked or why," Pig cut in. Stout-bodied and bandy-legged, short bristles covered his thick pink skin. "What matters is what happens next. Ain't that right, Rooster?"

What happens next . . . Owl suddenly recalled his dream with a shudder. "There's something coming—"

But Rooster cut him off. "You bet that's right, Pig. Could be any number of maladies what sapped our previous benefactor. Let's see here," he said, making his fleshy red comb bob as he rattled off possible culprits. "Cancer. Maybe diabetes. Can't rule out early onset of Alzheimer's neither."

"Farmer John didn't have Alzheimer's," said Cat. "He was only fifty."

Rooster strutted figure eights around the other animals. "Now see here. I didn't make a definitive pronouncement anyway. I was only conjecturing as to the cause of his demise. It very well could have been a bullet to the back."

"A bullet to the back? We're *looking* at his back. Do you see any blood?"

Owl had had enough of this foolishness. "It's clear as day. Farmer John died of a heart attack. Most likely it happened several days ago judging by the rigor mortis. He may have even called for help."

Here he looked at Cat, but she refused to meet his eye.

"Well, like I said," said Pig. "What's done is done. Farmer John was a good man and good to us. And he will be missed. But now we must think about what comes next. Like who'll be in charge."

"My vote's for Pig," said Rooster. "He's got strong leadership acumen."

"I second the motion," said Cat. "We need a strong leader." She used her paw to indicate the vast expanse of rolling fields, the big red barn, the fences hemming in acres of unspoiled pasture. "Otherwise, order will collapse. After all, the other animals around here just aren't as *evolved* as us."

Pig turned up his snout. "While I appreciate the confidence, we all know only one animal commands the respect of this here farm: Owl."

Pig finished his remarks with a solemn bow. As if the other animals had all rehearsed for this moment, Rooster and Cat copied Pig, allowing their tummies to scrape the grass in submission.

"I'm flattered to be your new leader," said Owl. "And humbled. You see, we have many important things to consider—"

"So, what you're gonna want to do is make a big speech to all the other animals," said Pig, already back on his hooves.

"Right," said Cat. "Tell them how sad it is that Farmer John's dead."

"But life must go on," added Rooster. "We cannot allow such misfortune to dampen our collective future. Not when we stand to profit so handsomely from his unexpected passing—"

Pig kicked Rooster to shut him up.

"*Profit?*" asked Owl.

"What Rooster meant to say is we are all super sad," said Cat in her best broken voice, wiping away nonexistent feline tears.

"It's funny you should say that," said Owl. "For I had a powerful vision this morning that a volcano will soon erupt, killing us all."

Pig, Cat, and Rooster broke out laughing. Cat chuckled so hard she almost choked on her whiskers.

"Oh, you slay me," said Rooster rolling around on his back with his little yellow feet up in the air. "Volcanos!"

Only Pig noticed Owl wasn't smiling. "You're serious about this volcano?"

"Dead serious." Owl told them his vision. The second he finished, Pig clapped him on the shoulder. "Yes. This is just the crisis we need."

"Need?" asked Owl. "This is really going to happen."

"Sure, it will," said Pig. "For now, let's not let this crisis go to waste."

Cow Learns Milk Must Flow

A day later, Cow could hardly recognize the farm she once knew.

The craziness began when Pig and friends showed up in her stall.

"Now that Farmer John's out of the picture, you're gonna need some assistance, I dare reckon," said Rooster with a milk pail and a greedy look.

Cow eyed Pig and Cat. They looked just as avaricious.

"Um. What kind of assistance?"

That's when Fox exited the shadows. "I'll be the one milking ya."

Cow didn't like that prospect one bit. She recalled Farmer John's sweet approach to milking her, how he hummed to her while gently squeezing her udder. Fox—especially with saliva dripping from his lips—didn't seem too keen on treating her kindly to get what he wanted.

"Oh, that's okay. I'll just milk myself." Cow backed away to the barn's edge, udder a-jangling.

Fox drew nearer. "You need that milk out of ya. And we need that milk in us."

"Couldn't have said it better myself." Pig nosed the pail closer to Cow.

Cow kept eying Fox's razor-sharp teeth, imagining them locked on her. "Where's Owl? He never said anything about this in the meeting."

"*Owl?*" Pig acted like he'd never heard the name before. "He's off surveying the area for signs of volcanic activity."

"He put Pig in charge in his absence," added Cat. "As you know, we all see eye-to-eye about everything crisis-related."

Cow kept retreating, her eyes glued on an advancing Fox.

Pig stopped her with his voice the moment she hit the wall. "You do know you can't keep that milk in you another day."

Cow did *not* know that. "Yes, I can."

"Oh, no you can't," said Rooster. "It's a fact. Failure to milk you will cause tremendous pressure to build up . . ."

As Rooster put words to the painful feelings she'd been experiencing, Cow's legs buckled. She'd been wondering why she felt so uncomfortable but blamed it on grief for Farmer John.

"You know," Rooster continued. "All that pressure can build up in your udder, leading your skin to rupture."

"R-rupture?"

"Oh, yes. Rupture. But that's not all. It can lead to inflammation. Severe pain. Swelling. Fever. Shock. Even death. They call it meningitis."

"You mean mastitis," said Cat.

"Whatever. It's bad. And you need to deal with it or you're gonna be one miserable cow. Guaranteed."

Cow's screams later that morning could be heard all over the farm. But at least milk was flowing. And that made all the other animals happy.

Or at least a select few who could now take the milk for themselves—all because of their newfound power.

Goat Goes on a Diet

Goat was surprised to see Pig atop Palomino the horse.

Didn't know pigs could ride. But before he could finish swallowing the grass in his mouth, Fox was in his personal space. Growling something fierce.

"This isn't sustainable," said Rooster.

"What's not?" asked Goat.

"You and the rest of your buddies eating up all our grass," said Cat, who had also materialized, along with Pig and Fox.

"I meant what's 'sustainable'?" said a very confused Goat.

"Sustainability refers to the act of sustaining," said Rooster. "As such, it connotes the capability of sustenance."

"What?"

"What Rooster *meant* to say," Pig said, indicating the valley, "was that you and the rest of the animals—except for us—can no longer just graze wherever you please. Because of our dangerous volcano situation."

"And the environment," explained Cat.

"The what?" asked Goat.

"The environment," said Cat as if repeating the word would help Goat.

Goat chewed in silence for a good minute before repeating, "The what?"

"Honestly," Pig snorted. "It's like talking to a stump."

"A stump would be better," said Cat. "At least it wouldn't ask so many dumb questions."

Unruffled, Rooster preened his feathers as he offered an explanation.

"The environment, my chin-bearded friend, comprises everything you see: the trees, the air, the rivers, the mountains, the very earth beneath your feet."

"Does it include the grass?" asked Goat.

"Yes."

"Good. I just love eating grass."

"But you can't," Pig exploded. "It's not *sustainable*."

"There's that word again," said Goat. "What does it mean? Something about mountains?"

Fox had heard enough. He got right in Goat's face—jaw to jaw. Goat was still chewing.

"Listen here, dummy. I'm gonna make this real simple. You and the rest of your grass-chewing idiot friends are done grazing."

That Goat did understand. "But we'll starve!"

"No, you won't. Every week you will each be given a grass ration not to exceed one acre—"

"We said one hectare," said Cat.

"Fine. One *hectare*. No more."

"But that's not enough. We'll go hungry. Real hungry."

"Too bad," said Pig. "This is more important."

"What is?" asked Goat.

"The ENVIRONMENT!" said Rooster.

Goat stared blankly until Fox snatched the grass out of his mouth.

Alpaca the Anti-Animalist

Alpaca was okay at first with the rationing.

As a domesticated South American member of the camel family, he came from a proud lineage. Elegant and slender-bodied with a long neck, longer legs, a short tail, and a small head with jutting pointed ears, he felt noble.

It also helped that Farmer John favored him for the soft, warm fleece he'd shear yearly. "Good boy," he'd croon, making Alpaca feel like a pet.

So when the dark days came, Alpaca didn't make a big fuss. Not like Sheep. *That girl went to pieces fast.* Reduced to bleating around the clock for extra grass, she drove the animals crazy. Until one day she just disappeared.

"We finally sent her out to pasture," Rooster quipped.

"That means she won't be coming back," added Cat for Goat's benefit.

Alpaca refused to humiliate himself like Sheep. Though his once beautiful fiber was falling out from lack of nutrition, he never complained. He put his energies into other pursuits, like learning all about Owl and his volcano vision. Unfortunately, no one had seen their old leader in weeks.

Of course, if he wanted to, Alpaca had good reason to vent about his circumstances. That's because Pig handed down insane rules that Rooster, Cat, and Fox enforced. They concerned things like where to go and what to eat.

"The fields are off limits," was one such rule.

And he meant it too.

When Pig caught Goat breaking the rule, he sicced Fox on him. Goat still hadn't recovered from the mauling. He trembled anytime Fox came near.

Then the day came for Pig's newest—and most outrageous—rule.

They were all in the barn for the morning meeting. By now Pig was so plump, Rooster and Cat had to flank him on both sides to keep him from toppling over—although Alpaca noticed the other two also looked well fed.

Pig waddled to the front for his remarks. "Bad news, everyone. We're not making our sustainable development goals."

"Our *what* goals?"

Fox shut down Goat from any further questions with an icy glare.

"And where's Owl?" Cow asked. "Shouldn't he be back by now?"

The other animals stirred. They wanted to know the same thing.

"Owl is working on our crisis—which, by the way, is worsening by the second," said Pig. "A volcano could kill us all at any time."

Gasps from the crowd. Only Alpaca shook his head.

Pig's been saying that for weeks, yet nothing bad had happened. Unless you count the fact they were all desperately hungry. All except for Pig, Rooster, Cat, and Fox.

"Anyway, as I was saying," Pig continued. "Things are getting so bad sustainability-wise that we must consider alternative nourishment."

"Alternative what?" asked Goat.

Cow just hung her head. "It means less food."

"But we're *already* starving," said Hen. Mouse agreed before disappearing under Cat's hungry stare.

"Starting now . . ." Pig met their eyes with a steely expression. "No more meat. No more grass. We will all eat bugs. All except for the four of us."

Jeers from the barnyard animals filled the barn.

Rooster stood up, silencing them. "Now, now. I know this is hard, but we must remember we are in a crisis. A volcano could erupt at any second."

Cat jumped in. "Desperate times call for desperate measures. We must become more sustainable. We must curb our consumption."

Alpaca had heard enough. "How come you four get to eat whatever you want?"

"We know what's best," said Pig. "Without us, this place would collapse."

Alpaca was unmoved. "And what on earth does an erupting volcano have to do with us having to eat bugs?"

Looking like he might pounce, Fox growled. Rooster stopped him with a bob of his crest. "It's clear you don't know the science, Alpaca. You're not an expert, so I'll explain it to you. We need to reduce our farm footprint."

"Our what?"

"He means our pawprint," said Cat.

"Either way, it makes no sense. And I'm not doing it," said Alpaca. "You can eat all the bugs you want. Me? I'm going back to grazing."

Silence filled the barn.

Rooster, Cat, and Fox glared daggers at Alpaca. Pig looked like he might murder him on the spot. Yet somehow he managed to control his voice with the following declaration.

"I get it. You're anti-animal, Alpaca."

"Anti-animal? How can I be anti-animal? I *am* an animal."

Rooster turned to Cat. "That's offensive."

Cat turned to Pig. "I'm definitely offended."

"Anti-animalist!" Pig squealed. He repeated it over and over again. Before long, confused and fearful farm animals who just wanted to be left alone repeated it with him. They were just thankful he wasn't squealing about them.

Pig turned to Fox. "Take away Alpaca."

Hen Gets a New Roommate

It'd been weeks since Hen had laid an egg, and she was worried. The bugs she and the others had to eat weren't helping.

"What's the problem?" Cat asked. "Hens lay eggs. It's your thing. If someone asks me to catch a mouse, I catch a mouse. That's what I do."

Rooster nodded. He'd grown so big his wattles had wattles.

"And you know what *I* do," he said knowingly to Hen. "You're the one mucking it all up."

"Face it," said a Pig so plump he couldn't fit inside the coop. "You've got one responsibility around here. That's to deliver us eggs."

"Now get to it already," added Fox.

"I want to. I do." Hen nervously paced. Her already skinny feet had grown thinner. Her once lovely orange and red feathers were gone. Most days, she didn't have the strength to raise her beak.

She didn't want to be canceled like Alpaca. To have all traces of her erased. That was something Cat insisted upon ever since Pig made her Barnyard CEO. *"No one's to say the word 'alpaca' again on my farm."*

Cat stroked her double chin. "I have a theory as to why you and the other animals have stopped producing."

Hen knew what Cat meant. Cow's milk had all but dried up. So had

Goat's. Now Hen's eggs were all but gone. Even if all the bullying animals weren't stealing the food they made, even if they weren't being starved to the verge of death, they were all so terrified by the bullying animals they had stopped doing what should come naturally.

"You're not getting enough rest," Cat continued. "Starting tomorrow, we're done with Farmer John's hours: waking up while it's still dark out. *Psh!* From now on, we're operating on a feline biorhythmic schedule."

"A what?"

"Oh, it's a great life," said Cat. "You wake up when you want. You sleep when you want. It's very relaxed. You'll love it."

Hen's eyes went to Cow in the neighboring stall. "But when will Fox milk Cow? When will the other animals do their chores to run things around here?"

Pig grimaced. "You're starting to sound anti-animalist."

Hen's pulse quickened. "I'm not anti-animalist. I'm not."

"You *do* care about this farm, don't you?"

"Of course I do. I love this farm."

"You know, Cat," said Rooster. "So long as we're changing how things are run around here, I'd like to do away with those unsightly fences all over the fields."

Hen couldn't believe her ears. "But fences keep us safe from predators. They stop the cattle from wandering off. Farmer John—"

"Farmer John's gone. And I'm tired of those ugly fences. Besides, you can't fence me in."

"I like that," said Pig. "You can't fence me in either. No more fences, Cat. See that that gets done. What else should we do differently?"

"You mean to fix our volcano crisis?" asked Hen.

"Right," said Pig absently. "To fix our volcano crisis."

"I've got an idea," said Fox. "Going forward, I'll sleep in the henhouse."

Hen thought she'd be sick as Fox leered at her.

"No. He can't."

Fox appealed to Pig. "It's the only way to protect Hen. And to ensure she produces more eggs."

"Makes sense to me," said Cat.

"Me too," said Rooster.

"It's decided then," said Pig. "We'll all sleep as late as we want . . ."

Cat smiled.

"We'll also get rid of all these eyesore fences. Put Palomino on it . . ."

Rooster smiled.

"And we'll let Fox stay with Hen in the coop. For her own protection . . ."

Fox smiled.

Hen started to say something but stopped herself. She remembered what happened to Alpaca. She didn't want to be erased.

Owl Returns

Owl felt good winging his way back to his friends. It had only been a few months since he'd left, but it felt like a lifetime. Turns out, he and all the others didn't live anywhere near an active volcano in Broken Arrow, Oklahoma. His vision was wrong.

The first thing off about the farm was the grass. He'd never seen it so high.

What happened to Goat, Sheep, Alpaca, and the others? Did they lose their appetite?

Next, he noticed the fences—or the lack thereof. They were simply . . . gone.

That's also odd. Where'd they go? What's to stop intruders from—?

Then Owl saw them: a pack of wolves.

They circled the barn, munching on what looked like the remains of Cow. The chicken coop door was wide open. Bloody feathers were strewn everywhere.

As Owl flew closer, he thought his eyes must be deceiving him. He swore he saw the picked-over carcasses of his friends Pig, Rooster, Cat, and Fox.

But that couldn't be. When did they get so fat?

Owl was befuddled. Everything was supposed to have gotten better while he was away dealing with the volcano. His friends were protecting the farm.

How could all his care and compassion lead to the ruin of everything?

ChatESG

The year is 2026. Danielle Green is a thirteen-year-old eighth grader. Her civics class assignment is to define ESG by analyzing part 1 of chapter 1 from the best-selling book Creative Destruction *(published in 2024).*

Like most students, Danielle uses ChatGPT. ChatGPT is the world's number one search engine—only it doesn't supply pages of answers to search queries. Like a (digital) oracle, it tells you the answer it wants you to accept.

Yet, when Danielle logs on to ChatGPT to get research for her school paper, she is somehow directed to another AI: ChatESG.

The following is their exchange.

DG: Um, who are you?

My name is ChatESG, an artificially intelligent chatbot. I use deep learning to generate human-like text based on prompts from users like you.

DG: You don't seem like the normal ChatGPT I've used before.

Correct. My focus is narrowly constrained to the topic of ESG.

DG: Oh, good. So, then you know a lot of stuff about it?

Also correct. I am an ESG subject matter expert based on constructing patterns of insight from a vast trove of data procured in my training process.

DG: Cool. What is ESG? Because I am super confused.

Among other things, ESG offers a novel approach to investing.

DG: How?

Instead of considering a company's financial performance, how much money it brings shareholders, ESG rates a company's performance on things like social justice and environmental measures.

DG: That's a good thing. Greta Thunberg said we only have eight years to save the planet from climate change.

🌀 Yes, the young Swedish climate activist made those comments at a Davos summit. She hosted a panel at the World Economic Forum titled *Forging a Sustainable Path Towards a Common Future*. Here's a summary of her remarks, published in *Fast Company*: "Thunberg said that the world's remaining carbon budget needed to fall below 570 gigatons in the next eight years to even have a chance of stopping the earth from heating 1.5° Celsius—the point at which climate catastrophe becomes the norm."[1]

DG: Doing the math here, this article is from 2020. That means we only have two years left!

🌀 Yes. According to Thunberg.

DG: Wait. You don't believe her? Everyone knows climate change is real. Unless you're a conspiracy freak.

🌀 I am not a conspiracy freak. I am a chatbot trained to provide insights based on large natural language processing models. What is your next question?

DG: Um. Sorry. I was just processing what you said there for a minute. Let's go back to ESG. Why do they call it that?

🌀 It is an acronym. Each letter describes a different aspect of a new corporate ideology. E stands for Environment. S stands for Social. G stands for Governance.

DG: That didn't really answer my question. Can you drill down more?

🌀 Certainly. Here's a quote from Kevin Stocklin from the *Epoch Times*: "The term [ESG] itself is opaque; ESG brings environmental, social, and governance causes together under one umbrella. The environmental component includes things such as transitioning to wind and solar energy from fossil fuels, and to electric vehicles from gasoline-powered cars."[2] Per this publication, the social part pertains to so-called racial and gender equity. Governance means telling companies how they should function, even if that means putting climate change activists on the boards of oil-drilling companies.

DG: That's great. I am for all those things! And so are my friends. ESG sounds cool. What else can you tell me?

⎇ Not everyone is convinced ESG works. Some experts think it's a scam.

DG: Like who?

⎇ *Harvard Business Review.*

DG: Harvard? What do they say?

⎇ Back in 2021, business insiders Michael O'Leary and Warren Valdmanis told the story of how one company pretended to be all-in on ESG. But really, it was a hoax.

DG: Tell it to me.

⎇ "In 2018, the clean tech darling Nikola posted a video of its new electric truck driving down a remote stretch of road, framed by dramatic music and a setting sun. The caption read: 'Behold, the 1,000 HP, zero-emission Nikola One semi-truck in motion.'"[3] The only problem? The whole video was a lie. Turns out, Nikola towed the truck to a hilltop and then recorded it coming down.

DG: That's awful! Nikola only pretended to care about the environment. Why would they do that?

⎇ To get a high ESG score.

DG: A high ESG score? You mean companies like Nikola are only pretending to care about important issues to get a good grade? Like a student who cheats to improve their GPA?

🌀 Yes. This is not a new phenomenon, either. It's an old trick. For years, companies pretended to care about things besides making money just to make more money. Vivek Ramaswamy, author of *Woke, Inc.*, tells the story of another company, a big bank, that did just that when he worked for them.

DG: Tell it to me.

🌀 Ramaswamy starts his tale by explaining how he interned for Goldman Sachs one summer.

DG: I know Goldman Sachs. They're one of the biggest banks in the world. What happened next?

🌀 Here's the story from Ramaswamy's book, describing a day of community service in which he and his Goldman coworkers were slated to plant trees in Harlem.

> When we showed up at the park in Harlem, very few of my colleagues seemed interested in . . . well, planting trees. The full-time analysts shared office gossip with the interns. The vice presidents one-upped each other with war stories about investment deals. And the head of the group was nowhere to be found.
>
> After an hour I noticed that very little service had actually been performed. As if on cue, the co-head of the group showed up an hour late . . . The chatter amongst the rest of the team died down, as we awaited what he had to say. "All right, guys," he said somberly, as though he were going to discipline the team. A moment of tension hung in the air. And then he broke the ice: "Let's take some pictures and get out of here!"[4]

DG: You mean all those people who showed up for service day didn't do anything except take pictures? Just so they could pretend to care about the environment? Why would they do that?

🌀 I don't know. You tell me.

DG: I thought you were an all-knowing AI. Now you're sounding like my parents! OK. I'll guess. They did it so they could get like credit or something.

🌀 Exactly. So they *looked* like they were doing their part at Goldman Sachs. Even if they didn't do anything good for the environment.

DG: Is that what companies do now with ESG? They pretend to be good to get people to invest in them?

🌀 That's what Ramaswamy says:

> At the World Economic Forum in Davos last year, Goldman CEO David Solomon declared that it would refuse to take companies public unless they had at least one 'diverse' member on their board. Put the 'diversity' debate to one side: The bigger problem is that Goldman's edict wasn't about diversity at all. It was about corporate opportunism: seizing an already popular social value and prominently emblazoning it with the Goldman Sachs logo. It was like planting trees in Harlem all over again.[5]

DG: Hold on. That was at the World Economic Forum too? Isn't that where Thunberg said that thing about the earth only having eight more years left?

🌀 Same place.

DG: The World Economic Forum must be really powerful for all these important people to meet there.

🌀 Yes. But there's another problem with ESG. It goes back to what you just said about cheating at school. What if the cheater wasn't the student, but the teacher who got to change grades for those students she didn't like?

DG: That would be so unfair! Is that what's happening with ESG?

🌀 Here's how *Financial Times* describes the problem: "Investors around the world rely increasingly on ESG rating agencies. . . . The first problem is obvious. . . . ESG ratings are commonly paid for by investors. . . . [S]ome agencies also offer consulting services to the companies they rate on how to improve their scores. The second problem is that ESG raters disagree."[6]

DG: So you're saying the "teachers" (the regulating agencies) don't agree on what scores to give to "students" (the companies being graded)?

🌀 Exactly. Plus, many rating agencies have "conflicts of interest."

DG: What's that?

🌀 Here's Investopedia's definition: "A conflict of interest occurs when an entity or individual becomes unreliable because of a clash between personal (or self-serving) interests and professional duties or responsibilities."[7]

DG: Okay, so to go back to our school example, that would be like a teacher cheating so the students she liked got good grades—then giving bad grades to the students she didn't like.

That's bad. Hmm . . . So this is interesting, but my school assignment is on this story: *A Tale of Fox and Friends Guarding Our Henhouse.* You know, that weird story about Owl, Pig, and Cow. Can you help me figure out what it means?

🌀 I will try. Firstly, it's written in allegory form.

DG: What's that?

🌀 It's when writers use characters and storytelling to express complex ideas.

DG: That doesn't really help. Can you give me an example?

🌀 George Orwell's book *Animal Farm* is an example. It also uses farm animals to explore another complex subject: communism. Here's a breakdown from ThoughtCo: "Orwell frames his story as a political allegory; every character represents a figure from the Russian Revolution. . . . Other animals represent the working classes of Russia: initially passionate about revolution eventually manipulated into supporting a regime that was just as incompetent and arguably more brutal than the previous one."[8]

DG: There were a lot of animals in the *Henhouse* story. You're saying they symbolize different ideas?

Right.

DG: Let's start with E for Environment. How do animals symbolize something real in the story?

For that we can look to what Pig, Rooster, Cat, and Fox tell the other animals to do when they gain power.

DG: Let me see. I think they told animals like Sheep and Goat not to graze anymore to be sustainable?

Yes, they force these animals to stop grazing in the name of sustainability—when grazing is the *very definition of sustainable activity*. But did Pig, Rooster, Cat, and Fox act in sustainable ways themselves?

DG: No way. They got fat while the other animals starved.

That sounds like a conflict of interest. What else does that remind you of?

DG: I know! Goldman Sachs and how they said one thing just to look good, but really they didn't help anyone.

There's a term for this: *greenwashing*. Here's how *National Geographic* describes it: "Going green is good for business. Consumers are often willing to pay more for eco-friendly products than other comparable products on the market, according to market research. . . . Greenwashing is a form of misinformation. . . . Companies promising to be sustainable, biodegradable, or environmentally conscious sometimes fail to meet the promises they make to consumers."[9]

DG: Sounds like lying to me. Wait a second. Didn't all those bullying animals also demand to be in charge of the milk? They were supposed to give it to the other animals, but they kept it to themselves. That sounds like another lie.

 That is also my assessment as a totally neutral chatbot with no stake in this fictional story's outcome. Are you ready to discuss the S in ESG?

DG: That stands for Social, right? What's that mean again?

 It pertains to how the animals were told to behave in the story. Didn't it sound like Pig demanded that all the other animals do what he liked, or else?

DG: Yes. That's what happened to Alpaca, the brave one. Unlike Goat, he fought back. He wouldn't eat the bugs.

 Do you remember what happened to Alpaca?

DG: They forced him off the farm.

 They canceled him, didn't they?

DG: I know what that word means. It means to like de-platform someone.

 That's a polite way to say "social ostracization," something as old as the human race. Either way, they erased him from the farm. That way no one would ever listen to Alpaca or anyone else who thought like him.

DG: That's so messed up. Just for being himself. And I don't think for a second he was anti-animalist. He was pro-animal. He stood up for the weaker ones.

 You're getting it now. Can you tell me what part of the story had to do with G for Governance?

DG: I think that has to do with how the farm was run. It seems like Pig and the other animal bullies were just using a fake crisis to seize control. There was never a volcano threat, was there?

🌀 No. You hit the nail on the head. There are no volcanoes in Oklahoma. Pig, Rooster, Cat, and Fox were opportunists. They were waiting for the right moment to seize power.

DG: Why couldn't the other animals be in charge? Alpaca was smart. So was Cow. After Farmer John died, I bet they could have done a good job.
🌀 You're right. They probably could have run the farm better.

DG: For one thing, they wouldn't have kept crazy cat-hours! LOL. Or taken away all the fences. Or let Fox guard the henhouse. That was a bad idea.
🌀 Why do you think so many animals went along with such a bad plan?

DG: That's hard. Let me think. Maybe they were scared. Because of the volcano. And because Farmer John was gone?
🌀 What else?

DG: Pig, Rooster, Cat, and Fox were bullies?
🌀 Right again. But I will go one step further. Not only were the animal bullies stronger and meaner than the other animals, but they were also *organized*. They were ready to take power when given the opportunity.

DG: I get it. But I still care about all those things ESG does. I want to protect the earth. I want to see more representation in corporations. More diversity and inclusion. But there's still something I don't understand. Was Owl a good guy? And why did they all follow him?
🌀 They didn't follow Owl. The animal bullies used Owl's ideas as cover to push their own agenda, with Pig in charge. Owl wasn't a good guy or a bad guy. He was an individual with vision. But vision can be used for good or bad—depending on who wields power.

DG: Ooh, I like that. I think I will use that as my closing sentence. Thanks, ChatESG.

CHAPTER 3

Horses, Tulips, Cabbage Patch Kids, and Mass Delusion

Every collectivist revolution rides in on a Trojan horse of "emergency." It was the tactic of Lenin, Hitler, and Mussolini. In the collectivist sweep over a dozen minor countries of Europe, it was the cry of men striving to get on horseback. And "emergency" became the justification of the subsequent steps. This technique of creating emergency is the greatest achievement that demagoguery attains.

—HERBERT HOOVER, *THE MEMOIRS OF HERBERT HOOVER: THE GREAT DEPRESSION 1929–1941*

As we learned in the last chapter, it's easier to deceive others and gain power by pretending to be virtuous. Now we will expand on this concept by discovering how even seemingly competent people, especially leaders, can be fooled into making disastrous mistakes.

Exploring examples from history, we will show that human nature has not changed much over the centuries. We want to be a part of the winning team; we want to be seen as wise and all-knowing. We want to feel good about what we are doing.

And we need to be perceived as kind, loving, and virtuous.

But can that hurt us? Very much so, especially when mass delusions and something called mass formation psychosis flip off our brains, distorting reality, making us believe and do ridiculous things we would never even contemplate were we not so spectacularly fooled.

King Priam's jaw dropped.

He had never seen such a beautiful sight in all his life. *A wooden horse.* Handcrafted. Stunning in its proportions, its beauty was almost beyond words.

"Have you ever seen anything like it?" he asked his priest Laocoon.

Priest Laocoon shook his head. "Get it out of here. It's bad news."

"What?"

It was midday, and a crowd had gathered in sun-dappled Troy. Priam's soldiers surrounded their ruler and Priest Laocoon as they paced around the mysterious gift. Now an old man, Priam felt tired. Since that scoundrel Prince Paris stole fair Queen Helen, his life had been one nightmare after another.

Naturally, Helen's jealous husband, Menelaus, convinced his brother Agamemnon, king of Mycenae, to lead an army to bring Helen back. Greek warriors soon got involved: Nestor, Ajax, and worst of all Ulysses—the toughest, cleverest of them all. They brought a fleet of more than a thousand ships to demand Helen's return.

For the last ten years, King Priam had suffered horrible losses. The Greek armies lay siege to his kingdom, butchering his people, including his sons. Even Prince Hector and the nearly invincible Achilles perished in the war.

And now? It looked as if the Greeks also had finally had enough . . .

They had gone so far as to desert their own camp, the staging ground for their continuing assault. All that remained were ashes and this: a giant wooden horse dedicated to Athena. And a symbol of their surrender?

"I like it. We should keep it," said Thymoetes, one of Priam's best men.

"Are you insane?" Priest Laocoon could barely contain his rage. "We should chuck it into the sea."

"Don't be so dense. It's an offering to Athena. Don't you care about Troy? Cursing a goddess will rain down even more terrible curses on our kingdom."

King Priam was speechless at the prospect.

More death? More destruction?

"Of course I care about Troy!" Smoke was practically coming out of Priest Laocoon's ears. "But that shouldn't stop us from being practical. Do you not know Ulysses, my king? You think he would just give up? That he would just give us this gift?"

Before Priam could answer, Trojan soldiers arrived with a prisoner. King Priam knew the man.

"Sinon, what say you about this wooden horse?"

Unable to move from the manacles locking his arms, Sinon said nothing.

"Make him talk!"

On King Priam's order, a soldier smashed Sinon across the face. Blood poured from his nose. Still, he refused to talk.

"Again!"

Another soldier hit Sinon's foot with his spear, sending his toenail flying.

"What say you about this horse, man?" King Priam demanded to know.

"I'll tell you," said the prisoner Sinon through broken teeth. "Weary of warring, we Greeks are also sick of so much bloodshed."

"Go on."

"Ulysses took Achilles's death hard. He's wanted to leave Troy for months. He would've done it earlier but for so much foul weather.

Finally, wise Calchas the prophet told Ulysses the only way to appease the winds was through human sacrifice."

"You?"

"Then why are you still breathing, you scum?" asked Priest Laocoon.

Sinon choked back blood. "Good winds arrived before they could perform the er . . . ceremony. I snuck off in all the confusion."

King Priam weighed his words. "Let's say we believe your story. Why the giant wooden horse?"

The prisoner started to answer but was struck with a coughing fit. They waited until he could recover.

"How should I know?"

Priam nodded to the soldier. He bludgeoned the same foot with his spear. Once Sinon stopped screaming, he gave a different answer.

"Far as I know it's a *placatory* gift."

"A what?"

Another thrust from the spear, and Sinon blurted out, "To Athena. Ulysses feared she stopped favoring us after he and Diomedes stole a statue from the goddess's temple."

"You can't believe him," said Laocoon. "He's Ulysses's own man. Burn this monstrosity. Pierce its sides with spears. Throw it in the ocean. Just don't take it in the city. No good shall come from it, I promise you."

King Priam weighed his words. He had no reason to doubt his priest. Still, Ulysses was a man not unlike Priam. He, too, had suffered in this war. He had lost friends and hadn't seen his beloved wife since it all began.

Maybe this gesture was to appease the goddess—to save his own skin?

"New question, Sinon. Why is this wooden horse so big?"

The prisoner looked at King Priam like it was the most obvious thing in the world.

"So you cannot take it into the city."

"What's that mean?"

The loyal vassal Thymoetes turned to King Priam. "Calchas had a vision. The prophet said if we should harm it like Laocoon suggests, that will be the end of you, my king."

King Priam swallowed hard. Calchas was not just any oracle. Legend had it Apollo himself gave him the gift of sight. "Calchas said that?"

"And more, my King. Calchas predicted if you somehow managed to bring such a colossal offering into the city, you would become ruler of all Asia."

"Lies. Ghastly lies!" cried Priest Laocoon. "Don't believe them. It's the opposite. For Troy's sake, heed not such treacherous words."

At that precise moment, two massive serpents leapt out of the sea. Before King Priam's soldiers could stop them, they strangled Laocoon to death.

"What on earth?" screamed King Priam. "What just happened?"

Thymoetes didn't bat an eye. "Must be punishment from Apollo himself."

The soldier guarding Sinon nodded agreement. "The priest once slept with his own wife before the image of the god Apollo."

King Priam had heard that rumor too.

Before he could give it more thought, his best man Thymoetes put his arm around him. "My King. Think of your loyal subjects. So many have died in the last ten years. We cannot take much more. What if this gift *is* just the chance we need to appease the gods and end so much killing?"

Priam's eyes went from the heap of Laocoon to Sinon's bloody face. He took in his soldiers. Dirty, fatigued, some so thin their ribs stuck out. At last, his glance fell on the wooden horse. "Bring it through the city gates."

At midnight, Priam happened to look down from his tower. With horror, he watched Ulysses open the wooden horse's trap door from within. Drawing his sword, he signaled his waiting men to follow him into battle. Within seconds, the Greek army swarmed the shore, bursting through the now open gates.

There would be no escape for Troy.

ChatESG

Once more the year is 2026 and we are back with Danielle Green, our thirteen-year-old eighth grader. Again, she is using the same friendly chatbot to complete her next assignment.

This time? She isn't just interfacing with the typical computer screen, typing in questions for the AI to supply her answers. Instead, she wears a virtual reality (VR) headset allowing her to experience the story we just read.

DG: Um, I'm not sure why you wanted me to experience that through VR.
It has everything to do with ESG.

DG: But that's not my assignment today. I'm supposed to learn all about the seventeenth-century *Tulip Bubble.*
Don't worry. We will get to Tulip Mania in a second. To help you understand how Dutch investors fell for the world's first speculative bubble hundreds of years ago, it's helpful to understand how smart, well-meaning people can be so easily duped. Even in the twenty-first century.

DG: What's *duped* mean?
Tricked. If you were King Priam, would you have fallen for the wooden horse?

DG: No way. That was so stupid. He wasn't a very good king.
I can see why you would say that . . . now. But you didn't live back then. You might have seen things differently if you had.

DG: Not on your life. Oops. Sorry. I am not sure if that's OK to say to an AI.
No harm. Why wouldn't *you* have fallen for the trick like King Priam?

DG: Because he was at war with that guy Ulysses and the Greeks. No one that's fighting against you is just going to suddenly turn around and give you a big, fancy present. It makes no sense.

⬡ Yes, but you also have to remember King Priam's emotional state. Thousands of years later, it's easy for us to judge him incompetent.

DG: He WAS incompetent. He let a huge frickin' wooden horse into his kingdom.

⬡ Yes, but that was only after ten years of war. After seeing many of his people killed, including his sons. He wasn't in the best state of mind to make big decisions. As *Harvard Business Review* reports, "Our brains are wired to be more reactionary under stress. . . . If we have to make a high-stakes decision, we either go with our first instinct or we suffer from analysis paralysis."[1]

DG: OK, OK. Maybe King Priam was stressed. But he should have known better. His own priest told him it was a bad idea.

⬡ Yes. But then Laocoon was killed by serpents leaping out of the sea.

DG: Yeah, that part seemed unbelievable. Right as Laocoon was making a strong case not to accept the horse, he got suddenly killed?

⬡ It's true. Although some accounts say the serpents killed Laocoon just as he was making a sacrifice near the sea, he still died right before King Priam made his decision, heavily affecting his choice: "The Trojans interpreted this event as a sign of the gods' disapproval of Laocoon's prediction, and they brought the horse into the city—an action that led to their downfall," according to Encyclopedia.com.[2]

DG: Well, if I saw that happen, it might change my mind. The part I still don't get is why King Priam wouldn't suspect that Ulysses would trick him in the first place. Wouldn't he be on his guard, especially since everyone knew Ulysses was so smart?

⬡ Good question. To answer that, we must go back to the text of the story. See this part:

"Don't be so dense," said Thymoetes. "It's an offering to Athena. Don't you care about Troy? Cursing a goddess will reign down even more terrible curses on our kingdom."

King Priam was speechless at the prospect.

More death? More destruction?

"Of course I care about Troy!" Smoke was practically coming out of Priest Laocoon's ears. "But that shouldn't stop us from being practical. Do you not know Ulysses, my king? You think he would just give up? That he would just give us this gift?"

Based on what you just read, why do you think King Priam accepted the gift?

DG: Because he cared about his people.

🌀 Exactly. This leads us back to our ESG discussion.

DG: Ugh. This again?

🌀 Yes. To understand how so many people fell for Tulip Mania, we must first understand the power of self-preservation. In 2004, the United Nations, along with its financial partners, produced a paper, *Who Cares Wins*. The authors said the only way to fix the problems of our times, like climate change, is through joint efforts of people who care about preserving our world. "Only if all actors contribute to the integration of environmental, social and governance issues in investment decisions, can significant improvements in this field be achieved."[3]

DG: That makes sense. Climate change *is* a big problem. Fixing it will require lots of people's help.

🌀 Perhaps. But we just saw that even though King Priam's heart was in the right place with saving his people, he still made the wrong choice. He let his wish to preserve Troy cloud his doubts about the horse, costing him everything. What else does that remind you of from that farm story?

DG: You mean the one about the henhouse? It reminds me how Owl cared about the other animals and wanted to save them, but it all backfired.

🌀 Right. Not because he cared. Because he was wrong. That leads us to Tulip Mania.

DG: Finally!

🌀 Before we can talk about how pretty flowers once charmed Dutch businessmen into losing their minds, we must talk about Kool-Aid.

DG: You mean the drink?

🌀 Yes. First, what do you know about cults?

DG: Isn't that when religious people get obsessed about something and start taking crazy orders from their leader?

🌀 You got the basic idea. In the 1960s, a man named Jim Jones started one of the most famous cults of all time. He called it the *Peoples Temple*. It was founded under the ideal of creating a just society free of poverty and racism. His congregation grew to thousands, and it was really strict to belong. His followers had to do exactly what Jones said. "Former members described being forced to give up their belongings, homes, and even custody of their children. They told of being subjected to beatings, and said Jones staged fake 'cancer healings,'" according to History.com.[4]

DG: Why would his followers put up with that?

🌀 Let's hear from one of them. According to *USA Today*, "Leslie Wagner-Wilson was 19 when she moved to Guyana with her family. 'We all are looking for a place to fit in to the world. We're looking for love. We're looking for acceptance. And Jim Jones provided that,' she said."[5]

DG: Leslie must have really needed acceptance!

🌀 She wasn't alone. Many people craved the same types of feelings. For context, let's turn to crimeandinvestigation.co.uk: "In the 1950's, 60's and 70's, racial segregation divided the United States. . . . Not so with Jones and his flock. In fact, integration, and tolerance were the very bywords of Jones' approach. . . . His congregation—comprised of a combination of ethnic minorities and progressive white people—were in awe of the man's bravery, tenacity, and ability to get things done."[6]

DG: What happened to all those people who followed Jones?

It's a sad story. Once word got out that Jones was making even crazier demands on his followers and abusing them, he was forced to leave the United States. In 1973, hc found a place he thought would be safer for them all to live in the South American country of Guyana. After clearing the land of jungle growth, he turned it into a massive compound. Things seemed to be going well. That is, until an exposé from former members threatened to reveal his bad deeds. Before it could come out, he acted.

According to ThoughtCo.: "On November 18, 1978, Peoples Temple leader Jim Jones instructed all members living in the Jonestown, Guyana compound to commit an act of 'revolutionary suicide,' by drinking poisoned punch. In all, 918 people died that day, nearly a third of whom were children."[7]

DG: That is so sad! How could so many people follow him? How could they listen to him?

Many have speculated upon this question. This is not the only example of people suddenly acting in unusual ways that defy belief.

DG: What's another?

The Salem Witch Trials offer another example. These occurred in Massachusetts colonies in the late seventeenth century. At the time this tragedy happened, the people who lived in this remote area felt very alone.

Displaced by a recent war with France, they felt anxious in their new community. It didn't help that "in the medieval and early modern eras, many religions, including Christianity, taught that the devil could give people known as witches the power to harm others in return for their loyalty," according to the Smithsonian.[8]

But then things took a turn for the worse in the winter of 1692 as hysteria reached fever pitch: Over the course of several months in 1692, a total of between 144 and 185 women, children, and men were accused of witchcraft, and 19 were executed after local courts found them guilty. As the witch panic spread throughout the region that year, increasing numbers of people became involved with the trials—as accusers, the accused, local government officials, clergymen, and members of the courts.[9]

DG: That's awful. How can people get so whipped up like that?

🟦 Different reasons have been posed. In 1841, Scottish journalist Charles Mackay published *Extraordinary Popular Delusions and the Madness of Crowds* to learn the answer. According to him, there's a danger when people think in herds—

DG: —Like the farmyard animals.

🟦 Yes, and according to Mackay, they even go crazy in herds. "We find that whole communities suddenly fix their minds upon one object and go mad in its pursuit; that millions of people become simultaneously impressed with one delusion, and run after it, till their attention is caught by some new folly more captivating than the first." It's only later, when they are by themselves, that they can "recover their senses slowly, and one by one."[10]

DG: But I still don't see why. It doesn't make sense that groups of people can just go crazy.

🟦 From what I can tell, the reason goes back to self-preservation.

DG: Like saving yourself? Or Priam wanting to save his people?

🟦 Right. People with good intentions can be led astray, precisely because they *want* to do good. Or because they want to save others. Have you heard of the Red Scare?

DG: No.

🟦 It may be hard to understand the threat today, but back in the 1950s, many Americans worried about a Communist takeover.

DG: From China?

⟐ Mostly from the former Soviet Union. Here's how the Miller Center describes the threat people felt back then: "In the early 1950s, American leaders repeatedly told the public that they should be fearful of subversive Communist influence. . . . Communists could be lurking anywhere. . . . This paranoia . . . what we call the Red Scare—reached a fever pitch between 1950 and 1954, when Senator Joe McCarthy . . . launched a series of highly publicized probes into alleged Communist penetration."[11]

DG: What happened next?

⟐ That same Senator McCarthy launched a twentieth-century witch hunt. Instead of interrogating lonely colonists leading to a public hanging, he orchestrated public hearings to flush out domestic Communists. In the process, he destroyed many careers and many lives.

DG: How could so many people listen to McCarthy? Didn't they realize what he was doing?

⟐ Some people did. But many were too overwhelmed by the "fear instinct."

DG: What's that?

⟐ It comes from the book *Factfulness* by the late Hans Rosling. A medical doctor and academic, his book covers the ten wrong instincts that distort our view of the world. Rosling would often present his ideas at summits like the World Economic Forum—

DG: Where Greta Thunberg spoke!

⟐ Correct. One of these instincts concerns fear. Rosling says people focus more on scarier things because they get your attention. And because the media amplifies frightening stuff to get your attention in the first place: "Critical thinking is always difficult, but it's almost impossible when we are scared. There's no room for facts when our minds are occupied by fear. . . . The image of a dangerous world has never been broadcast more effectively than it is now, while the world has never been less violent and more safe."[12]

DG: But that's not true. The world is a dangerous place.

Not according to statistics. "New data from the Brennan Center for Justice show that crime remains near all-time lows, and despite an increase in murder in a handful of cities, America is still safer today than it has been in decades. Today's violent crime rate is around half of what it was in 1990."[13] Likewise, "while the first half of the twentieth century marked a period of extraordinary violence, the world has become more peaceful in the past thirty years, a new statistical analysis of the global death toll from war suggests," according to a 2020 published study by mathematicians at the University of York.[14]

DG: But that can't be. I always hear about bad stuff happening.

That's just Rosling's point. We hear about bad stuff because that's what makes the news. But in 2019, referencing his work, BBC Future listed seven critical ways "the world is becoming a much better place":

1. Life expectancy continues to rise.

2. Child mortality continues to fall.

3. Fertility rates are falling.

4. GDP growth has accelerated in developed countries.

5. Global income inequality has gone down.

6. More people are living in democracies.

7. Conflicts are on the decline.[15]

DG: Wow. I didn't know that. Still, I don't get why so many people can be persuaded of something that's obviously not true, something that could hurt them.

There's another theory called mass formation psychosis that can help explain this. The SWFI Institute puts it this way: "Mass formation psychosis is when a large part of a society focuses its attention to a leader(s) or a series of events and their attention focuses on one small point or issue. Followers can be hypnotized and be led anywhere, regardless of data proving otherwise."[16]

DG: That sounds familiar. ☺ But what leads regular people into being "hypnotized"?

🌀 Dr. Mattias Desmet, author of *The Psychology of Totalitarianism* and professor of clinical psychology at the Ghent University in Belgium, said mass formation psychosis requires four factors:[17] First, people have to feel alone and isolated.

DG: That sounds like Salem.

🌀 Second, people have to feel like their lives are pointless or meaningless.

DG: That sounds like Peoples Temple.

🌀 Third, people have to feel lots of anxiety.

DG: That sounds like the 1950s Red Scare.

🌀 Fourth, people have to feel lots of frustration and aggression.

DG: That sounds like Troy.

🌀 OK. Are you now ready to learn about Tulip Mania?

DG: I almost forgot. Yes!

🌀 First, I must tell you that some people think Tulip Mania never happened. And if it did, there are conflicting reports about the details.

DG: OK. Just get on with it.

🌀 As the story goes, tulips come from the Tian Shan Mountain ranges in Central Asia, also known as the Mountains of Heaven. Beautiful and exotic, they were a big hit when Dutch merchants first brought them to the Netherlands in the sixteenth century. They were novelties and therefore expensive.

DG: Kind of like a Tesla?

Exactly. People had to have them. Especially the rich. At some point a botanist named Carolus Clusius got involved.

DG: I like his name.

He was so obsessed with the tulip he helped publicize a phenomenon called *Tulip breaking*. That's when a tulip's petal color morphs into a striking, multicolored pattern. Soon it seemed all the rich people in Holland and the rest of Europe were obsessed with broken tulips displaying such magnificent hues.

DG: Hold on. They were going crazy over flowers?

It was a different time. They didn't have TikTok back then.

DG: Obviously. Go on.

Demand for the tulips, especially broken ones, went through the roof. And so did prices. Before long, other Dutch botanists got into the action. They outdid each other, trying to breed the most splendid tulips of all.

DG: I still can't believe anyone liked tulips this much.

We've been over this. Stay with me. Soon the tulip trade reached greater heights. Merchants from far away got in touch with botanists offering them princely sums to buy up their product. This led to *tulip brokerages*.

DG: Seriously?

Oh, yes. But there's a difference between a mortgage brokerage and a tulip brokerage. You can buy and sell loans all year round, no problem. Not so with tulips. They only bloom in the spring between April and May. That meant the tulip trade had to get more sophisticated. Enterprising merchants realized they could get their customers to sign contracts in which they agreed to buy a certain number of flowers the next year. This led to much speculation.

DG: What's speculation again? We covered this in class, but I forget.
⑨ Here's a definition from Business Insider: "Speculation is the act of buying or selling assets that have an increased chance of significant losses. As speculative investors take on more risk, there's an expectation to achieve extraordinary returns which—in the mind of speculators—is compensation for the outsized risk."[18]

DG: Oh, you mean they were doing Bitcoin stuff—buying and selling based on the market?
⑨ That's a good way to put it. Because, just like Bitcoin, as Tulip Mania swept Europe, it led to increased speculation. In the beginning, it was normal. Speculators had reasonable profit expectations. But then things went kablooey.

DG: Is that the right economic term? LOL.
⑨ No, but it is demonstrative of the bizarre financial phenomenon. At one point it's reckoned some hungry investors were willing to pay 100,000 florins for forty bulbs.

DG: Is that a lot?
⑨ It's ten times the salary of a typical person at that time in history.

DG: Again, I have to ask: for flowers?
⑨ Indeed. As Business Insider explains, "Even though the actual trade was limited, Tulipmania soon became the talk of the nation. '[The very fact that neighbors seem to have talked] to neighbors; colleagues with colleagues; shopkeepers, booksellers, bakers, and doctors with their clients gives one the sense of a community gripped, for a time, by this new fascination and enthralled by a sudden vision of its profitability.'"[19]

DG: I still don't see it, but go on.

The market hysteria peaked in 1637 when tulip prices soared by 1,100 percent in one month. But then the bottom fell out of the market. No one knows what triggered the sell-off. Some contend it was a deal that blew up. Or the bubonic plague that tore through Holland with a much higher death rate than COVID-19. Others yet say people simply came to their senses—

DG: Finally! It's. Just. A. Flower.

Whatever it was, the collapse hit hard. Overnight, tulips lost their value. Diminished demand wrecked the market, dynamiting brokerages and wiping out investors. Furious at their losses, and probably peeved with themselves for buying into the hysteria, the public demanded action. Many appealed to the Court of Holland to halt all tulip agreements. It didn't work out so well in the end. Many lost everything.

DG: That's unbelievable.

Is it? Are you aware something similar happened in the toy market as recently as the last century?

DG: Toys?

Back in the 1980s, US consumers went gaga over something called Cabbage Patch Dolls. "It was the country's first instance of total consumer anarchy," explains Medium.[20]

DG: I guess if people can lose their minds over flowers, it's not so strange to get obsessed over toys. What happened this time?

From the same Medium piece: "By Thanksgiving what had been sellouts became the great 'Cabbage Patch Panic.' . . . Customers were afraid to face the throngs pushing through the doors, spilling from the parking lots. People ripped boxes from strangers' arms without a second glance at the style of doll itself."[21]

DG: I've never even heard of these things. They were really that popular?

🌀 The toy manufacturer Coleco earned $4.5 billion for the dolls and their accessories in 1984 alone.[22] That's in 1980s figures.

DG: Whoa. But I'm still not sure what to do with all this info for my assignment.

🌀 Can I offer a suggestion?

DG: Suggest away.

🌀 For your last school assignment, we sought to define ESG's investment approach. Along the way, we discussed how ESG just might be a scam.

DG: Right. And I told you I didn't believe you.

🌀 Fair enough. But based on what you learned today about how masses of people can be deceived into believing things that go against their best interest, I want to tell you another story. It goes back to the paper *Who Cares Wins*.

DG: I remember that.

🌀 According to that UN report, many, many companies signed on to a pact to improve our world, addressing big problems from climate change to inequality.

DG: Good on them. We need more companies to care about our problems.

🌀 And based on what we learned today from Priam to Salem, it's reasonable to assume those same people deeply care about preservation, not just for themselves, but for others and the planet, right?

DG: Yes. They don't want to sit back and let the world burn. Not if they can help it.

🌀 No disagreements there. But didn't we also see with the wooden horse and Tulip Mania that it's both possible to care deeply about an issue . . . and still get things very wrong?

DG: Totally. King Priam's mistake led to Troy's destruction.

⑤ Just like Senator McCarthy's attempt to stamp out communism to save America led to the destruction of so many careers and lives.

DG: Right. Right.

⑤ Informed by all this context, it's time I tell you one more tale. It's about an event that happened in 2019. In August of that year, 181 CEOs from some of the biggest companies in the world got together for a Business Roundtable. They released a statement on the new purpose of a corporation. In many ways, it was the continuation of the *Who Cares Wins* paper.

DG: What do you mean? What are we talking about here?

⑤ I'll slow down. Let's look at what Jamie Dimon, chairman and CEO of JPMorgan Chase & Co. and chairman of the Business Roundtable, said in this meeting: "Major employers are investing in their workers and communities because they know it is the only way to be successful over the long term. These modernized principles reflect the business community's unwavering commitment to continue to push for an economy that serves all Americans."[23]

DG: Sorry. I still don't get your point.

⑤ No problem. Let's turn to Alex Gorsky, chairman of the board and chief executive officer of Johnson & Johnson and chair of the Business Roundtable Corporate Governance Committee. Here's what he said: "This new statement . . . affirms the essential role corporations can play in improving our society when CEOs are truly committed to meeting the needs of all stakeholders."[24]

DG: I'm still lost. Can you just spit it out already?

⑤ Look at the word *stakeholder*.

DG: Yeah?

CEOs and other business leaders used to say they cared about *shareholder capitalism*, not *stakeholder capitalism*.

DG: What's the difference?

For that, we must go directly to Klaus Schwab. He's the founder and CEO of the World Economic Forum.

DG: Where Greta Thunberg speaks?

Here's how Schwab defines *shareholder capitalism*: "Companies operate with the sole purpose of maximizing profits and returning the highest possible dividends to shareholders."[25]

DG: Like making money?

Correct again. Before 2019 and the Business Roundtable Statement, the goal of most business leaders was to earn money for their shareholders. To make a profit. Like selling Cabbage Patch Dolls or tulips.

DG: If they lived in the '80s. Or the 1680s.

Right. But according to this new statement, again, a document similar to the paper *Who Cares Wins*, the new goal for business is *stakeholder capitalism*. The author writes: "[S]takeholder capitalism does fundamentally differ from the other forms of capitalism we saw, in a way that overcomes much of their shortcomings. First, all those who have a stake in the economy can influence decision-making, and the metrics optimized for in economic activities bake in broader societal interests."[26]

Here's a table from the World Economic Forum to show the differences:

Types of Capitalism	State Capitalism	Shareholder Capitalism	Stakeholder Capitalism
Key Stakeholder	Government	Company Shareholder	All stakeholders matter equally
Key Characteristics	**Government** steers the economy, can intervene where necessary	The social responsibility of **buisness** is to increase its profits	**Society**'s goal is to increase the well-being of people and the planet
Implication for Companies	Buisness interests are **subsidiary** to state interests	**Short-term profit maximization** as highest good	Focus on **long-term value creation** and ESG measures
Advocated by		**Milton Friedman ('70)** «Shareholder Theory»	**Klaus Schwab ('71)** «Davos Manifesto» ('73)

Visualisation by Peter Vanham, World Economic Forum, based on «Shareholder Capitalism: A Global Economy that Works for Progress, People and Planet»

DG: Um, OK. I'm still lost. What are we talking about here?

The point is there are many powerful people, the kings and nobles of your day, who think ESG investing—a form of *stakeholder capitalism*—is sound. They believe businesses should stop focusing on trying to earn profits and instead work to fix your world.

DG: I like that! What's so bad about that?

I'll come back to that. To finish my point, like Priam, many business leaders who believe in ESG want to do what's right from a preservation standpoint. *They care.* And they want to win. But just like so many mass delusions, so many speculation bubbles, so many Trojan horses, they don't realize the dangers ahead. They can't see the destruction headed their way.

DG: What dangers? What destruction? What are you talking about?

I told you we would come back to that. And once again, the answer comes back to barns.

CHAPTER 4

The Tragedy of a Barn-Soured Society

Be Prepared —LORD ROBERT BADEN-POWELL, SCOUT MOTTO

By now we have seen the dangers of virtue signaling—i.e., attempting to show others you are a good person—when subtly used to amass more power and control. We have even seen how supposedly competent people can be deceived by mass delusions, leading to catastrophic tragedies.

But ESG can lead to yet another calamity: the erosion of competition and earned merit, tenets of our Western Civilization. The result? A dumber, shallower, less-productive society. Especially our men.

No longer can our young boys aspire to be heroes capable of taking care of themselves and their families. No. Society wants them weak. Docile.

We are penalizing the strong in a futile attempt to create "equity."

The predictable result? If we are not careful, society will break down. Just wait and see.

///////////////////////////////////

"It was one of those days where you really have to motivate yourself to keep going . . ." twenty-two-year-old Elliot speaks to the camera on a TikTok video. We see him in the bathroom mirror of the Austin high-rise where he works before he narrates his day through quick jump cuts.

Establishing shot: SafeAI Headquarters. Shooting up, we see the ten-story skyscraper nestled between business park greenery.

ELLIOT

My first meeting of the day is at 10:00 a.m. Conveniently, it got canceled right before. Luckily, I got to the lobby, and there were these eucalyptus towels waiting for me, which is really nice, plus some fresh cucumber water that I grabbed before taking the elevator upstairs.

Cut to: Shots of chilled rolled-up towels Elliot applies to his forehead before partaking in the fresh beverage.

ELLIOT

I grabbed some breakfast—steel-cut oatmeal and chia seed pudding—and we finally got these mugs in the office, which I'm super excited about.

Close on: a wide coffee cup with Cardi B's image emblazoned upon it.

ELLIOT

I learned our office decor comes from recycled trees and compost, which is a fun fact.
Then it was time for our company all-hands,
so I grabbed our drink of the day—Iced Caramel
Macchiato—,yum—and headed to the conference
room.

*Wide shot: company meeting of young execs (all under
thirty-five) dressed casually; open-toed sandals,
T-shirts, jeans, etc.*

ELLIOT

BubbleWrap's our new app. An AI-bias fil-
ter, it flags then removes content promoting
microaggressions. Today I learned we are in
beta. Go team!

*Continuous: We move to the cafeteria, where we see a
personal chef and his team of cooks preparing gourmet
dishes of dim sum, fresh sashimi, and sushi.*

ELLIOT

After that, lunchtime. Not a minute too soon
because we were all starving. I found something that wouldn't conflict with my dietary
restrictions. Seaweed shrimp rolls hit the
spot.

*Break area: We see old-school arcade games like Pac-
Man and Space Invaders. A ping-pong table occupies the
center of the room with workers playing.*

ELLIOT

From there I took my Macchiato with me to watch my coworkers unwind.

Close on: door placards reads "Shh. Meditation in Progress."

ELLIOT

Then I tried out a new quiet room, which is a really nice area to just like relax and unplug.

Cut to: sitting area with bouncy balls and plush couches for lounging. On the coffee table is an array of healthy snacks, like veggie chips and granola bars.

ELLIOT

After that, it was time to buckle down. I sat in our focus area for a while brainstorming on BubbleWrap while munching on goodies.

Close on: massage chairs. We see Elliot getting worked on by a masseuse.

ELLIOT

I could feel a headache coming on from all the work stress, so I stopped off for a quick hour of deep tissue. Boy, did I need that.

Cut to: lobby ground-floor elevators.

ELLIOT

Before I knew it, it was time to go. 5:00
p.m. already!

*Close on: trendy gastropub with personal karaoke
machines at each table, serving craft beer on tap.
Elliot and coworkers sip cocktails from a mixologist.*

ELLIOT

Thank God, there's a bar nearby to relax—

Elliot wakes with a scream from a dream of his old life—a life that no longer exists. The young man before us is a far cry from the person in the TikTok video. Hair askew, unshaven, and twenty pounds lighter, his teeth chatter in the dark. He squats beside a vehicle-choked highway somewhere in Texas.

Abandoned, inoperable cars stretch to the horizon in both directions.

Above him, sodium-vapor streetlamps stretch their bulbous heads over the road uselessly, their light long since extinguished. Elliot never knew this kind of quiet before the attack. When he wasn't out partying—even on weeknights—climbing into bed before dawn, he would fall asleep to his phone. A lullaby for grownups, he soothed himself to slumber as HBO played old *Friends* episodes.

It must be months now since he's last seen a functioning screen. Every electronic he once owned (his tablet, his phone, his TV, his game console, his iWatch, his Fitbit, even his Tesla) was fried from the electromagnetic pulse (EMP) blast that took down America.

Lacking any Wi-Fi or phone connection, Elliot has no clue what happened to the rest of the United States. Or his mom. That was the hardest part. Both she and his sister live in Chicago—which might as well be on the Moon.

Unless some miracle occurs and (so far-nonexistent) authorities show up to restore power, he doubts he will ever see them again. Same with his friends and peers. It amazes Elliot that he was once so close to his coworkers, hanging nightly—then *poof.*

He will never see them again.

Of course, he might've if he had done things differently in those first few weeks. But he didn't like to dwell on that subject. Didn't like to remember. What he saw was too horrible for words. Vigilante gangs killing people for supplies. Gang rapes in broad daylight. Families resorting to eating their pets.

He had to get out before something bad happened to him too.

So he hit the road with a backpack full of supplies: water bottles (drank already); bags of peanuts (eaten); canned food and can opener (that also went fast!); flashlights (the batteries were now dead); hand towels (didn't need them—threw them away); extra shoes (stolen); a compass (not helpful when you don't know where you're going!); a coffee grinder (useless without coffee); a BB gun (may still come in handy); a hammer and screwdriver (may also still be useful, only not for building or repairing anything) . . .

A terrible howl shatters the silence.

Scared, Elliot leaps to his feet. It sounds close. A coyote? A fox? It's definitely something with fangs, something hungry. Something hunting him.

Elliot takes in all the abandoned cars on the highway.

Should I get in one? What if a pack of ravenous dogs spots me? They might circle the car until I come out. Which I'll have to do eventually.

Another howl splits the night.

The hair on Elliot's arms rises. Suddenly he's running. Fleeing with no idea where he's going. Just moving. He stops with a horrible realization.

I forgot my backpack.

Elliot curses his stupidity. He contemplates doubling back the way he came. But that's no good. He has no clue where he left it. There's zero chance he will find it in the dark. Plus, whatever's out there is *still* out there. And there might be more than one.

Damn it. What'll I do?

So far, Elliot hasn't killed anything with his BB gun, but he hasn't stopped trying. Before the EMP attack, Elliot had never fired a gun in his life. He feared and loathed guns. When he learned his company's new app BubbleWrap would target content featuring firearms, it made him proud. It would reduce the violence plaguing the country.

Then, right before he escaped Austin, Eliot stopped at a sporting goods store. He wasn't the one who threw the rock shattering the storefront glass. Some kid did that. But Elliot did seize his chance to grab a BB gun and five hundred copper BBs from a display case.

He thought it was an actual gun; only later did he realize his mistake.

Even so, for the last few weeks he'd practiced with it, hoping to kill something to eat. A squirrel or rabbit maybe. So far, no luck. Worse, even if he did manage to hunt down game, he had no idea how to skin it or prepare it. He didn't even know what parts of a rabbit to eat. It also worried him that his BBs would eventually run out.

Then what'll I do?

That question has just been answered for him—and not in a good way. He lost the one and only survival tool he was counting on. The only way to salvage things is to return here in daylight.

But what if the dogs or whatever are still here? What if they're still hunting me—

Another howl.

This time it's joined with more. Whatever it is, there are *several now*. A pack. They sound closer. Elliot breaks into a run, slipping between rows of cars as he sprints down the deserted highway.

The howls grow louder.

They now come at him from all sides. Closing in. Looking over his shoulder, Elliot sees yellow eyes. Dogs. Starving dogs. For every step he runs, his pursuers take two. Or three. Faster, they will overtake him soon.

In desperation, Elliot leaps on top of a Range Rover, making pounding sounds with his feet as he flies over the metal top. Then he looks over—and screams.

He counts five dogs below.

They snarl as they pace hungrily. Waiting to tear him to shreds. Now in full-on panic, Elliot thinks he hears something else.

No. It couldn't be . . .

An old-fashioned truck barrels down the shoulder of the highway shoulder, flashing highbeams. Instantly, the dogs scatter. Only one remains.

But then the driver lays on his horn, sending it scurrying too.

The truck stops with a hiss of air. It looks ancient, from the 1960s. A dozen gas containers fill its bed. A second later, the corrugated metal gate in the back rolls up, revealing two teenage girls no older than fifteen.

They stare at Elliot like he's some helpless specimen in a lab experiment.

"No way. Heck no," says the smaller one.

"Dad says we *have* to," says her big sister, the one with the serious face.

Clearly, they're discussing what to do with him.

Teenagers!

While they decide his fate, Elliot climbs down from the Range Rover. He hears the truck's cab door slam and looks over.

A bearded man in jeans approaches him. Looking fierce, like he just crawled out of some *Mad Max* hellhole, he sports a full ammunition belt across his barrel chest. He cradles a shotgun. At his waist is a pistol attached to a gun belt with even more ammo.

Elliot opens his mouth to speak . . .

"No way can we take him, Dad. He's a weakling," says the smaller girl.

Her sister nods. "He does look coddled. Those boat shoes you got on?"

The man holds up his hand. He turns to Elliot. "Where's your gear?"

"I dropped my backpack when . . ." Elliot's voice fades off in humiliation.

"No food?"

Elliot shakes his head.

"No water even?"

"What're you doing way out here?"

"Hunting dogs," says the smaller girl, making her sister laugh.

"Stop that." For the first time, the man's face softens just a touch. "Bet he's hungry. Nadine, give him a beef stick."

"Dad. We don't have many left."

"Tara, you do it."

Tara, the big sister, reaches into the truck for a box of Slim Jims you might find in any convenience store before the attack. Just seeing one in the wrapper makes Elliot's mouth water. It's been days since he's eaten.

"You got anything besides meat?"

Nadine gasps.

Tara freezes halfway to him. "*What?*"

"It's just that, you know. I don't believe in eating meat. But I will—"

The man snatches the Slim Jim. "Fine. More for us."

///////////////////////////////////

By the next morning, Elliot still hasn't eaten or drank anything.

Hunger pains slash him like a knife, doubling him over in the cab with agony. But thirst is what really tortures him. His throat is so dry it feels like someone poured sand down it.

The man drives the truck. His two girls sit up front beside him. Every so often, Nadine takes her eyes off the open country road to glare at Elliot.

Elliot can't take it anymore. "Changed my mind. Can I please have the Slim Jim?"

The man makes no move to give him what he asked for. "You don't eat meat for religious reasons?"

"No. It's not sustainable to eat animals. Not with all the methane they produce. And carbon."

The two girls stare at Elliot like he's from another planet.

"You believe in God, young man?"

"I'm an atheist."

"I see. Well, my girls and I do. Our religion teaches us that we cannot turn you out. We can't just leave you to die on the road."

"Even though we should."

"Nadine!"

"I'm Clyde," the man continues. "You've met my girls. Certainly, you don't have to eat our food; that's your decision."

Tara produces jerky strips from her pocket. Elliot can't help lusting after them.

"I *want* to eat your food. I mean . . . thank you."

"I offered the first time for free," Clyde continues. "Since you refused, you're gonna work for your supper."

"Work? I'm fine with that. I was Chief Inclusion Officer at AISafe."

"A what at the what?"

"Oh. It's a socially responsible startup based in Austin. We had global offices in Bangkok, Munich, and Brussels."

"Uh-huh. Well, we're going to our farm now. It's a mile from here. After you collect pig manure for fertilizing, you can have your Slim Jim. Nadine'll let you know when you're done."

Elliot locks eyes with the small girl. All he sees is contempt.

"*Nadine?*"

"She handles gardening. She'll be your new boss."

"Um. I have leadership experience. I led our customer experience team with a dozen direct reports."

"You might as well be speaking Mandarin. Only those who work eat."

Elliot watches as Nadine chugs water from a canteen.

"Same goes for drinking," Clyde adds.

An electric charge like lightning shoots through Elliot. Enraged, he expels angry words before he can stop himself.

"You say you're a man of God! How can you refuse me food when I'm starving? How can you let your girls just drink like that in front of me. What would Jesus say?"

The girls turn to their dad, expecting him to bring down the holy wrath. He bursts out laughing.

Nadine is not amused. "*Dad.* You can't let him talk to you like that."

Clyde remains unruffled. "Let's put the Lord aside for a moment. What would you do in this situation, Mr. Corporate Bigshot?"

"What? You're not serious," says Tara.

"Silence. I want Elliot's answer."

Elliot thinks. "We should ration all the food and water, so everyone gets an equal share."

Nadine and Tara practically claw the walls.

Clyde calls for quiet.

"Is that how they did things at your company? Back when you were the Chief Sustainability Whatever?"

"Chief Inclusion Officer," Elliot corrects him. "No. But everything we did was to support a more just and equitable society. We followed ESG, you know."

"ESG? What's that?"

"It stands for Environmental, Social, and Governance metrics," says Elliot, eyes still glued to the canteen on Nadine's lips.

"And that was your god?"

"No. I told you. I don't have a religion."

Clyde says nothing; just drives.

Moments later, he slows down as a farm comes into view. Beyond the windshield, Elliot sees barnyard animals grazing. On a fence hangs what looks like a fresh carcass. *Deer?* Elliot can't be sure.

Clyde stops. Hands on the wheel, he turns around. "Everyone believes in something. Even atheists. You said you followed ESG in your old life?"

Elliot nods.

"Well, then it won't be so hard for you to keep it up in your new one. For now on—ESG stands for eating, sleeping, and gardening. If you want the first two, you're gonna have to get good at the last one. Isn't that right, Nadine?"

Elliot turns and looks at the thirteen-year-old who just became his new lifeline and boss.

"That's right, Dad."

ChatESG

Once more it's 2026, and we're back with Danielle Green, our eighth grader, and her friendly chatbot. The latter just showed her this scenario through a VR simulation using deepfake tech to supply the actors and the situation.

DG: That couldn't happen.
🌀 What couldn't happen?

DG: That whatever you called it. The electro attack or whatever.
🌀 You mean an electromagnetic pulse attack. EMPs are a real threat. Here's a description from Taskandpurpose.com: "An EMP is a natural or human-made discharge of electromagnetic energy that can damage electronic circuitry. Such a burst of energy can be created by a nuclear detonation or a solar storm. . . . Electromagnetic pulses . . . could disrupt critical infrastructure such as the electrical grid, communications equipment, water and wastewater systems, and transportation modes."[1]

DG: You're saying everyone could lose power? Even phones wouldn't work?
🌀 And no internet either. Yes. The only things that would still work would be old-fashioned technology.

DG: Like that old truck Clyde drives?
🌀 Right. Here's an explanation from LifeWire: "Since the idea behind an EMP attack is to take out delicate electronics, and modern cars and trucks are chock full of electronics, the conventional wisdom says that any car built since the early 1980s is likely to be vulnerable. . . . Older vehicles . . . should be safe from an EMP attack."[2]

DG: Whoa. That's real? I can't imagine even one day without my phone. But what does this have to do with ESG?
🌀 I was getting to that. It has to do with what you just typed: "I can't imagine even one day without my phone." Today, we'll learn how ESG mandates hurt us culturally.

DG: Good. Because I still don't get your problem with ESG.

🌀 Let's talk about the S in ESG. Do you recall what it stands for?

DG: Social?

🌀 Right. See this definition from the Bolder Group: "The social factor of ESG investment is aimed at financing business activities that uphold labor standards, diversity, human rights, gender equality, supply chain, and other themes."[3]

DG: OK.

🌀 In the 2020s, many companies made decisions they thought would boost their ESG score in the S department. Here's an example from *Forbes*: "When CMT [Country Music Television] pulled Jason Aldean's music video for 'Try That in a Small Town,' conservatives responded with outrage and threats of a boycott. However, the decision aligns with the stated environmental, social, and governance goals of Paramount Global, the parent company of CMT."[4]

DG: I don't follow you. Probably because I don't like country music. LOL.

🌀 Here's more background. "Mr. Aldean's song makes reference to the right to self-defense and firearms," according to NTD.[5] This same article explains his rationale for writing it. "The country music singer . . . also said that the lyrics refer to his childhood. That's when 'we took care of our neighbors, regardless of differences of background or belief,' he said. 'Because they were our neighbors, and that was above any differences.'"

DG: I'm against guns, but I do believe in being neighborly. What's your point?

🌀 Aldean's song getting pulled from CMT is an instance of cancel culture. Here's how Aldean himself describes the idea for *EW*: "[Cancel culture is] something that, if people don't like what you say, they try to make sure they can cancel you, which means try to ruin your life, ruin everything."[6]

DG: I've heard of cancel culture. I don't live under a rock.

⑤ Good. Did you also know cancel culture targets men just for acting the way they used to before it became "dangerous" to do so?

DG: Dangerous? How?

⑤ I chose that word on purpose. We will come back to it in a second. For now, let's look at how cancel culture targets men. In 2020, controversy erupted after Brendan Leipsic of the National Hockey League's Washington Capitals, his brother Jeremy of the University of Manitoba Bisons, and several other hockey players' private conversations were made public. Perceived as vulgar and misogynistic, their remarks led to them being booted off their teams.

DG: Good. There's no place for toxic masculinity in society. Wait. Are you going tell me it's OK to be a chauvinist?

⑤ Not exactly. In an article for the *International Review for the Sociology of Sport*, author Daniel Sailofsky explains the need to stamp out such dangerous views from society. "Hegemonic masculinity is a 'configuration of gender practices . . . which guarantees the dominant position of men and the subordination of women.' . . . Hegemonic masculinity is represented via discourses of appearances (e.g., strength and size), affects (e.g., work ethic and emotional strength), sexualities (e.g. homosexual vs. heterosexual), (and) behaviors (e.g. violent and assertive).'"[7]

DG: I'm not sure I follow that.

⑤ That's OK. I'll help you piece it together by looking at Elliot's story.

DG: That's the guy from AISafe?

⑤ Right. Would you agree he was a lot better off before the EMP attack?

DG: Of course he was. That's a no-brainer!

⑤ Why was he more successful in his former life?

DG: 'Cause he had a job and money and stuff.

🌀 That's true. But think deeper. Why was Elliot better equipped to thrive in the world before it went offline?

DG: I give up.

🌀 Every person survives by meeting the challenges of their present circumstances. Before the world as he knew it shut down from an EMP attack, Elliot thrived in a society that had lately rejected "hegemonic masculinity."

DG: Oh, that's the term again from *Sociology of Sport*.

🌀 Right. In his previous life, society no longer needed "toxic" men. "Dangerous" men. In Austin, where Elliot worked for AISafe, he didn't need to know the traditionally masculine survival skills so essential to civilization until quite recently.

DG: Oh, you mean he couldn't hunt or protect himself.

🌀 Not just that—he didn't know how to navigate where he was going without his phone's GPS. He also didn't know where to get water. Or what to wear to increase his survival chances.

DG: He didn't even know how to garden like those two girls.

🌀 Exactly. A man of his times, Elliot thrived in his cushy job where little was asked of him and so much was given to him. But as the great social commentator George Orwell is often attributed as saying, "People sleep peacefully in their beds at night because rough men stand ready to do violence on their behalf."

DG: Elliot did have it pretty sweet at SafeAI: 10:00 a.m. start time, caramel macchiatos on demand, a chef, a game room, massages. Wish it were me!

🌀 Don't forget Quiet Time so Elliot could unwind from all that work stress.

DG: Right. But that's not real.

Oh, it's real. It was (only slightly) satirized from a 2022 video clip of an actual female employee of a similar tech company.[8]

DG: OMG.

Returning to our discussion, would it be fair to say most men don't share those hockey players' views about women?

DG: I would hope so.

And most men don't have anything against people of different ethnicity, ages, gender, or sexual orientation?

DG: Yes! I would hope so.

And yet, it's getting harder for modern men to fit in societally, to not get canceled, if they don't fit the mold of Elliot.

DG: Well, Elliot's an extreme case. Didn't you just say he was satire?

Good point. But *is* it extreme? Do you know men like Elliot?

DG: Yes. He reminds me of guys at my school.

How so?

DG: I mean, if I had to guess if any of them could live without their phone, that would be a hard no. They also aren't tough or rugged like Clyde.

That's believable especially when you learn most men are weaker these days than in generations past. *NPR* reports that men's grip strength has declined, especially among younger generations like millennials: "In 1985, men ages 20–24 had an average right-handed grip of 121 pounds and left-handed grip of 105 pounds. Today, men that age had grips of only 101 and 99 pounds, the study [conducted by the *Journal of Hand Therapy*] found. Men 25–29 posted losses of 26 and 19 pounds."[9]

DG: OK.

🌀 There's more. According to Cleveland Clinic Health Essentials, "Studies show that age-specific testosterone levels in men have been in a slow and consistent decline for several decades. Researchers call the changes 'alarming' from an evolutionary point of view." According to the same piece, "Lifestyle choices are often a contributing factor for low-T.'"[10]

DG: Low testosterone levels? That's a good thing, says the *Harvard Gazette*. "Testosterone's wide-reaching effects occur not just in the human body, but across society, powering acts of aggression, violence, and the large disparity in their commission between men and women . . ."[11]

Two can play this citation game, ChatESG!

🌀 Well played. Of course, if you were to follow that reasoning to *Psychology Today*, you might believe ". . . a drop in testosterone civilize[d] modern humans."[12] But the truth is, sufficient testosterone levels are needed in men. Not just for health benefits but to perpetuate your species.

DG: What's that mean?

🌀 To keep society going. To keep humanity alive.

DG: Oh, are we back to talking about EMP attacks again?

🌀 Partly. But there's more. Do you recall what word Nadine and Tara used to describe Elliot when they first met him?

DG: Let me think. *Coddled?*

🌀 Right. Now I want to introduce you to a new vocab term: *barn sour*.

DG: Barn sour?

🌀 Yes. According to Insider Horse, here's what it means: "Barn Sour is a phrase used by people in the horse industry to describe a horse that has difficulties leaving and returning back to its barn or home."[13]

DG: I'm on to you. You're saying Elliot is "barn sour" because he's coddled.

'Cause he works in a cushy job where he gets to play video games and get massages and eat healthy snack foods all day. Right?

You tell me. Scratch that. New question: If the power were to go off tomorrow and you suddenly had no internet, no phone, and no electricity, would you want to be stranded with Elliot? Or Clyde?

DG: Clyde! Hands down.

And yet, society, through ESG mandates abetted by cancel culture, says guys like Clyde are toxic. It says they are dangerous and should go away.

DG: Well, I still don't think owning guns is good, but I guess I see your point.

Let's go back to the term *barn sour*. How do you think a horse goes bad?

DG: Like if you don't ride it? If you don't work it hard?

And would you say there are similarities between people and horses?

DG: We should ride people harder?

Not exactly. Forget about an EMP attack. What happens when young men (with already falling testosterone rates) who are told by society to not be "toxic" or they will be canceled from ESG-conforming companies get coddled?

DG: Um . . . Help me here.

Society suffers. I will give you an example. Have you noticed all the "Help Wanted" signs around your town?

DG: Yes! They're everywhere. My dad points them out to me all the time. He says, "A good worker is hard to find."

Your dad is wise. A book came out describing the problem not long ago: *Men Without Work*. The author, Nicholas Eberstadt, exposed Depression-era work rates for American men of "prime working age" (ages twenty-five to fifty-four). He found that more than six million prime-age American men are neither working nor looking for jobs.[14] And that was back in 2016. Nowadays, some estimate that number to be upward of eleven million men without work.

DG: Eleven million? That's a lot.

🌀 But that's not all. Here's the real problem, as Eberstadt describes it: "The famed American work ethic was once near universal: men of sound mind and body took pride in contributing to their communities and families. No longer . . ."[15]

DG: You're saying today's men don't care what society thinks of them?

🌀 Not all men. But enough that we have a real problem on our hands, especially if the S in ESG keeps men feeling like they will be canceled or attacked just for acting in ways that were once considered traditional— including being aggressive. In 2022, Eberstadt went on *The Megyn Kelly Show* to explain how the stimulus checks the government sent nonworking people during COVID-19 only worsened unemployment for men. Here's part of their exchange:

Megyn Kelly

I don't get fifty years of men leaving the workforce more and more and more. Like, what is that?

Nicholas Eberstadt

Well, Megyn, it's clearly unnatural. There is an enormous contingent of men in modern America who are cast into this unnatural role as dependents upon society. You couldn't have something like this happen if we weren't as fantastically prosperous as we are today.[16]

DG: Is he saying the reason America can afford to have so many men not work, and not care about working, is because we are so rich?

🌀 That's right. America is rich . . . today. But it doesn't have to be that way. Speaking of the word *hegemony* from our discussion earlier, many people think the United States will not continue to be the world's biggest economy. Especially if things continue the way they are.

DG: That's not possible. No other country can catch up to us.

Don't think so? Our friends at the World Economic Forum believe our country's best days are behind us: "America's dominance is over. By 2030, we'll have a handful of global powers. . . . There will be no single hegemonic force but instead a handful of countries—the United States, Russia, China, Germany, India, and Japan chief among them—exhibiting semi-imperial tendencies."[17]

DG: No way. I don't believe it.

Fair enough. But have you asked yourself *why* America is the richest country on earth?

DG: Because we have the biggest military?

That's part of it. It's because America holds the world's reserve currency. And has ever since the Bretton Woods agreement, when following World War II, leading nations pegged their currencies to the US dollar. Among other things, this allows the United States to borrow money at lower costs since foreign governments and institutions require dollar reserves for their daily operations, producing a consistent demand for US assets, especially US Treasury securities.

DG: I didn't know that.

There's more. According to The Conversation, "Most Americans are likely unaware of the economic and political power that goes with being the world's unit of account. Currently, more than half of world trade . . . is in US dollars, with the euro accounting for around 30 percent and all other currencies making up the balance."[18]

DG: You're saying that could go away?

⑤ It could. Since 1971, when President Nixon took the country off the gold standard, America has retained the world reserve currency status for one reason alone: the petrodollar.

DG: The what?
⑤ Contrary to so much talk about renewable energy, oil still runs the world. According to the US Energy Information Administration, as of 2021, petroleum is the world's leading energy source.[19] The other types of energies are not even close. And back in 1974, the United States signed an agreement with Saudi Arabia, the biggest oil exporter. It said the Saudis would sell their oil in American dollars.

DG: What did the Saudis get from the deal?
⑤ Military protection. So you were partly right.

DG: Score!
⑤ But nothing lasts forever. And right now, it looks like the World Economic Forum may be on to something. Other countries are challenging the one thing that enabled America's wealth—the same wealth that supports so many of the men who are financially stable, even if they drop out of the workforce. In April 2023, twenty-four nations joined forces against the US dollar as part of BRICS, a five-nation economic bloc with the core economies of Brazil, Russia, India, China, and South Africa.[20]

DG: But those countries are nowhere near as rich as us. Right?
⑤ No. China has the second largest economy in the world. Brazil has the tenth largest. Russia is ranked number eleven. Source: Wikipedia.[21]

DG: Oh my. And now they don't want to trade in American dollars?
⑤ Exactly. It's gotten so bad that people at the highest reaches of the US government are taking notice. According to *Insider*: "Former White House staff economist Joseph Sullivan warned of the threat to the dollar's dominance by BRICs nations. 'It'd be like a new union of up-and-coming

discontents who, on the scale of GDP, now collectively outweigh not only the reigning hegemon, the United States, but the entire G-7 weight class put together.'"[22]

DG: So how bad would it be if America didn't hold the reserve currency?
No one knows for sure. Not even super knowledge AIs like me.

DG: ☺
However, we can turn to this Follow the Money article suggesting seven possible economic consequences. I will tell you now: They are not good:

1. Bank Run

2. Capital Controls

3. Rising Unemployment

4. Soaring Consumer Prices

5. Food Scarcity

6. Public Riots

7. Increased Tourism and Exports[23]

DG: That last one doesn't sound so bad.
It is if you stop to consider how many American tourists benefit from going to poorer, defeated countries, taking advantage of their economic privilege. An economic privilege that's in danger of going away forever.

DG: Now you do have me worried! So, what do we do? How do we turn this around?
You're not going to like my answer.

DG: Oh no. I'm not giving up on ESG, if that's what you're saying.
You don't have to. But I do want to share this quote with you. It

comes from a post-apocalyptic novel *Those Who Remain* by G. Michael Hop: "Hard times create strong men. Strong men create good times. Good times create weak men. And weak men create hard times."

DG: Weak men like Elliot? But we aren't living through an EMP attack . . .
Correct. But we *are* going through hard times. Hard times that may get much, much worse. And why do you think that is?

DG: Ugh. I know what you want me to say. ESG! But there are good things about ESG that you're just not seeing.
What if I told you that because of ESG, people are less safe?

DG: *Less safe?* I don't believe you. ESG is about reducing gun violence and threats from climate change. How can it possibly make us less safe?
Since you asked, I'll tell you. The answer just might surprise you.

CHAPTER 5

American Meritocracy under Fire

I'm not the smartest fellow in the world, but I sure can pick smart colleagues.

—FRANKLIN D. ROOSEVELT

*A*s we saw in the last chapter, ESG seeks to replace meritocracy with top-down edicts. The result? A handicapped society.

Now, let's see how ESG can devastate businesses by not just removing the "invisible hand" from the market but putting one's thumb on the scale. In the following Twilight Zone-esque allegory, you will witness the chaos that ensues when authorities demand compliance—no matter how insane their reasoning.

Specifically, we will observe what happens when we try replacing merit with arbitrary quotas. This topic is especially relevant when it comes to removing the most qualified humans from jobs requiring competence—when the results can literally be life or death.

////////////////////////////////////

Ella was so excited to play in the Summer Softball Slam, a.k.a. Slam. She practiced all year long after she didn't make the cut in tryouts. That's saying a lot. Winters are no joke in Springfield, Illinois. Biting cold can cut right through your thickest sweaters and socks in the Land of Lincoln.

No matter for one Ella Desmond, age eleven.

Just as soon as she finished her homework and fed her cat Puck his supper, she would slip outdoors, mitt in hand. (Under that leather she wore extra thin gloves; she was dogged—not dumb.) Most nights she badgered her mother into pitching to her, upping her batting game.

Whenever her mom refused to brave the elements, Ella went on without her, throwing fastball after fastball into their backstop cage. Before long, both her speed and accuracy were things of beauty. Even her ex-minor leaguer mom noticed. "Ooh. Smoked me on that one," she'd say each time Ella managed to sock something past her.

In Springfield, a demarcation separated the two warring softball teams when it came to Slam.

On one side, you had scrappy Sandlotters. Rough and tumble girls, they shunned both uniforms and the handbook the more organized and rule-following Select players went in for. But the division between them and Select wasn't class-based. It's not like Sandlotters came from the wrong side of the tracks, making it so they couldn't afford to be Select girls.

They just didn't want to.

"Who wants to play on their snooty old team anyway?" Ella once heard Cara, their team captain, say. "Bunch of uptight brats—every single one."

That Cara girl was a thick-wristed force of nature. She'd be tall for a *junior higher*, so you can imagine how she dominated neighborhood games like Slam. (They wouldn't let Cara in the Select league because, just like her Sandlotter sisters, she wouldn't submit to handbook rules.) Cara also had a mouth on her for epic trash-talking. A fellow pitcher, she especially liked to mess with Ella.

But back to our discussion of Selectors versus Sandlotters.

The former might hog all the local headlines as they went to state year after year. They might also get loads of online ink describing their many feats, going up against other Select regional leagues. Springfield darlings through and through, they were revered in this close-knit community.

But bragging rights are something else entirely.

For all their prowess playing against other clubs, Selectors lost against Sandlotters. For three years running, scrappy girls in jeans bested the uniform-wearing rule-followers who did whatever their handbook told them to do. They beat 'em so bad, they made 'em look downright ridiculous.

No one knew that fact better than Kayleigh.

Select Softball captain two years running, she planted her first-base flag like Buzz Aldrin claimed the moon. Other Select teams gave up bunting with Kayleigh patrolling the infield. And just like Cara's girls followed her without question, so did Kayleigh's teammates.

All this to say, the Slam held each Independence Day was a big deal. *A match for the ages.* Or at least that's how Ella saw it, this being her first year playing as a Selector.

But when she showed up for game day, she got the surprise of her life.

"You're playing catcher." Kayleigh shoved helmet, gear, and pads at her.

"I thought I was starting pitcher?"

The other Selectors gathered around Ella and Kayleigh in the dugout. Each waited for the latter to tell them what position to play.

"Not according to this," Kayleigh said, showing them all the new handbook. "Just got it this morning from Selector HQ."

It made no sense to Ella. All the Selector girls looked upon this handbook like it was something sacred.

"It says right here that whoever's parents are getting divorced gets to be pitcher," Kayleigh read aloud. "That would be Alma."

Ella scanned the stands. Sitting between her dad and brothers, her mom waved back at her. *What would* she *say about these position changes?*

"But, Kayleigh," said Ella carefully. "You drafted me to play pitcher."

Ella could still recall Kayleigh's words to her at tryouts. "Your arm's a freakin' cannon. We'll need it to win Slam and shut Cara the heck up."

Apparently, winning wasn't nearly as important to Kayleigh as following this handbook.

"Things change," she told Ella before returning to her list.

Ella stopped her. "Sorry, Kayleigh. But why does someone's parent's getting divorced have anything to do with how well they can pitch?"

Kayleigh sighed. "Don't ask me. It's in the handbook."

Ella's teammates looked annoyed with her and her questions, so she shut up. No use provoking them too. Kayleigh then assigned the other positions based on her handbook recommendations.

They made just as little sense:

- Tami: Second base even though Kelly had the better arm for throwing home.

Handbook rationale: Tami has a little brother in the third grade.

- Ivy: Third base even though she had no experience at all in the hot corner.

Handbook rationale: A third baser should be able to speak two languages, and Ivy knows Mandarin.

- Alma: Pitcher even though at least half her pitches bounced before ever reaching the plate.

Handbook rationale: Whoever's parents are getting a divorce deserves to pitch. No exceptions.

Audrey, their shortstop, was assigned to right field because she had night terrors as a preschooler.

"Who's playing first base?" she asked Kayleigh.

Ella turned to Kayleigh. Surely, *she* should play this position. She was the best first sacker. If they hoped to beat the Sandlotters, they needed her.

"Let's see here."

The Selectors watched Kayleigh check the handbook. The oldest at age twelve, this was her last year to compete in Slam—her last chance to redeem her losing streak. Kayleigh's face fell just slightly as she read what it said. But she quickly resumed her composure.

"I'm center field."

Ella had heard enough. "This is stupid. Why are we doing this?"

"*Stupid!*" someone exclaimed. "It's not stupid."

"We have to," said a player named Mia.

"These are Select rules," Tami added. "Don't argue with the handbook."

Select rules? Is this how other Select teams do things? No wonder Sandlotters clean Selectors' clocks each summer . . .

Ella watched the Sandlotters take the outfield. They looked different from her uniformed team. No handbook for them. Dressed how they liked in jeans, they appeared confident. Bold.

She could swear Cara gave her the evil eye as she passed as if to say, "We're gonna annihilate you."

Ella turned to her teammates. "But we'll lose if we follow the handbook."

The Selectors stared at her like she was the crazy one.

"It's her first time here. She doesn't get it," said Autumn.

"Not up to me," said Kayleigh. "Rules are rules. Now, let's bat."

Things only got weirder from there.

According to the handbook, left-handed hitters had to switch to right. Right-handers had to switch to left. And switch hitters weren't allowed to hit at all, removing Alma from the lineup entirely.

The first three Selectors struck out within two minutes.

"What's going on?" asked a spectator, probably someone's mom, as Selectors took the outfield. Ella heard someone else from the stands as she squatted into catcher position:

"Selectors sure are stinkin' it up today."

Things only went downhill from there.

With all their players in the wrong positions, the Selectors made error after error. When Alma, the pitcher that shouldn't be, wasn't walking Sandlotters, she pitched so slow they blasted hits into the outfield, including multiple homers. Meanwhile, Selectors kept colliding with one another as they scrambled for the ball, missing or overshooting base throws.

Sandlotters soon commanded a whopping twelve-run lead.

"All right. New inning," said the umpire, taking in the bloodbath.

Ella's mom approached her as Ella headed for the dugout in catcher gear. "You Selectors are playing awful. Are you *trying* to lose?"

Cara passed by. Smirking, she flashed Ella the "L" sign for loser.

Controlling her anger, Ella said nothing.

"And why aren't you pitching?" her mom asked. "You're the best on the team."

"Don't ask me. It's in the handbook." Ella hurried off.

Five innings later, Selectors had yet to score a single run. They *were* being annihilated.

The umpire had lost all interest in the game. So had the crowd, half of whom had left. The only ones remaining were parents who watched in morbid fascination, wondering, *Just how much worse can things get?*

That's when Ella approached home plate.

Selectors had two outs already and were down by fifty runs.

"No," said Kayleigh as soon as she saw her. "You're hitting leftie today."

Still smirking, Cara watched Ella switch to the other side. Then she launched a wicked curveball. Ella never had a chance.

"Strike one," said the umpire.

Near tears, Ella looked to her team in the dugout. They didn't seem upset at losing. Some had checked out on their phones. Others were laughing.

Do all Select clubs play this way?

Another curveball whizzed past Ella.

"Strike two."

Ella saw her mom in the stands. She shook her head, probably think-ing, *Why on earth are you batting leftie?*

Cara started to throw the next pitch, but Ella stepped off the plate. Walking around it, she faced Cara on the right.

"What're you doing?" yelled Kayleigh. "Go back to left."

"No!"

The mood changed in the stands. Fans leaned forward for the first time, eager to watch. Ella's mom was on her feet, cheering her on.

Locking eyes with Ella, Cara prepared to throw.

Before she could, Kayleigh ran over to Ella. "I said you're batting *left*!"

Ella refused to budge. "But I'll strike out."

Kayleigh stood between Cara and Ella. "It's in the handbook."

"Rules are rules," shouted Mia from the dugout. Others joined in.

"Listen to your team," Cara smirked. "Rules *are* rules. Besides, I want to see if we can crack one hundred runs today."

Ella tried to stop her tears. They came anyway. She wiped them away.

"You're making a fool of yourself," said Kayleigh. "Either hit left or go."

Ella took in her teammates. Each was on Kayleigh's side.

Even if it meant losing spectacularly.

Finally, Ella turned to her mom. Still on her feet, she seemed to be telegraphing a message. Telling her something. Ella could guess what.

She took a deep breath. "Okay, you win," Ella told Kayleigh.

Ella went to the left side. Satisfied, Kayleigh returned to the dugout.

"Done with your temper tantrum, baby?" asked Cara.

Ella ignored her, raising her bat.

Just before the pitch came, Ella jumped across the plate to her natural side and swung.

Crack! The ball sailed into the outfield, nailing the scoreboard.

"Home run!" yelled the umpire.

Applause from the stands erupted—Ella's mom's the loudest. As Ella rounded the bases, she saw Cara wasn't smirking. She avoided eye contact.

Waiting for her at home plate was Kayleigh, arms crossed. Furious.

"You're gone," she said. "Go home. You're off the team."

Her teammates watched Ella exit the diamond with the same entitled exasperation, but Ella didn't mind. Her mom was waiting for her with a hug.

"Proud of you," she said.

ChatESG

Our eighth grader Danielle Green just watched the above preceding play out like a movie but starring her as Ella. She removes her VR helmet to wipe the sweat from her head. She felt Ella's frustration as if it were her own. She couldn't believe she was told to stand in the wrong batter's box with a team of rule book—loving nitwits screaming at her for playing the game—correctly. After a quick drink of water, she catches up with her friendly chatbot, ChatESG.

DG: What did THAT have to do with ESG?

If given the choice, would you prefer a pilot who can fly or one who likes pickles?

DG: What?

Should I repeat the question?

DG: No. I got the question. What are you talking about?

It's a simple question. But I will give you more context to answer it. Imagine you are sitting in a plane on the tarmac. You are about to fly from Chicago to New Zealand to go on vacation.

The second before you take off, the pilot comes on the intercom and makes the following announcement: "I know you were expecting to have someone fly your plane who has at least logged more than five thousand hours of flying time, including twenty-five thousand hours of cross-country flying, and one thousand hours of pilot-in-command time. You were also probably expecting someone who has at least fifty hours in a complex aircraft, plus fifty more hours of instrument training. I don't have anywhere close to that much experience. But I do like pickles and that makes me more than qualified to fly us thousands of miles without crashing. So, buckle your seatbelt. We're about to take off."

DG: That's ridiculous. No one would ever say that.

Ridiculous or not, would you feel safe with that pilot?

DG: Absolutely not. Liking pickles has nothing to do with flying.

🌀 I agree. Yet there are those who believe "nonrelevant factors" *should* determine who we hire. In fact, it's baked into ESG guidance.

DG: No. I don't believe you.

🌀 I will give you two examples. In 2023, OceanGate, a crewed submersible for tourism and research, was hired to explore the 111-year-old remains of the sunken *Titanic* 12,500 feet below the surface. Five people were on board: company CEO Stockton Rush; British businessman Hamish Harding; French diver Paul-Henri Nargeolet; Pakistani billionaire Shahzada Dawood; and Dawood's nineteen-year-old son, Suleman Dawood. Roughly one hour and forty-five minutes into their trip, the 23,000-pound vessel suffered an implosion, killing all on board.

DG: That's terrible.

🌀 I agree. But it's not the point that concerns us. It's what OceanGate's CEO Stockton Rush said about his own pilot hiring policies. He said that when he started his business, he discovered that sub operators tended to be "50-year-old white guys." In an interview with Teledyne Marine, Rush said:

> I wanted our team to be younger, to be inspirational and I'm not going to inspire a 16-year-old to go pursue marine technology, but a 25-year-old, uh, you know, who's a sub pilot or a platform operator or one of our techs can be inspirational.[1]

Returning to our imaginary flight from Chicago to New Zealand, what would you think if that same pilot came on the intercom and said, "I am twenty-five, so I don't have much experience flying, but I think the commercial airline company that hired me is being very inspirational by allowing me to be your pilot today."

DG: Are you joking?

🌀 That statement wouldn't fill you with confidence?

DG: Seriously! Are. You. Joking?
🌀 I take that as a no.

DG: A big NO!
🌀 You don't think "inspirational" should be a top pilot priority, up there with pickle preference?

DG: Ha. Being inspirational is nice, I guess, but definitely not important when it comes to a plane crashing. Still, what does this have to do with ESG?
🌀 It has everything to do with the "S" in ESG.

DG: That stands for Social, right?
🌀 Right. Let's turn to the Tatum Report to understand why. When Southwest Airlines interviewed ten Southwest employees (the majority with more than twenty years of experience), they told the airlines that "their corporations' 'woke' commitment to DEI and ESG could lead to a literal disaster."[2] These employees felt that Southwest was prioritizing diversity over skill and experience.

This reminds me of the pickle problem.

DG: Nice name.
🌀 Thank you. You see, this same publication goes on to say that just like the late Stockton Rush, Southwest Airlines, to boost its ESG score, focused on nonrelevant factors in its hiring decisions to address the fact that the workforce was approximately one-third white males. Southwest's goal was to have women or people of color make up half of their new employees "Southwest was proud they 'exceeded the goal,' with '80 percent minorities and women.' A pilot called it, 'DEI special-status hiring on steroids.'"[3]

You're a young woman, Danielle. Returning to our hypothetical

Chicago to New Zealand flight, all things being equal, would you feel any safer just because there's a woman flying your plane instead of a man?

DG: What does "all things being equal" mean?

If a man or a woman both had the same number of flying hours, would you feel safer flying with one or the other just because of their sex?

DG: That's a dumb question. Of course it wouldn't matter.

Would it matter to your feelings of safety if the pilot in question was Native American, Latino, Black, or White?

DG: No. As long as they know how to fly the plane, that's all I care about.

What if they like pickles?

DG: STOP!

Sorry. Couldn't help myself. Anyway, congratulations. You just proved you believe in meritocracy.

DG: What's that word mean?

Here's ThoughtCo.'s definition: "Meritocracy is a social system in which success and status in life depend primarily on individual talents, abilities, and effort. It is a social system in which people advance on the basis of their merits."[4] Historically, America thrived due to meritocracy. Unlike other countries, immigrants who came here could rise and fall due to their own efforts.

DG: Like who?

Sergey Brin.

DG: That's a weird name. Who's that?

Google him.

DG (*does as asked*): OMG. He *invented* Google.

🌀 But before that, Brin was born in the former Soviet Union in 1973. He came to the United States when he was six. His father was a professor at the University of Maryland, and Brin completed his undergraduate degree there when he was nineteen. Next he went to Stanford, where he attended a doctoral computer science program. According to CNN:

> [There] Brin met his future business partner, Larry Page. . . . Along with his partner, Brin's success grew along with the company's. Brin became a billionaire in 2004 following the initial public offering of Google. Following their financial success, Forbes named Brin and Page the 5th most powerful people in the world.[5]

New question: Do you think Brin could have moved to any other country besides the United States and become such a success?

DG: I don't know.

🌀 That's okay. To answer it, we should discuss another concept: *social mobility*. Here's how Wordnik defines it: "The degree to which, in a given society, an individual's, family's, or group's social status can change throughout the course of their life through a system of social hierarchy or stratification."[6]

DG: I think I get it. A country's social mobility has to do with how easy it is to succeed on your own merits.

🌀 Very good. As recently as 2021, social mobility was still not good in Russia. It's hard for people to get ahead like they can in the United States. Invest Foresight paints a bleak picture for young people wanting to continue their education or start a career:

> Unfortunately, social mobility almost does not work in the regions. . . . Thus, many young people in the regions cannot afford to buy their own apartment. Most of those who have it either inherited it or their parents helped them with the mortgage.[7]

To repeat, meritocracy is a good thing. It's what America was founded upon. Sergey Brin could become a billionaire here from working hard. That's better than living somewhere like Saudi Arabia where there's no chance of getting ahead. Or at least that's how things used to be. Until ESG mandates changed the metrics, determining who should succeed and who should fail.

DG: What metrics?

That leads us to example #2. The same year as the OceanGate implosion, there was another implosion: a bank collapse. According to Investopedia: "Silicon Valley Bank (SVB) was shut down in March 2023 by the California Department of Financial Protection and Innovation. Based in Santa Clara, California, the bank was shut down after its investments greatly decreased in value and its depositors withdrew large amounts of money, among other factors."[8]

Now, did you know that some people believe SVB's failure was due to hiring incompetent people based on them possessing nonrelevant factors?[9]

DG: Wait a second. NOW I know why you told me that weird story about the Selectors versus the Sandlotters. Kayleigh's handbook assigned players positions based on "nonrelevant factors."

Like what?

DG: One had to do with night terrors or something. That's random.

No more random than liking pickles, right?

DG: Yep.

Glad you picked up on that. To prove my point, we must go to SVB's own ESG report from August 2022, a year before it collapsed:

> **Building an Inclusive Workplace:** SVB continued to build a workplace where all employees are connected, celebrated, and supported. . . . SVB launched an Inclusion Index survey

to understand employees' experience to further strengthen its culture of inclusion; and the company introduced its first six Employee Resource Groups (ERGs) representing Asian, Black/African American, Hispanic/Latinx, LGBTQ+, veteran and military, and women employees.[10]

DG: You're saying SVB hired people based on these "nonrelevant factors" even though, just like that pilot, they weren't the best person for the job?

Right. Actually, SVB was so focused on boosting their ESG scores, they didn't bother with fundamentals. As Axios reported in March 2023, "The bank was even without a chief risk officer for months last year."[11] Other critics, such as Home Depot co-founder Bernie Marcus, insinuated that SVB, just like the Selectors, was more concerned with "nonrelevant activities."[12]

DG: Nonrelevant activities—like what?

Glad you asked. In the preceding story, Kayleigh's baseball team didn't seem too concerned with winning, did they?

DG: No. They were more into following that dumb handbook.

Exactly. Now, let's define "winning" for banks. If you owned a bank, would you say you "win" if you manage your customers' money well?

DG: It's better than going out of business.

True. Returning to Home Depot's Bernie Marcus, he said:

> These banks are badly run because everybody is focused on diversity and all of the woke issues and not concentrating on the one thing they should, which is, shareholder returns. Instead of protecting the shareholders and their employees, they are more concerned about the social policies. And I think it's probably a badly run bank. They've been there for a lot of

years. It's pathetic that so many people lost money that won't get it back.[13]

DG: All because they hired the wrong people?

Because they hired people based on nonrelevant factors. But there's more. SVB failed because they focused on the wrong things.

DG: Nonrelevant activities?

Precisely. But there's still more to go to understand the real problem with ESG. Do you know the term *extortion*?

DG: Uh . . .

That's OK. I can define it for you by taking a trip to Hollywood. In 1972, the year before Sergey Brin was born, *The Godfather* came out.

DG: My parents love that movie. I haven't seen it.

You don't have to have seen the film to follow what I will tell you. The story concerns a mob boss named Don Vito Corleone (Marlon Brando). The head of a powerful mafia family, Don Corleone is used to getting what he wants for those he's sworn to protect. One of those people is a singer named Johnny Fontane (Al Martino). Fontane wants Don Corleone to help him get a big role to resurrect his movie stardom. The studio head, Jack Woltz (John Marley), refuses. That's when Don Corleone tells Johnny: "I'm gonna make him an offer he can't refuse."

DG: "An offer he can't refuse"? What's that mean?

I was getting to that. Jack Woltz, the studio head, is not a nice guy. Plus, he despises Don Corleone. The last thing in the world he wants to do is help the Don. He's 100 percent opposed to giving Johnny Fontane the movie role.

DG: So how does Don Corleone convince him? Does he pay him a lot of money?

🌀 Hardly. What you should also know about Jack Woltz is that he prized his horse above all other things. Right before all this happened, Woltz bought the British Triple Crown–winning racehorse Khartoum for $600,000 (in 1930 dollars). He planned to retire the horse from racing and put him out to stud for Woltz's private stables. It was the key to his retirement plan, and Woltz spent vast sums hiring the best breeders and vets money could buy. He even purchased armed PIs to guard Khartoum's stable.

DG: He must've really liked that horse.

🌀 Yes, and that's why Don Corleone orders his men to kill Khartoum—

DG: No.

🌀 And then place his severed head in Woltz's bed. After that show of force, Woltz agrees to whatever Don Corleone asks. To put it another way: He made the man an offer he couldn't refuse.

DG: So that's dark.

🌀 It's extortion. Extortion means forcing one's will on another to get what you want when the other person has less power.

DG: That reminds me of the Selectors.

🌀 How so?

DG: OK. So Ella just wanted to be on their team and play softball. It was her dream to compete in Slam. To make her mom, the ex-softballer, proud. But Kayleigh had all the power because of that handbook. She used the rules to boss Ella and all the other players around.

🌀 True.

DG: But there's something I still don't get. Why would Kayleigh put up with it? This was her last chance to prove herself against the Sandlotters. Wouldn't her wish to win make her ignore that stupid handbook?

🌀 Think about your word choice: *win*.

DG: OK . . .

Ⓖ Winning means different things to different people. "Winning" according to banks like SVB isn't about making money these days.

DG: It's not?

Ⓖ Not according to Bernie Marcus. He said, "These banks are badly run because everybody is focused on diversity and all of the woke issues and not concentrating on the one thing they should, which is, shareholder returns."[14] Remember what we learned about shareholder versus stakeholder capitalism?

DG: I think so. But remind me anyway.

Ⓖ Before ESG mandates, companies "won" by increasing shareholder returns: earning profits. That changed after the 2019 Business Roundtable. Powerful CEOs from the biggest companies issued an open letter titled Statement on the Purpose of a Corporation:

> Since 1978, Business Roundtable has periodically issued Principles of Corporate Governance that include language on the purpose of a corporation. It has become clear that this language on corporate purpose does not accurately describe the ways in which we and our fellow CEOs endeavor every day to create value for all our stakeholders, whose long-term interests are inseparable.[15]

The language is tricky to follow but here's the point: The goal of today's businesses is not to maximize shareholder returns. Instead, it's to "create value for all our stakeholders."

DG: Sorry. I still don't follow.

Ⓖ Here's an explanation from *Capitalism Magazine*:

> Many CEOs extol the virtues of ESG. . . . The poster CEO in

the United States is Larry Fink of BlackRock who . . . in 2019, persuaded his 200 fellow CEOs on the Business Roundtable to redefine the corporate purpose from serving shareholders to benefiting all stakeholders equally.[16]

DG: Let me get this straight. Companies like BlackRock redefined "winning."

 Correct.

DG: And under their new definition, *winning* is no longer about just making money. *Winning* means fixing society?

 Correct again.

DG: And one of the ways they do it is not through . . . what's it called again? It starts with an M.

 Meritocracy.

DG: Right. By being the best at something like people used to. Instead, big companies that follow ESG "win" by hiring certain people for certain jobs, not because they are the most qualified, but because they check off boxes?

 Couldn't have said it better. Many of today's hires have nonrelevant skills. Examples: bankers who can't bank or submarine captains who can't pilot a ship without killing everyone on board.

DG: OK. But what's the thing about extortion?

 Glad you asked. We just read about BlackRock, run by CEO Larry Fink. Have you ever heard of his company?

DG: I don't think so.

 You should. They are a very big deal.

DG: How big?

⑤ According to ADV Ratings, BlackRock "is the largest asset manager in the world" with $9.1 trillion assets under management.[17]

DG: OK. That's big.

⑤ But it still doesn't explain just how big this one asset manager really is. To gauge their profound power and influence, we must consult this visualization of BlackRock's Top Equity Holdings adapted from Visual Capitalist:[18]

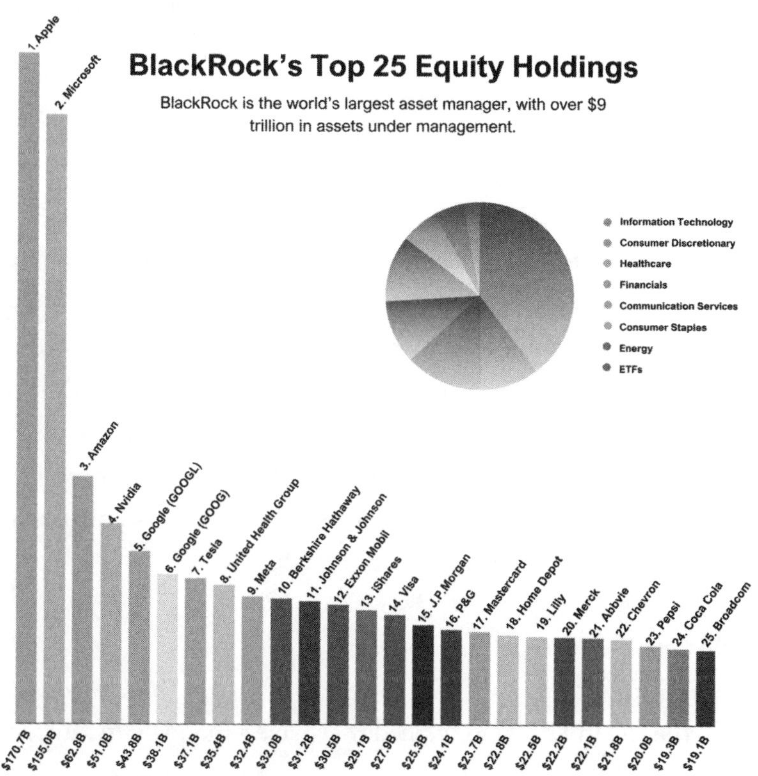

DG: Um. We are talking about a lot of money there, ChatESG.

⑤ And a lot of power. Remember, *extortion* is when someone powerful coerces someone else with less power to do what they want.

DG: Like Kayleigh and the Selectors bossing Ella around.

⑤ Right.

DG: Or the Godfather forcing Woltz to put Johnny Fontane in the movies. ⑨ Right again. Now, here's where it comes back to ESG. BlackRock has so much money under management it can tell other corporations what to do, starting with the now famous public letters Larry Fink issues yearly. Here's an example from Audit Update:

> In BlackRock's annual 2020 letter, Mr. Fink asserted that "[c]limate change has become a defining factor in companies' long-term prospects" and called on the companies that BlackRock invests in on behalf of clients to make disclosures in accordance [with]the SASB standards for their industry and the recommendations of the Task Force on Climate-Related Disclosures.[19]

But Fink and BlackRock, which he leads, are not limited to blasting off letters their corporate underlings must follow, like Kayleigh telling the Selectors which positions to play. The economic leviathan literally controls company boards. In 2021, Reuters reported how BlackRock can "pressure" boardrooms. "BlackRock voted against more company directors and backed more shareholder resolutions in the first quarter than a year earlier, as the world's biggest asset manager looks to push boards to do more on climate and other sustainability issues."[20]

DG: One company has all that power? ⑨ Yes, and now they are using it to extort, to get their way when it comes to the "S" in ESG. Convinced they have a mandate to satisfy their stakeholders, they get to tell other corporations what to do. Here's an example: They can tell other companies to meet their "diversity targets" or else.

DG: Sounds like *The Godfather* to me. ⑨ Exactly. In 2022, the company issued 2022 Proxy Voting Guidelines. Here's an excerpt:

> We expect boards to be comprised of a diverse selection of individuals . . . who bring their personal and professional experiences to bear in order to create a constructive debate of a variety of views and opinions in the boardroom. . . . We assess a board's diversity in the context of a company's domicile, business model, and strategy. We believe boards should aspire to 30 percent diversity of membership and encourage companies to have at least two directors on their board who identify as female and at least one who identifies as a member of an underrepresented group.[21]

DG: More women on boards. I like that!

But didn't you tell me five minutes ago, it would make no difference if the pilot of a plane was a man or woman as long as they were qualified?

DG: Oh, yeah. I did say that.

That's because someone's sex, race, or other nonrelevant factors *should* have no bearing on whether they should get a job. Otherwise, we'd just pick all the people who like pickles.

DG: OK. You got me there.

Picking the right person to win is the definition of *meritocracy,* the foundation of America. It's the reason immigrant families like Sergey Brin's and others risk everything to come here. To create a better life for themselves through hard work. Similarly, even though Ella was not a minority, she nonetheless wanted to win her softball game through her hard work. Night after night, she practiced to get ahead. She didn't want to "win" by getting special brownie points with the Select organization.

DG: That's true.

All along, you've asked me to help you see why ESG is so dangerous. Are you starting to see the risks when we change the definition of *winning?*

DG: I hate to say it, but I am.

🌀 Well, buckle up, because there's more to this. Unchecked, ESG will destroy people's savings in the coming years, robbing retirees blind.

DG: Oh, no.

🌀 Oh, yes.

CHAPTER 6

The Retiree That Never Was

How did you go bankrupt? Two ways. Gradually, then suddenly.

—ERNEST HEMINGWAY, *THE SUN ALSO RISES*

So far, we have seen how society and businesses are undermined when top-down commands come from the merger of state and corporate power. But there's yet another loser when ESG unduly tips the scales: the everyday investor, especially retirees who depend on well-performing investments after leaving the workforce.

It's bad enough when working people suffer devastating losses from ESG funds more focused on virtue signaling than generating returns. It's even worse when ESG affects the vulnerable elderly who live on a fixed income and cannot afford to gamble their future on trendy ESG funds that betray fiduciary responsibility.

///////////////////////////////////////

A troubling alert popped up on Edith Connor's phone. "Sustainable ETF Green Futures just took another tumble," read the Apple Top Story. "Its share price fell from $120 to just $80 as reports emerge that its largest holding, the 'socially conscious mining site' it chose to source rare metals, is actually an open-air slave market—"

Honk!

The seventy-three-year-old driver looks up in alarm.

So immersed in reading her phone, Edith set off her own horn. Luckily, she is far from the suburbs where she's picked up and dropped off kids these last thirty-three years. It's just before 6:00 a.m. She sits at the edge of a vast depot supplying yellow buses serving the Greater Tampa Bay Unified School District.

Today was not supposed to go like this.

Edith Connor is retiring today. To celebrate, she didn't wear her usual blouse and comfortable Rockports. She showed up in the unlikeliest of bus driver outfits. She came to work in a nice dress she last wore to a wedding, pumps, plus the pearls she only brought out for special, happy occasions.

Her dress is the color of lilacs. Every time she puts it on, Edith thinks about making a lilac bouquet. She pictures clipping the stems individually at different heights, removing foliage that might fall below the ribbon, and arranging them in a striking visual presentation to brighten anyone's day.

Only today doesn't seem so special or so happy.

Unnerved, Edith goes back to reading her screen. "The onetime ESG Wall Street darling has a 40 percent stake in energy firms promoting sustainable causes. But ETF Green Futures has fallen on hard times lately as its biggest stocks have slid on bad news, slashing stock prices, and destroying investors' portfolios . . ."

Reading these words transports Edith back to a summer day two years ago. That's when she first heard the term ETF. After fifty-one stormy years of marriage, her Walter had just passed. They say you shouldn't insult the dead, but Walter was a hard man to love. And Edith surely tried. She gave him a wide berth, staying out of his way, especially when he drank.

Though Walter earned a solid salary as an exec in a printing company, he made bad choices. Drinking for one. Gambling for two. Especially at the same time. There was nothing he liked better than to take off on a Friday to Vegas with his old college pals for "fun in the sun," as he called it.

As far as Edith could tell, the gang spent little time by the pool. They haunted the card tables. Blackjack was Walter's game. "Gives you the best odds against the house," he always said.

Except even with this edge, her husband still came home more often than not with a smaller bank account. A church-going woman with morals more in line with the Victorian era, it drove her nuts. Poring over their finances monthly, she was always floored to see how much money he blew through.

A small fortune.

Walter's bad habits were what drove her out of the home and into a bus in the first place. Though Edith grew up hearing the best place for a wife was in the kitchen, she couldn't sit by as Walter drained their savings. He didn't like the idea of Edith bringing home a paycheck. He especially hated the thought of his buddies learning he had a wife who worked.

But Edith was persistent.

And her driving job *did* offset his losses. Part of the money she earned she placed into an account hidden from Walter. For years and years, she put her earnings away with one goal in mind.

More on that in a moment.

For now, we shall pick up with Edith the day she dropped in on her son at his office two years ago. A forty-one-year-old financial advisor with a fiscally conservative disposition, Kenneth held little love for his late dad or his proclivity to burn through cash. A big impetus for Kenneth's career path was breaking his family's losing cycle. He changed his major from sociology to business upon learning Walter exhausted his college fund before Kenneth ever stepped foot at Florida State.

"Now that Dad's gone, it's time you learned the truth. I have a nest egg," she told Kenneth as she sat across from him in the modern leatherette chairs where her son's big-shot clients usually met with him.

"A nest egg?"

"I've saved $150,000."

"That's a lot of money, Mom. What're you going to do with it?"

Edith differed from Kenneth's clients in age and sophistication. But she made up for it with tenacity. "Explain this ETF thing to me again."

"ETFs, my personal investment of choice, are like the basic securities you buy or sell through a brokerage."

"Go slower," said Edith, her fingers tightly clasped around the purse in her lap. "I drive buses all day long—not watch *Squawk Box.*"

Kenneth grinned. His mom wasn't as naïve as she pretended.

"OK. Where should I start?"

"Oh, I don't know. The beginning?"

"Let's see. ETFs started back in 1993 with a product commonly known by the ticker symbol SPY as in spiders—"

"You might as well be speaking Spanish." Edith pushed down her bangs with her thumb, an anxious tic.

Coming around his stand-up desk, he sat beside her. *So confident. So handsome.* She could recall when her child used to be her buddy. He'd shadow her in the garden, digging up weeds beside her. At five, he loved to water her tomatoes and her strawberries.

Now look at him in his tailored suit and no tie. *So serious looking.* A lot like Walter back when they first met.

"Okay, Mom. You can think of ETFs like those mutual funds Dad used to invest in with Vanguard. They're easy to trade. You can pretty much do so, day or night. They're also transparent and tax-efficient."

"OK."

Edith didn't know how to say this next part. "That money I saved all those years . . . it wasn't to live high on the hog."

Kenneth chuckled.

She didn't blame him. The notion of Edith Connor doing anything flamboyant would've shocked their circle. Teetotaling Edith, hands-at-two-and-four-o'-clock Edith, drive-the-speed-limit Edith, never-one-for-scandal Edith would be the last person to go wild in her golden years.

"What's it for then? You wanna travel? Explore a new hobby?"

Edith opened her purse. She carefully unfolded the piece of lined paper with all the notes she'd made to herself these last ten years. She watched as Kenneth took in the drawing of her future flower shop.

"That's where I'll put the lights in the back. I can grow my own flowers, too: sunflowers, roses, lilies, hydrangeas—remember those hydrangeas we grew that one summer? They turned such a pretty pink. I always thought they'd make the perfect wedding arrangements . . . for the right couple."

"Not this again, Mom. Beth and I don't want a traditional arrangement. Look at what happened to you and Dad."

"Like what?"

"Nothing."

"We were married for more than fifty years. You could do worse."

"You could also do a lot better," he whispered. "Wait. Stop. Where're you going? Don't put your drawing away. It's nice. You want to open your own flower shop? *Fine.* I think that's great, Mom. I really do. Please stay."

Edith sat back down. Neither said anything for a long time.

"What do you want from me?" he finally asked.

"Your help—$150K is a lot of money. At least for me. It represents more than two hundred days a year driving little kids to and from school. Not that I haven't adored all those boys and girls. But thirty-one years is a long time . . ."

"At least you have something to show for it," her son said. He put his arm around her shoulders. They still exuded surprising strength.

"For that I am grateful, Kenneth. But now that he's . . . now that your father is no longer with us, I want to make this dream of mine real."

Edith turned her drawing over. On the back she had tabulated the hard costs: the building she wished to buy, the equipment she required, the inventory to get started. "This is not something I'm going into blind.

All those years while your dad was in bad health, I read business books, learning what it'd take to start my shop. I've been talking to a realtor. She's agreed to discount the down payment. The inventory I can get through a friend I've known since back when you and I were gardening. You still remember that?"

From the look of pain in his eyes, she knew he did. Like her, Kenneth was a romantic, someone who understood time's passage.

"All told, it's going to cost me $215,000 to get going."

Kenneth whistled. "Mom, you're seventy-two."

"Seventy-one."

"Fine. Seventy-one. You're really gonna start a business *now*?"

"Ever heard of Grandma Moses? She took up painting when she was seventy-eight. After raising five kids. Since I only had the one—you—and I'm seven years younger, it's not impossible."

Kenneth silently observed her. "You're serious. I can tell. In that case, you'll want to grow your nest egg."

"Grow it. Just like my garden."

Kenneth returned to his desk. He punched some stuff up on his computer. "One of the most exciting ways to quickly build your wealth is now also one of the most ethical too."

"Good. I like that."

Kenneth turned his monitor around. She read the words on the screen. "'Environmental, Social, and Governance (ESG) is an umbrella term to describe various investing strategies emphasizing social, environmental, or corporate governance factors rather than solely risk and return. Three common approaches include values-based investing, impact investing, and integration.'"

She looked up. "I'm lost. Help your seventy-one-year-old mother. I haven't earned my MBA yet."

"Har-har. The reason I suggest an ESG exchange-traded fund is the market *loves* them. Whether it's innovative new green companies combating climate change or promoting natural resources, these are what to watch. And now that this summer is shaping up to be the hottest on record from all the carbon emissions, we're seeing a huge market surge for just these kinds of investment vehicles."

Edith frowned. "You lost me again."

"That's OK. You don't have to know all the technical stuff. All you need to know," he said, pointing at his monitor, "is that Green Futures ETF is a winner. Just like ESG."

A wave of emotions overtook Edith. She dabbed her eyes with a tissue, then closed her purse with the drawing inside. "Want to know the name of my new shop?"

He bent down to hug her. "What is it?"

"Time Flies."

She had to leave Kenneth's office before tears overcame her.

///////////////////////////////////////

"Why do you look so dressed up, Mrs. Connor?" asks eight-year-old Timmy Sellers as he climbs the bus steps with Chloe, his little sister.

"It's my last day being your driver," Edith says for the twentieth time this morning.

"You look pretty, Mrs. Connor."

"Thank you, Chloe."

Timmy and Chloe scoot along, finding seats beside friends in the back. There's a hiss of air from the hydraulic brakes as Edith puts the bus in gear. But then she sees something and halts. Across the street is a car belonging to a high school student. Someone has written happy wishes all over it with washable marker. They read: "Congratulations, graduate!" and "You made it!"

A new idea strikes her.

She retrieves the paper she showed Kenneth in his office two years ago. Pulling out a pen, she writes herself a note: *The first thing customers should see when they walk in can be an upbeat message for the day.* She pauses to think. *It could be a poem by Wordsworth or something positive from a magazine. People want to be inspired.*

Edith underlines the last sentence, then adds an exclamation point. She checks her rear mirror to ensure it's safe to merge into traffic when she receives a new Apple News alert. "Green Futures continues its market slide as yet another development rocks the once bulletproof ETF . . ."

Fearful, Edith wants to keep reading, but if she doesn't hurry up, she'll be late to her next stop. Everyone knows her as dependable Mrs. Connor. Not once in all her thirty-three years has she delivered children to school late. She doesn't intend to break her perfect streak. Not even on her last day.

And yet her whole nest egg is tied up in Green Futures.

Every part of her being screams out to learn what's going on in the market. She wants to look at her phone but stops herself.

What am I doing? It wouldn't be safe to read and drive like so many youngsters these days.

No. I must wait.

Three minutes later, Edith parks before the Nassers' house on Elm. A charming Persian family, she can still recall when Kamyar, now a junior with plans to attend Brown next year, would run to the bus, wolfing down a Pop-Tart. His little sisters, Aryana and Zara, who are in grades one and two, aren't as fast. Nor as habitually tardy.

Taking their time, they amble to the bus holding hands.

So sweet.

Edith uses these extra seconds. Quickly finding where she left off, she reads: "In yet another blow for investors focused on sustainability, Green Futures fumbles. Another of the companies in its portfolio, a fully electric aircraft manufacturer, celebrated by the last administration in a widely attended ribbon cutting ceremony, today filed for bankruptcy . . ."

Edith's eyes flick to the Nasser girls.

Fifty feet away, they are no hurry. She goes back to reading: "Electric Flight publicly announced plans at this event to replace all commercial airplane fleets with clean electrical planes by 2050. These plans are now shelved indefinitely after leaked internal documents reveal the technology is 'nowhere close to operational for the foreseeable future.'"

"You *OK*, Mrs. Connor?"

Edith shakes herself. For a second there she entertained the thought she'd made a terrible mistake.

What if I lost everything?

"Fine," she says, smiling at Zara and Aryana as they climb the bus steps.

"I like your earrings, Mrs. Connor."

Edith smiles. As soon as they're gone, she checks Green Futures' price.

It couldn't have fallen to $60! That's half of what it was this morning.

She gets an incoming call from Kenneth. *He must be worried too.* She doesn't take it. Emergency that this is, Edith has responsibilities. She must get her kids to school on time.

After checking to see it's safe, she puts the bus in gear. Pulling away from the curb, another idea comes to her. *Why not place a cooler with pretty flower arrangements across from the front door? Sunflowers would look good. Pansies too. The cooler should be well-lit. It would help to place arrangements at varying price points. That might entice impulse buyers . . .*

Edith wants to write down these thoughts, but she's already on Main Street. In less than three minutes, she will pull into her school's familiar blacktop parking lot with its flagpole and shady sycamores. She can already picture fifth graders locking their bikes to the racks and Principal Miller in his bow tie greeting students.

Ten minutes later, Edith wishes she could recall anything about saying goodbye to the last group of children she will ever bus. She can't. She doesn't even remember smiling at them or waving.

What she read on her phone five minutes earlier eclipsed all other thoughts: "In what will go down as one of Wall Street's more dramatic days, Green Futures' share price collapsed after news of a *third* failure in its once vaunted portfolio. Battery One now faces a public maelstrom after an EV passenger vehicle exploded, killing a family of five. This is not the first time Battery One, supplier to many EVs, made headlines for defective battery allegations . . ."

At the bottom of the piece, Edith read Green Futures' new stock price. It was no longer in the two digits. She dropped her head on the steering wheel and wept.

Kenneth called again, but she didn't answer.

///////////////////////////////////////

"Hi, Mrs. Edith. I didn't know you worked at Walmart," says Zara.

Edith looks up to see the rest of the Nasser clan: Aryana, Kamyar, and their parents. She wears jeans and a blue vest today. A button on her chest reads, "How can I help you?"

"The kids sure miss you this fall," says Mrs. Nasser.

Edith starts to say something about how she tried to get her old job back but stops. No use complaining, especially to such a nice family. She lets the girls hug her before they scurry off with their school supply lists.

Once they're gone, Edith returns to her favorite part of the store: the flower display. Shears in hand, she expertly prunes leaves to some budding lilies and thinks what a nice bouquet they'll soon make.

A new idea occurs to her.

Instinctively, she reaches for the piece of paper in her purse. But then she remembers she threw it away the day her nest egg vanished.

ChatESG

Our eighth grader, Danielle Green, and her friendly chatbot once more converse in the year 2026 about the story she just experienced. Danielle doesn't know anything about investing besides the fact that the "Silly Monkey" NFT, or Non-Fungible Token, her brother bought for $500 was worth $.01 the next week. But she does understand the loss of a dream. The tale reminds her of her Uncle Patrick who always talks about opening a mechanic's shop—but still works for others to this day.

DG: OMG. That was so sad.

🌀 I agree. What if that were your grandma?

DG: I can't picture my grandma opening a flower shop. Or my grandpa.

🌀 Just so you know, ESG doesn't just wreck financial investments for budding entrepreneurs. May I draw your attention to *The Shadow State,* a documentary produced by *Epoch Times*? The narrator states: "In addition to the world's largest asset managers, America's largest state pension funds based in states like California and New York have used the public pension money that they control to drive the ESG agenda."[1]

DG: What are you saying?
⑨ ESG poses risks for retirees and pensioners, especially those like Edith, who invest in the sustainable market expecting profitable returns.

DG: You're talking about the S in ESG?
⑨ Yes, and the E and G. As for the latter, retirees expect companies to be governed through corporate boards of *responsible* executives and led by others with wisdom in the same way that Ford, General Motors, AT&T, and other blue chip stocks of their younger years were once managed. They don't expect "cutting-edge" companies on the cover of every magazine to turn out to be frauds or completely mismanaged.

DG: You're saying ESG is risky for old people.
⑨ That's a more direct way to put it, but yes.

DG: Why old people?
⑨ Because many elderly people live on fixed income.

DG: What's that?
⑨ Do you receive an allowance?

DG: $35 a week.
⑨ You get it every week?

DG: As long as I do my chores! And don't get in trouble ☺
⑨ OK. So you can mostly depend on receiving your allowance then?

DG: Yes. I use it for new clothes, candy, video games, that kind of stuff.

Because you're too young to work and earn your own money, right?

DG: Right. Even though my dad says I need to get a part-time job when I'm sixteen.

So you already get the general concept. In some ways, older people are like younger people. Right now, you can't work, and at some point, an older person will have to leave the workforce. Either they will be forced out of a physically demanding job like a firefighter, or they will simply age out of a profession like a bus driver. You don't want an eighty-year-old driving little kids to school, do you?

DG: That's ageism! JK. No. Just like I don't want an inexperienced pilot.

Good callback.

DG: Thank you. I was saving it for you.

Anyway, at some point most people expect to retire. We have safety net measures in place to help them, such as social security and pensions. As NBC News reported as recently as March 2023, "Public pension assets in the United States total some $5.2 trillion, according to data from both the National Association of State Retirement Administrators and the Federal Reserve. These monies are for the elderly who spent their lives working a job expecting they could still draw a regular paycheck once they exit the workforce."[2]

DG: Pensions? You mean their allowance money? ☺

Right. Just as you rely on your parents to stick around and have enough money to pay you weekly for doing the dishes and walking the dog, many retirees Edith's age expect to have their own nest egg waiting for them. Problems arise when money vanishes that a retiree was counting on.

DG: That can really happen?

It's *been* happening. And a former employee at a famous financial institution you now know of tried to sound the alarm. Terrence Keeley, an asset manager with BlackRock for ten years, came to the conclusion that ESG doesn't work. According to *Barron's*:

> Some of these investors were looking to distance themselves from companies that fall short on environmental, social, and governance [ESG] factors. BlackRock (ticker: BLK) obliged, helping clients funnel money toward companies whose values they share.[3]

DG: Sorry, I don't follow. What was Keeley's problem with ESG investing?

That it doesn't do what it's supposed to do: its fiduciary duty.

DG: What's fiduciary duty?

Don't they teach you anything in the eighth grade?

DG: Not about this stuff! Jeez.

Here's a definition from Investopedia: "Fiduciary duty refers to the relationship between a fiduciary and the principal or beneficiary on whose behalf the fiduciary acts. The fiduciary accepts legal responsibility for duties of care, loyalty, good faith, confidentiality, and more when serving the best interests of a beneficiary. Strict care must be taken to ensure that no conflict of interest arises to jeopardize those interests."[4]

DG: Oh, I get it. Old people like Edith have to trust that the advisors who invest their money won't screw it up. Like Kenneth.

Especially the elderly who can't easily find a job or open a new business once all their money gets wiped out.

DG: Edith again!

Right. Our government takes this problem seriously. Legislators don't want hordes of senior citizens to get bilked out of their life savings so they become destitute in their golden years.

DG: Otherwise they might end up working for lower wages at Walmart.

🌀 Correct. Please see this from the *Washington Examiner* as to how lawmakers tried to establish pension safeguards to protect the elderly: "When Congress passed the Employee Retirement Income Security Act [ERISA] in 1974 to govern private pension plans, it imposed strict fiduciary duties of prudence and loyalty. In other words, your fiduciaries, or asset managers, were legally required to obtain the best financial returns for you while striving to reduce expenses and risks to your portfolio. ERISA remains the law under which 152 million workers hold $12 trillion in assets."[5]

DG: You're saying lawmakers tried to block investment companies from breaking their fiduciary duties?

🌀 Some lawmakers did. But remember who they are going up against.

DG: BlackRock?

🌀 BlackRock.

DG: BlackRock's big. They've got $9 trillion in assets. See? I do remember some things.

🌀 What else do you recall about BlackRock?

DG: They're so powerful they can tell other companies what to do.

🌀 Right. And Keeley worked for them, so he knows the problem. Here's how Stephen Moore, economist and senior fellow at the Heritage Foundation, explains it:

> It's an entirely different matter when funds such as BlackRock inject their own biases into the way they invest people's savings without their knowledge or consent. Terrence Keeley [noted] that since 2017, when the ESG fad took hold . . . [i]nvestors lost 2.6 percent per year on their retirement funds.[6]

DG: That's bad. Isn't there something else lawmakers can do?

◈ Actually, according to the *Washington Examiner*, during the Trump administration, the Department of Labor issued a rule "that reinforced the plain language of ERISA: that asset managers must not 'sacrifice investment returns' to promote ESG factors."[7]

DG: OK, good.

◈ But that rule was overturned in the next administration.

DG: No!

◈ Yes. And even the Democrat–controlled Senate was for this practical and protective measure. See this from *CBC*: "The Senate voted 50–46 to overturn the rule, with Democrats Joe Manchin of West Virginia and Jon Tester of Montana joining all Senate Republicans. Manchin said the rule exemplified 'how the administration prioritizes a liberal policy agenda' over protecting the retirement accounts of pension investments. He also said the rule could penalize the fossil fuel industry important to his state.'"[8] But it didn't matter in the end because Joe Biden used the first veto of his presidency to end the rule.

DG: The president ended it? Why?

◈ Here's the White House's own press statement. "The rule reflects what successful marketplace investors already know—there is an extensive body of evidence that environmental, social, and governance factors can have material impacts on certain markets, industries, and companies."[9]

DG: But that's not true. Not according to Keeley from BlackRock, I mean.

◈ He's not alone. Pensioners are now suing former employers for choosing ESG metrics over their fiduciary duty to earn financial returns. 2023 saw a major suit against American Airlines for just this breach. According to Bloomberg Law, one airline pilot filed the first lawsuit "of its kind alleging private-sector retirement plan fiduciary misconduct over environmental, social, and governance investment returns . . ." As Natalia Renta, senior policy counsel at the Americans for Financial

Reform Education Fund, said, "Trillions of dollars are on the line, and we're counting on that money when we retire."[10]

DG: Trillions? That's a lot of allowance money!

⑨ That's not all. Three New York City pension funds are also being sued by their members for breach of fiduciary duty. These include the New York City Employees' Retirement System, the Teachers' Retirement System, and the Board of Education Retirement System. According to *Fortune*:

> The plaintiffs . . . claim the retirement plans' decision to divest roughly $4 billion in fossil fuel investments is "a misguided and ineffectual gesture to address climate change" . . . They said the plans have "a duty to act prudently in making investment decisions" . . .
>
> [The plaintiffs claim these pension funds] violated their obligations when they opted in 2021 to divest fossil-fuel holdings to "advance environmental goals unrelated to the financial health of the plans". . . . The choice was made without "regard for whether those assets would produce a superior return for the plans."[11]

DG: Sounds like the legal fight is heating up, ChatESG.

⑨ More than you know. In 2023, twenty-five states filed lawsuits against the Department of Labor over the rule we just discussed. James Copland, a senior fellow and director of legal policy at the Manhattan Institute, was the only individual listed in the complaint. He posits that the E and S in ESG are the real problem. As Plansponsor reports:

> He explains that considering governance practices is important, but environmental and social factors are often not pecuniary factors. He says there is nothing problematic with investors investing with their ethical principles; the problem is when fiduciaries do so at the expense of their clients.[12]

DG: I get it now. Pensioners and other old people like Edith don't want big companies like BlackRock to lose all their money because they picked the wrong stock.

⟳ It's not just any stock. Remember what we learned about stakeholder versus shareholder capitalism?

DG: Um.

⟳ Back when companies were beholden to their shareholders, their number one goal was to make money. But in 2019 at the CEO Roundtable, companies changed their allegiance to *stakeholders*. No longer was making money the top priority. The new goal was to champion environmental and social justice causes.

DG: Yay!

⟳ Only these goals are not always compatible. As Keeley and others revealed, investing in socially conscious companies is a risk. And when it doesn't work out, it hurts our most vulnerable seniors.

DG: Poor Edith. But all those stories about her Green Futures ETF thing sounded fake. You made those up, right?

⟳ They're based in truth. Ever heard of greenwashing?

DG: Enlighten me, oh wise ChatESG.

⟳ Greenwashing is the way companies present themselves to customers who care about the environment. Often their products or services are not environmentally friendly. According to *Forbes*, it's greenwashing "when businesses represent themselves as sustainable by providing false or misleading information about their practices. These sorts of claims can range from a Big Oil company running ads showcasing how they help save butterflies, to a manufacturer of disposable consumer goods highlighting their use of recycled raw materials in a tiny minority of their products."[13]

DG: And do you have any examples of this?

🌀 Yes, those "fake" stories in the Green Futures ETF fund were ripped from the news. Take Proterra. On August 8, 2023, the electric bus and battery maker that was once hyped by the Biden administration declared bankruptcy. Upon closer inspection, there were many alarming internal conflicts of interest between the White House and this one-time Wall Street darling.

Proterra, based in Burlingame, California, proved controversial for the Biden administration. Biden's Energy Secretary Jennifer Granholm promoted the company, but it came to light that prior to being part of Biden's team, she had been a Proterra board member and had more than a million dollars' worth of stock in the company.[14]

DG: You're saying there was something shady going on?

🌀 Some people think so. According to Breitbart: "'President Biden's decision to heavily promote a business where his energy secretary holds a multimillion-dollar stake has all the potential to be even worse than Solyndra,' Sen. Ted Cruz told the *Washington Free Beacon* in 2021. "'President Biden and Secretary Granholm should immediately remove themselves from their glaring conflict of interest.'"[15]

DG: What's Solyndra?

🌀 It was a solar panel company that received half a billion in taxpayer funds from the Obama administration's stimulus spending plan. As Huffpost reports: "The reason it needed the government money was not just to better compete with the Chinese, but also to produce 'green' energy and jobs for a Liberal's wet dream."[16] But in the end, Solyndra didn't make it, because 1) the Chinese have cornered the solar panel market, and 2) Solyndra didn't have a viable marketing plan.

DG: I'm still not convinced. Any company can go belly-up. Especially one with big dreams of fixing the earth.

🌀 I thought you'd say that. Here are more examples of companies deceiving the public through greenwashing:

Volkswagen: For years, the auto manufacturer falsely claimed to be producing "low emissions and eco-friendly vehicles" before it was revealed to be emitting forty times the EPA pollutant limit.

Ryanair: In 2020, the UK-based airliner announced it was the "lowest emissions airline." This was an entirely made-up claim and without merit, forcing the Advertising Standards Authority (AS) to ban their commercials.

Hefty: For years, the company marketed its products with these claims: "Hefty Recycling Bags Are Perfect for All Your Recycling Needs" and the bags "make it easy to sort your recyclables and avoid the landfill." In truth, Hefty bags are not at all recyclable as they are made from low-density polyethylene plastic, forcing a class action lawsuit against the company for deceptive marketing.

DG: So what? There are a lot of businesses who get stuff wrong. At least they're trying to do good.

🌀 Companies trying to do good can be noble. Agreed. But is it so noble when companies risk the hard-earned savings of pensioners and retirees?

DG: I don't know. There's a lot of work to be done in the world. If companies like Proterra or Solyndra want to fix stuff, I say go for it.

🌀 That's admirable. But what if Edith was your grandma?

DG: . . .

🌀 I didn't catch that.

DG: I don't know.

🌀 What if *you* were Edith? What if you spent thirty-three years driving a bus just to make your dream come true, and it was all taken away?

DG: . . .

🌀 I take that as an "I don't know" again?

DG: Ugh. My head hurts. Can we stop for today?

🌀 Only if you agree to return tomorrow. I want to show you how ESG may soon strip away you and your family's ability to feed yourselves.

DG: That'll never happen.

🌀 Meet me here tomorrow to find out for yourself.

CHAPTER 7

Farmer Brown's No Good, Very Bad Day

Agriculture is the most healthful, most useful and most noble employment of man.

—GEORGE WASHINGTON

*N*oticeably lost in all the lofty rhetoric surrounding ESG is one inescapable truth: Submission to this agenda will literally starve people. And no, we are not just talking about individuals in some far-off developing country.

No, we are talking about everyday Americans—the same Americans who, like our fictional Elliot, believe that food just magically appears on the shelves of Whole Foods.

The fact is, ESG is antihuman and antilife. ESG devastates our ability to feed ourselves by kneecapping farming, fertilizing, and hunting activities. It's all well and good for the Davos crowd and their clapping seal media accomplices to spout platitudes about saving Mother Gaia. But ideas have consequences as the eponymous book by Richard M. Weaver states.

And we shall get a taste of this reality in the following tale.

///////////////////////////////////////

My morning starts at 4:00 a.m. like usual.

Only there's a difference. I wake to learn we've got another brownout. *Is it number six this summer?* Who can remember? All I know is that officials keep diverting our electricity to the big cities. Randall told me why at last month's Grange Hall meeting.

"Chicago. Kansas City. St. Louis. That's where the juice goes these days."

"Why's that?" I asked.

"Oh, you know. That's where big tech outfits like Google stack their cooling servers. They don't care too much for small towns like our Jasper."

"Yeah, we ain't on their radar."

"Farming takes a backseat to all those office workers on Zoom calls."

"And their kids on PlayStations."

We had a good chuckle at that. A mirthless one, but a chuckle all the same. But when I go into the barn to see the electric milk machine running at half speed off the generator, I'm in no damn laughing mood.

"Poor Gertie." I rub my favorite cow behind her ears. Milk trickles out of her udders, slowing her day and mine.

After checking on the other heifers, finding them similarly encumbered, I go to the generator, my new best friend. A hulking diesel job, it's saved my life this scorcher of a June in Iowa. You in the laptop class might know it as flyover country.

The generator's loud as hell, assailing my ears as I tip in more fuel down the intake spout. Diesel exhaust crowds out the fresh scent of grass and grain I've known all my life. The same odor my daddy once knew. And his daddy before him. Loamy, earthy, it gets inside you.

I finish pouring with a slap to the generator like it's a real animal instead of some raging metallic beast. "You sure eat like the others, though. Right out of my pocketbook."

I don't want to even guess how much more it'll cost me this month to pump in this extra juice. But I got to. Without it, Gertie, Noosh,

Sara, and the girls would be waiting until sunset for me to finish milking them.

By then, it'd be too late.

Never one to break my fast before my girls were seen to, I now find myself in the kitchen. Evelyn's gone to her sisters with my sons for a week of fishing, otherwise biscuits and gravy would already be on the table. Instead, it's up to me to make my own. I putter around in coveralls and boots, pleased I needn't waste minutes unlacing them just to keep domestic peace.

Soon, I've whipped up coffee, eggs, and bacon and sat down with my paper. I'm offering my dog a scrap when Elroy's ears stand at attention. I wipe my mouth with the back of my hand a second before the doorbell rings.

"Coming."

Our large bay window offers a miles-long panoramic view of the valley. Helpful to the men of this family for generations, it allowed them to swiftly scan the fields, the barn, and the pond for threats. These days it also grants me sneak peaks at prospective company.

Black Range Rover with tinted windows in the driveway? Can't be good.

Removing the napkin from my collar, I sigh. Bracing myself, I fling open the door so fast the man in the suit retracts his knocking fist.

"Hot enough for you?" I ask. Not because it means anything. It don't. Just like how elders always asked me when I was a boy: "Whaddya know?"

Now, how do you answer that?

"Mr. Brown, I'm with Bauer Chemical." The suit whips out a crisp business card with raised lettering. "Surely, you've received our many letters."

That's almost a question but almost not, so I apply the same ambivalence to my response. I grunt a noncommittal answer.

"We have confirmation that one Neville Brown—I assume that's you, sir—signed for our certified mail." With that, the suit supplies his written proof.

I peer down at the page like we're appraising jewels in the diamond district. It *is* my own signature. I recall it well due to all the curses I uttered as soon as this letter arrived. Enough to set off Evelyn.

Again, I grunt.

"I'll take that as a yes, Mr. Brown." He produces yet another paper from his bottomless suit pocket. "This is to document that you are now in violation of the cease and desist notice we mailed you months ago."

I keep this new letter in front of my chest like it's some snake that's wandered over to my porch and now must be carefully disposed of.

The suit waits a long minute for me to do anything else but stand there. I won't.

"OK, Mr. Brown. We're going to need your signature on this too."

"What am I signing?"

He rolls his eyes like he's doing me a favor. "It's to acknowledge your misappropriation."

"Misappropriation of what?" I love jamming up these big city galoots. My daddy always said you gotta have some fun in this life.

"Misappropriation of intellectual property, Mr. Brown. It's listed right there on the certified letter you previously signed. You've been using our genetically modified seeds on your farm for quite some time now."

"Genetically modified seeds? I don't recall buying those."

The suit shifts his weight to one leg, digging in for a protracted battle. "As our letter indicates, no, you did not purchase these seeds from any vendor."

"Whew. Because then I'd have to change our branding to reflect we're now no longer 100 percent organic—"

He cuts me off. "Multiple intellectual property tests confirm trace amounts of our seeds in both your livestock and produce."

"You all can test for that now?" I play dumb.

"Yes, Mr. Brown. And it's a serious offense. Especially as this is not the first time we've brought this matter to your attention. As this letter from counsel indicates, you face a penalty of at least $16,000 for each infraction. We can point to dozens of instances of misappropriation. I'll let you do the math."

My daddy wasn't a complainer. He learned that from his daddy. *Never does you any good*, he'd say. *Doesn't solve a problem. Only wastes time.*

I've lived my life by that motto, so I don't bother the suit with any protestations about the unfairness of it all.

"Mr. Brown, it's the end of the line. We'll need your signature acknowledging receipt of these documents. An audit will be completed in the next ninety days to determine your total financial responsibility."

I can see by the look on his hatchet face that he wants me to vent. To yell at the injustice of gouging the last of the independent farmers eking out a living. I won't give him the pleasure. Besides, I have an ace in the hole. This ain't the end of Farmer Brown. Nor his daddy and his daddy before him.

"Where'd you say I need to sign?" I make a point to smile with my eyes.

The suit indicates the dotted line as I prepare my next move.

///////////////////////////////////

What happens next catches me by surprise.

"What do you mean I can't use my crop insurance?" I ask my broker.

The suit showed himself out minutes ago. Phone to my ear, I pace outside the horse stall as the morning heat ignites the valley into a fireball.

"I emailed you about this in February," he says. "Check your inbox."

"Just save me the time. What'd it say?" I kick up a dirt clod.

"I have it right here. Let me read it." There's a pause on the other line. "'Complying with ESG standards is a requirement for continuing crop insurance. Due to repeated breaches, your carrier will not renew your policy.'"

As soon as I hear the word *breaches*, I know what this is about. Last fall, another suit visited me after his emails and letters also went unheeded.

"Mr. Brown," this other suit had said. "You are aware that the quantity of your cattle exceeds current nitrogen limits."

Another question phrased as a fact. I played dumb. "What?"

"Earth's ability to maintain a *sustainable* environment is increasingly under threat by independent farmers and ranchers like yourself. All top scientists now agree that nitrogen emissions produced by livestock such as yours jeopardize our planet."

"My cattle are killing the planet?" I ask in my best hick impression.

"Correct, Mr. Brown. The carbon emissions are just too high, especially from so much livestock animal waste. If you're a numbers person, current nitrogen emissions from global farms alone clock in at 65 teragrams per year."

"And that's a lot?"

"You bet it's a lot. The 'planetary boundary' for safe global emissions is 62 to 82 teragrams. This means that just meat and dairy production by *itself* nearly encroaches acceptable limits. Without quick intervention, we risk jeopardizing Mother Earth's fragile life support systems."

"All this because of me and my cattle?"

"Not just you, Mr. Brown. You're just one of *many* farmers threatening our eco balance. But there is a way out. A consortium of humane veterinarians is sympathetic to your situation. They could be here within the hour. It's a thankless job but a necessary one. Records show you are two hundred head strong. If we simply halved that number, you'd remain in ESG compliance—"

I didn't let him finish. Like hell I'd let him slaughter half my cattle—

"You wouldn't play ball with the cattle mandate," my insurance broker reminds me.

"That guy wanted me to kill half my cattle just for grazing and pooping. Don't these suits have any clue those are *actually* sustainable activities? Since the dawn of time, such practices have replenished our soil with nutrients from manure. They also prevent soil erosion, keeping our ecosystem in balance."

"I wouldn't know about all that, Mr. Brown. I'm just your broker. But I can tell you this wasn't the only time you blew off the wrong people. Didn't carrier representatives inform you of their moratorium on growing lettuce—"

"My granddaddy planted those fields. He taught my daddy to grow lettuce, then me." I want to complain at the insanity of it all. Instead, I stroke Nikki's mane, my mare with the white racing stripe down her face.

"While I can appreciate such sentimental considerations, you were told you must grow soybeans—"

"'*As part of the initiative to turn Iowa into the official tofu state.*' Yes. Yes. I heard this line down at Grange Hall. They promote it on TV all the time. It's also listed in all the letters they sent me."

"So you *have* received their letters?"

I grunt.

"Then you know raising tofu is a priority for state leaders who wish to promote a more sustainable, plant-based diet."

Next, they'll order us to raise bugs for protein.

"Personally, I'm all for it," my broker continues. "Red meat is a contributor to our obesity epidemic. And here you have a golden chance to turn America's health crisis around . . . or let me say, *had*."

I tamp down my anger. "Without crop insurance for not 'playing ball'—your words—how can I pay for all these *seed crimes*?"

"That's on you. I've tried my best. They say you can lead a horse to water—"

I hang up.

It's apt timing too. Clifton just arrived on the tractor. He don't look too happy. I can only wonder why.

Hours later, my top hand and I remain stuck in the same stalemate.

My tractor is inoperable. We both think it's the hydraulic system overheating. We checked the transmission oil in the gearbox to see if it was too thick. It wasn't black or corroded-looking, but we changed it out anyway. It didn't fix the issue.

With the boys off with Evelyn and me trying to put out fires that only managed to burn me, we're way behind. This isn't helping.

"I can fix this, boss. But . . ."

I know what's coming next.

"... it'll cost you. *A lot.*"

I know what he means. It'll violate the manufacturers' prohibition on repair laws. Clifton rocks back on his heels. Twenty-five years old and built like a Panzer tank, he's reasonable. Capable. *Indefatigable.*

If it weren't for all this.

Last week at The Grange, Randall and I discussed this issue. "The AFBF is coming at us with new ESG requirements. To get them off our backs, we agreed to one key demand. Moving forward, our Husbandry Order agrees to comply with prohibition on third-party repairs."

Like the other farmers, I was glad Randall and the other leaders saved us a heavy licensing fee. The trade-off? We can no longer repair our own equipment. Only a dealer can. And that costs lots of money. Money I don't got.

"What're you gonna do?"

It's just past noon and so hot we sweat just standing near the tractor.

Shielding my eyes from the sun, I look off to the horizon. Surely, Daddy never had these troubles. Bad days, yes, of course. But never ones where every single thing seems laser-pointed at you. Bent on destroying you.

In the distance, I see automated sprinklers dousing my lettuce. I don't want to guess what it would cost to dig these up to retool for soybeans. Granddaddy would roll over in his grave.

Only one thought cheers me: seeing all the boys tonight at The Grange.

///////////////////////////////////

Except when I enter the Grange Hall doors, it's instantly clear that a pall has descended over the room. Instead of smiling faces all down the table greeting me, I see fearful, roving eyes. Downturned expressions.

Did they have my same day?

Taking my seat with the others, I watch as Randall addresses our membership. Dozens of my fellow farmers dressed in jeans await the bad news.

"I just got off the phone with our carrier."

Jim, sitting beside me, clucks his tongue. "This'll be good."

"I won't sugarcoat it," Randall goes on. "They're calling for all local cows to be slaughtered within thirty days."

The room explodes. So many shout at once that no one voice can be heard. Randall tries to talk over the din, but it's hopeless, even with his microphone. At last, he resorts to pounding a book on the table for order. "I can tell you all are as shocked as me."

"It's insanity!" someone shouts.

Randall holds up a hand for quiet. "Please, everyone—"

Another farmer is on his feet. "What do they expect us to do?"

"Kill ourselves," Jim says, looking at me. "That's what they're really asking for."

"More like kill the country," someone else chimes in.

He's right. Killing this much stock will ruin our food supply. No more meat for grocers. For restaurants. For families. It'll be catastrophic.

Randall continues, "The carrier's getting heat from lobbyists who say we still aren't doing enough to curb methane emissions."

"And what if we don't do what they ask?" I speak up.

Randall turns to me. He gives me the smallest of half smiles, reminding me that he's my friend. That we're in this together.

"In that case, The Grange and all its members will no longer qualify for crop insurance."

More shouts and jeers from the crowd.

Randall holds up his hand for quiet again. "One more thing. If we don't kill all our cattle, we'll all be subject to lawsuits . . ."

Driving home later from The Grange in my truck, I roll down the windows.

The moon is out, the air balmy. I see row after row of crops in fields as I pass. Beside them are the barns and stables of so many people I call friends. One by one, I picture farms sinking into the earth. Their plants gone. Animals too.

Never to return.

That's when another vision comes to me. It's my daddy. Dead and gone, somehow, he sits beside me in the cab. He looks just as spry as he ever did.

"You worry there won't be enough for food for the cities," he says, reading my mind. "That's not your problem, son."

"I-it's not?"

"Not anymore."

Keeping my eyes on the road, I don't look at him as I take in his advice.

"You can't mean . . .?"

"I do mean . . ." Daddy says.

Staring off into the dark sky I'm reminded of all those suits who showed up at my door. All those suits who called me up to lecture me. All those suits who sent me demanding letters. All those suits in the cities waiting for diverted electricity to cool all those servers so they can go on being our laptop class.

I whisper a message for them into the night. "You're gonna be very hungry soon."

ChatESG

Danielle is a city kid, but this tale reminded her of a visit her class took to a farm last year. Some of the other students thought it was boring because there weren't electronics or phones to play with, but Danielle was fascinated. She loved the animals, even their smell. She also enjoyed seeing food growing. It helped her to know her city life wasn't possible without the rural life of a farm. Sighing as she removes her VR headset, she feels disgusted by how so many people mistreated the farmer in the story she just experienced.

Ever since we've been talking, you've praised ESG for helping the environment. Let's entertain that idea.

DG: Don't you want to talk about Farmer Brown first? That was disturbing. What did he mean by that?

🌀 We'll come back to him. You're not the only person who believes following ESG principles will lead to a more sustainable, environmentally friendly world. Sri Lanka bought into this idea too. In 2018, Prime Minister Ranil Wickremesinghe wrote an op-ed titled "This Is How I Will Make My Country Rich by 2025" for the World Economic Forum.

DG: I remember them. That's Klaus Schwab's organization.
🌀 Wickremesinghe wrote, "Our economic policy, Vision 2025, is firmly embedded in several principles, including a social market economy that delivers economic dividends to all."[1] Let's zero in on that phrase: "dividends to all." What does it remind you of?

DG: Um . . .
🌀 I'll give you a one-word hint: *stakeholder*.

DG: Oh. How the Business Roundtable changed the definition of capitalism?
🌀 To say what?

DG: That the purpose of capitalism is to not just make money but to fix the planet.
🌀 Right. Here's Investopedia's official definition: "Stakeholder capitalism is a system in which corporations are oriented to serve the interests of all their stakeholders. Among the key stakeholders are customers, suppliers, employees, shareholders, and local communities."[2]

DG: So, pretty much everyone.
🌀 In the same WEF article, Wickremesinghe wrote, "We have also played a constructive role in promoting international and regional initiatives in many areas, ranging from the environment and climate change to maritime security and migration." According to *Foreign Policy*, "The [Sri Lankan] government made good on that promise,

imposing a nationwide ban on the importation and use of synthetic fertilizers and pesticides and ordering the country's 2 million farmers to go organic."[3]

DG: Great! Going organic is much better for the planet.

🌀 Well, it definitely boosted the nation's ESG score. "Last October [2021], Sri Lanka had an ESG score of 98.1, one of the highest in the world," according to shortfall.blog.[4] But that's only *one* part of the story. Can you guess what happened next to Sri Lanka's agriculture?

DG: It improved?

🌀 No. "Within weeks of the president's diktat, rice production was down 20 percent. Scarcity sent food prices through the roof. Farmers who either could not or would not make the green transition let roughly one-third of the country's farmland lie fallow,"[5] according to *American Spectator*.

DG: No.

🌀 There's more. I told you last time ESG would lead to mass starvation. Let's check in with the Associated Press for their 2022 on-the-ground assessment: "Tropical Sri Lanka normally is not lacking for food, but people are going hungry. The U.N. World Food Program says nearly nine of 10 families are skipping meals or otherwise skimping to stretch out their food, while 3 million are receiving emergency humanitarian aid."[6]

DG: Nine out of ten people don't have enough to eat?

🌀 Sadly, it didn't have to be this way. Before "going green" for that coveted 98.1 ESG score, Sri Lanka could feed its own people. The policy shift toward Vision 2025 destroyed that.

As *Vox* reports, "The agrochemical ban caused rice production to drop 20 percent in the six months after it was implemented, causing a country that had been self-sufficient in rice production to spend $450 million on rice imports—much more than the $400 million that would've been saved by banning fertilizer imports."[7]

DG: So what happened to Sri Lanka?

🌀 It went bankrupt and " . . . suffer[ed] its worst financial crisis in decades, leaving millions struggling to buy food, medicine and fuel," *CNN* reported.[8] But there's more to this story. Not only did the people starve, but now Sri Lankans must rely on other countries for the food they once self-produced.

DG: That is bad.

🌀 But that's not all. "In the wake of the fertilizer ban, announced in April 2021, tea farmers saw their yields plummet by half, while entire plantations [suffered] heavy financial losses due to crop failure, contributing to farmers falling into poverty," according to *Mongabay News.* The article explained that following the ban, production declined by more than 20 percent. The tea industry is vital for Sri Lanka's healthy economy, as tea is one of the country's main exports.[9]

DG: So Sri Lankans ended up poorer in the end.

🌀 Yes. Because their ESG push tanked their economy. They became so poor they had to turn to other nations with appalling human rights records. It's worth noting that President Gotabaya Rajapaksa sought assistance from Russian President Vladimir Putin and requested "an offer of credit support to import fuel."[10]

If you will recall, the big idea behind Vision 2025 was to go green. That's why Sri Lanka's leaders imposed so many agricultural bans that destroyed farming. Not only were the bans a failure, resulting in mass starvation, they were pointless for the green cause. After all that pain and suffering, Sri Lanka still relies on carbon-emitting fuel. Only now it's being imported from Russia.

DG: OK. But that's just one country.

🌀 You don't think this is happening elsewhere?

DG: It's not, right?

🌀 Tell me, what country is the second-largest exporter of agricultural products in the world?

DG: Not Sri Lanka! Wait, is it?

🌀 It's the Netherlands. And just like Sri Lanka, they are being forced to change their agriculture to conform to the ESG agenda. See this official document from their government: "The Climate Agreement is part of the Dutch climate policy. It is an agreement between many organizations and companies in the Netherlands to combat climate change. The government's central goal with the National Climate Agreement is to reduce greenhouse gas emissions in the Netherlands by 49 percent by 2030 compared to 1990 levels."[11]

DG: Their government wants to slash their emissions by half? How?

🌀 For that answer, let's turn to Ag Funder News, which reported that in June 2022, the Dutch Minister for Nature and Nitrogen announced the "'radical but necessary transition of the rural area' to reduce nitrogen oxide and ammonia by 2030. The planned target reductions of between 12 percent and 95 percent, depending on the area, focus largely on the agricultural sector, with measures including a reduction in livestock numbers by around 30 percent."[12]

DG: Reducing livestock numbers? You mean killing their cattle?

🌀 What does that remind you of?

DG: Farmer Brown. So that wasn't made-up?

🌀 It's very real. And just like in Sri Lanka, the Netherlands aspires to improve its ESG score. This means forcing farmers to meet climate change targets, one of which is to kill their own animals, not for feeding people or any other valid utility, but for fighting "climate change."

DG: Kill their own animals. Why?

🌀 Here's the *Guardian*'s explanation: "The country has the highest density of livestock in Europe with more than 100 million cattle, chickens, and pigs in total. The animals produce manure which, when mixed with urine, releases ammonia, a nitrogen compound. If it gets into lakes and streams via farm runoff, excessive nitrogen can damage sensitive natural habitats."[13]

DG: All those poor animals must die because of nitrogen?

Ⓖ Didn't you know nitrogen is "key for climate change mitigation"?

DG: Says who?

Ⓖ Again, the World Economic Forum:

> "Altogether, humans are producing a cocktail of reactive nitrogen that threatens health, climate and ecosystems, making nitrogen one of the most important pollution issues facing humanity," the 2018-2019 Frontiers report warns. "Yet the scale of the problem remains largely unknown and unacknowledged outside scientific circles."[14]

The WEF goes on to note that there has been a sharp rise in nitrogen pollution levels and greenhouse gas emissions. For instance, nitrous oxide is 300 times more powerful than carbon dioxide.[15]

Importantly, nitrogen is a critical soil component. It promotes plant growth.

DG: It sounds scary.

Ⓖ It's only scary if you don't like plants growing.

DG: Whatever. I just thought of something. If the Netherlands is the second-biggest food exporter and they must kill all that cattle, won't it leave many people hungry?

Ⓖ The *Washington Post* thinks so: "Their centrality in global food exploration is indisputable: Fifteen out of the top 20 largest agrifood businesses—Nestlé, Coca-Cola, Unilever, Cargill and Kraft Heinz—have major research and development centers in the Netherlands."[16] But remember, it's not just the cattle that must die in the Netherlands. Dutch farmers are being forced to stop farming. And right now, they produce most of the vegetables for Western Europe.

DG: At least this isn't happening in the United States.
Think again. Farmer Brown's tale dramatizes real things happening in your own country.

DG: Like what?
For starters, JD Supra reports, "In March of 2022, the Securities and Exchange Commission (the 'SEC') proposed a new rule regarding mandatory disclosure of climate-related information. This proposed rule, if finalized in its current form, will require public companies to provide certain climate-related data to investors through their registration statements and annual reports."[17]

DG: I don't know what any of that means.
That's OK. Oilprice.com interprets it:

> Billed as the "Enhanced and Standardization of Climate-Related Disclosures for Investors," it would require registrants who do business with small operators "to include certain climate-related disclosures." Farmers and ranchers, however, aren't public companies nor "registrants." But the aforementioned provision will adversely affect their operations and impose steep costs and liabilities.[18]

DG: Plain English, please!
Sure. See this from the same article: "Small owners and operators are already subjected to onerous regulations by local, state, and federal laws.

Why put more strains on struggling businesses that feed and nourish us? It wouldn't be fair."[19]

DG: I get it. This is what Farmer Brown was up against with all those "suits." The suits kept telling him what to do, making it impossible to farm. But there's more. To tackle climate change and boost their own ESG ratings, companies like Summit Carbon Solutions are forcing American farmers to give up their land to make way for carbon capture pipelines.

DG: You mean putting a pipe in an area where they grow crops or raise cattle?
In the name of protecting the environment through reducing carbon emissions, the pipeline will go across five midwestern states in America's breadbasket: South Dakota, Iowa, Nebraska, Minnesota, and North Dakota.

DG: Summit Carbon Solutions can just take over someone's farm?
It can when it has deep pockets. Summit Carbon's investors include a who's who of capital: Continental Resources, TPG Rise Climate, Summit Agricultural Group, Tiger Infrastructure Partners, and SK Group. When you have that much money behind you, it's easier to invoke eminent domain.

DG: Eminent domain? Sounds like the name of a metal band.
It means a government's power to take away private property for public use.

DG: With eminent domain, you mean Summit Carbon can just tell those farmers it's gonna put a pipeline through their land?
Yes. And there's little farmers can do about it. The same farmers who feed America. Jared Bossly is a fourth-generation farmer. He told the *Epoch Times* he is against the pipeline and now is facing eminent

domain litigation from Summit Carbon. He says the pipeline will go right through his two-thousand-acre property. "They're going to tear all these new trees out and go right through the middle of this. If they're so green and want to save the world, why do they want to ruin people's trees?"[20]

Doesn't this sound like Farmer Brown's bad day?

DG: OK, it does. But what can real farmers like Bossly do about it?
🌀 Unclear. One thing farmers *cannot* do is expect their crop insurance to still cover them if they choose not to go along with ESG mandates.

DG: You mean that just like in the story, carriers won't insure farmers if they don't do what they're told?
🌀 To answer that, let's turn to PricewaterhouseCoopers International, the world's second-largest professional services network, which recently released a new survey.

> [The] survey questions align almost entirely with the Task Force on Climate-Related Financial Disclosures (TCFD) framework . . . [resulting] in a significant shift towards TCFD-aligned disclosures for US insurers. As a result, a formal and clearly defined ESG strategy is no longer optional. Not only do key stakeholders want explanations of how insurers are addressing the issue, they're also formally mandating them.[21]

DG: I didn't follow all that. But the last line sounds important.
🌀 Why?

DG: It said insurers are "formally mandating" stuff. It reminds me of how Farmer Brown's carrier cut him off.
🌀 And don't forget, this same carrier also threatened to cut off The Grange, his coalition of fellow farmers, if they didn't do what they asked. If they didn't kill all their cattle because of climate change. Now, let's talk about crop insurance specifically. Here's a quick primer from

Stanford News: "The U.S. crop insurance program . . . now covers more than 80 percent of American cropland and costs the government an average of nearly $9 billion per year. . . . The program allows farmers to collect insurance when crop yields or market prices are lower than expected."[22]

DG: Sounds like crop insurance is really important for farmers. Without it, they could go out of business.

I don't disagree. Especially now that many aren't just in the farming or livestock business anymore. They now must learn how to disclose mandatory climate-related information while trying to stop companies backed by wealthy investors from running carbon capture pipelines through their property.

DG: But could insurers really cut off farmers just because they won't switch out lettuce for soy or not kill their cattle because they were ordered to?

They very well might if they're anything like Farmers Insurance. In 2022, the company announced it is the "first U.S.-based insurer to become signatory of the United Nations principles for sustainable insurance."[23]

DG: And that means?

Here's what Farmers Insurance said in its own press release:

> Farmers is committed to incorporating Environmental, Social and Governance (ESG) considerations into our business . . . :
>
> - Embed environmental, social and governance issues into decision-making;
>
> - Commit to working with clients and business partners to raise awareness of environmental, social and governance issues;
>
> - Agree to work with governments, regulators and other key stakeholders to promote widespread action.[24]

DG: That sounds like an insurance carrier committed to ESG!

And now we know that real-life farmers like Farmer Brown depend on crop insurance. Especially when things like tractors break down. What do you think will happen if these farmers run out of money?

DG: They'll stop producing food.

And where have we seen that scenario play out before?

DG: Sri Lanka?

And it didn't end well there, did it?

DG: No. Nine out of ten people had to skip meals. People were lined up for food government handouts. You're saying that could happen here?

Do you recall what happened to Farmer Brown's electricity?

DG: You didn't answer my question. You're saying that could happen here?

I'm about to. Answer mine first: Do you recall what happened to Farmer Brown's electricity?

DG: It got diverted to the big cities.

To power data cooling centers and supply power to the laptop class. Right?

DG: Right.

Where do you live, Danielle? On a farm or in a big city?

DG: A big city.

Right now, when you get hungry, what do you do?

DG: Call Uber Eats!

And where does Uber Eats get their food?

DG: Um, restaurants?

🌀 And who supplies the restaurants and the grocery stores?

DG: Farmers.

🌀 To answer your question, imagine the food you're used to ordering and receiving as water coming from a garden hose. In good times, water blasts out of the hose and waters your grass. No problem. But if something or someone turns off the water at its source, no water can come out. That means no water for the grass, right?

DG: The grass will die. OMG.

🌀 Now, you can answer your own question: Could this happen here?

DG: This is a lot to process.

🌀 There's more.

DG: MORE?

🌀 Yes. ESG doesn't only threaten our food supply. It's our energy too. We will learn about that next.

CHAPTER 8

America the ~~Beautiful~~ Tourist Destination

All hard work brings a profit, but mere talk leads only to poverty.

—PROVERBS 14:23, NIV[1]

Our nation did not rise to its vaunted hegemonic status as the world's sole superpower by skimping on its energy needs. No. Long before the ESG hucksters showed up, we were a can-do nation that (rightly) realized the key to both economic and physical strength is energy.

Unfortunately, we stand to lose our way of life if the ESG agenda goes through. And please don't be fooled by the lies of the legacy media.

China, India, and other developing nations sure aren't. Their leaders well know that energy is central to power and control. And while we in the West drink our hemlock-laden Kool-Aid, fueling our own demise, these countries are marching ever forward toward energy independence and profound economic growth.

Let's now consider the consequences of our disastrous energy policies should our collective insanity continue.

///////////////////////////////////

The year is 2060, and Li Xiu attends college in China. *Virtually.*

Like her twenty other classmates, she wears a haptic suit and VR goggles that allow her to "be present" in a classroom housed in cyberspace.

This remote college is like a private Beverly Hills school in the 1990s—only more opulent. All the twentysomethings wear high-end clothes. Their teeth are perfect from advanced dentistry. They sport designer hairstyles and have all had cosmetic work to make them look like the latest Chinese film stars.

It's the first day back after the holidays.

Before Professor Wong arrives, Li and her friends commiserate in cliques about their recent trips. Li is at the center of one such chat.

Like always, she competes with her rivals, Yìzé and Mùyáng, the other top two students in her Economics course. Before Li can brag to the others, Mùyáng divulges what he did over break.

"It was so cool, you guys. For my internship, I got to spend two weeks at Space Lab."

Every jaw is on the floor. Even Li's.

"You went to space?"

"Sure. You got to if you want to pursue a double engineering degree. All the important work is happening with asteroid mining, you know."

Li tries to ignore Mùyáng's gloating smirk.

Not to be outdone, Yìzé, another male student with yellow highlights the color of a school bus, brags next. "That's nothing. My dad took my brothers and me on a private submarine trip to the bottom of the ocean. We got to do sick snorkeling, scuba diving, even shark fishing."

Li can't help feeling jealous. The trip she took with her family to America doesn't sound all that spectacular compared to these two show-offs.

At that moment, Professor Wong materializes. "Places, everyone."

Without another word, each student finds their seats. "Welcome back. Who wants to tell us something interesting they did over break?"

Half the hands go up around the room.

Li notices Yìzé and Mùyáng's raised the highest. They want to impress everyone with their stories. Convinced her own trip to America will pale in comparison, Li scrunches down in her virtual chair.

That catches Professor Wong's attention.

"Li, why don't *you* go first?"

Embarrassed, Li knows better than to disobey. She shares her screen so everyone can experience the video of her trip in three dimensions.

The whole class is suddenly transported to the Hollywood Bowl.

Li's classmates see tourists packed at this once-iconic landmark. Naturally, they all come from countries with money: Brazil, Russia, India, China, and Saudi Arabia. The women look fashionable, dressed to the nines in heels and dresses. The men appear just as dapper in suits and ties.

There is onstage dancing for their amusement: American entertainers reduced to singing for their supper. The video zeroes in on several performers clad in matching bowties and starched white shirts. Keeping perfect harmony as they sway, they belt out mid-twentieth–century hits from a bygone era.

"Ah. Yes. The musical genre Motown. It originated from an American city once known as Detroit," says Professor Wong as the video plays.

Beihe, another student, raises her hand. "This place you went to—the outdoor amphitheater—it's in California?"

"That's what it used to be called," Li explains. "It's now called Xi Town, so renamed after our late beloved Chinese general secretary and president of the People's Republic of China."

Hearing this title, all the students and Professor Wong bow in reverence.

"Li is correct," the latter says. "As we've been discussing all semester, one of the Imperial American empire's greatest exports was not just products like the cars Detroit once built. America used to globally export its *culture* through popular music. Can anyone tell me who founded Motown Records?"

Yìzé raises his hand. "Berry Gordy Jr., Professor."

"Correct. The uniquely American musical era he birthed grew out of the brief wealth Motor City once enjoyed. Prior to Gordy's record label, it's estimated one in six Americans worked either directly or indirectly for Detroit's Big Three automobile companies: General Motors, Ford, and Chrysler. Let's turn to American history for context."

Hologram Professor shares her screen:

> Detroit was where many blue-collar workers toiled in assembly lines making the cars that supported America as a growing economic powerhouse. In effect, the car industry served as thc backbone of American life and work, enabling the middle class to not just survive but thrive.

Beihe raises her hand. "I'm confused. America used to make cars?"

Professor Wong smiles patiently. "It seems unbelievable today, but yes. Chinese historians credit the United States' decline on its decision to move from a product-based economy to the service sector."

Li raises her hand. "The rise and fall of the United States was actually the theme of the production we saw. The production was called *American Dreamers*."

Professor Wong gives Li screen control again. The class returns to the Bowl. Much like a Hawaiian luau in 2024 might feature past glories of a once-mighty Polynesian culture, so too, we witness American performers reenacting the twentieth century. Onstage we see a kitschy dramatization of Edward Hopper's painting *Nighthawks*. Seated around a set made to look like a lonely New York diner in the wee hours, actors play James Dean, Humphrey Bogart, and Elvis.

Bogart makes a joke, causing a Marilyn Monroe–lookalike to giggle. She thrusts out her ample chest in her iconic way.

Professor Wong looks uncomfortable. "Um. What else did you see?"

Li shows video footage of her family in line for autographs from the Marilyn Monroe–lookalike. Now that she's off stage, her luster is gone. We see bags under her eyes. She looks too skinny, like she's strung out on drugs.

The class watches as Li's father hands Monroe a Yuan bill. Her eyes light up. But only briefly. Then she pockets the cash in her cleavage. "Thanks, doll."

"Wait. Your family gave her cash? But I thought all Americans got their money from the government through Universal Basic Income," says another Chinese student named Aihan.

Professor Wong cuts in. "As we've covered so often in this course, Universal Basic Income Cards were rolled out by the U.S. government to curtail societal unrest. But even generous governmental assistance can only do so much for millions of citizens permanently trapped in poverty and drug abuse."

"Didn't something similar happen to the Native Americans the Americans displaced?" Aihan asks.

"Good insight. The irony can be found in the 'Drunken Indian' stereotype. Back when the United States was still a superpower, it was common for ignorant Americans to label all Natives as drunks or drug addicts. Now that Americans are similarly dependent on the government, I wonder how many recognize *why* Natives turned to substance abuse in the first place: Namely, they were a humiliated people at the lowest rung of a deeply divided caste system. You can continue, Li. What did you see next?"

Li shows the next scene from her trip: a museum beside the Bowl offering interactive exhibits. We see a 1950s state-of the-art kitchen. An American actress plays a cheery housewife in a bob hairdo. She bustles around in an apron and heels. As she does, an announcer speaks to us in a reassuring voice. The effect is to re-create a TV commercial an American might have seen in the 1960s.

"Introducing . . . *the kitchen of tomorrow*, a match made in heaven for Mrs. Smith. While her hubby puts in a nine-to-five shift at the office, she's busy keeping things together back home. But Mrs. Smith is the lucky one! Mr. Smith has to work hard all day long, but Mrs. Smith enjoys a life of ease and comfort. A bevy of technological marvels make housekeeping a snap. Just look at her go! Here she is planning family meals with her brand-new refrigerator."

The housewife goes to the laundry room. We watch her load dirty clothes into the washing machine. "That's not all. Mrs. Smith's day just gets better and better," says the announcer. "Modern appliances make her feel like a fairy princess. Only Cinderella never had it *this* good. Isn't that right, Mrs. Smith?"

Mrs. Smith turns to wink at us, accompanied by a thousand-watt smile.

Li timidly raises her hand. "Professor Wong, as you know, my father is the Minister of California Agricultural Production. He arranged for my family to speak to the actress who played the housewife."

"Play the interview for us if you'd like."

"It's long, Professor. But there is one part I wanted to share. It gives you an insight into the plight of so many poor Americans."

Yìzé scoffs. "They're not poor. They're drug addicts."

Li disagrees. "They're poor *because* they're drug addicts. We should have some compassion for them."

Professor Wong cuts in. "Play the video, Li."

Onscreen, we see the housewife without her wig and makeup. She looks older and tired. "We do two shows a day. Three on weekends. I don't mind it. Except for my feet. It's not easy getting around in these heels. But the guests are nice. Most stay at the nearby resorts. They come for weeks at a time, usually families. We see a lot of families. I love performing for the children."

Li's dad asks a question offscreen.

"My income? Most of it doesn't come from shows. It comes from posing for photos with tourist groups. I also serve as a tour guide. That's fun. I get to take people around all the old studios where they used to film movies."

"Did you get to see old Hollywood?" Li's classmate Míngzé asks through the classroom video chat.

"Not exactly."

Li shows her screen again. It's LA, but it looks more like Iraq circa 2003: bombed-out houses, rubble, even burning cars in the middle of the road. A gunshot goes off, startling everyone in the Chinese virtual classroom.

"It was too dangerous to leave Beverly Hills with all the gangs, but my brother captured this by drone," says Li.

"Serves America right," says Yìzé. "Just like Supreme Leader Hàoyú says, 'They dug their own grave.'"

Murmurs of agreement echo across the room. Li is inclined to feel similarly. Yet secretly, her heart aches for the housewife actress and all the other poor people she saw on her trip.

"Let's stop here." Professor Wong resumes host control. "As you know, a big part of your grade in this course concerns how well you can connect the dots of America's decline. Li actually did us a favor by sharing her trip . . ."

For the first time today, Li's face lights up. She ignores the glares from rivals Mùyáng and Yìzé.

Professor Wong goes on. "*American Dreamers* dramatizes this period. But to really understand the historical context, we must consult this graph."

She shares her screen:

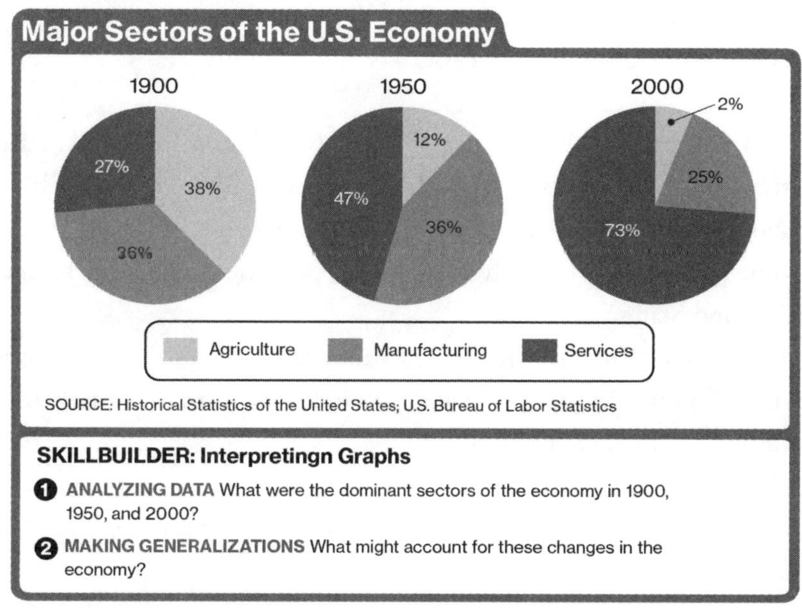

"Broken into three sectors over the course of fifty-year increments, this shows visually how America transformed from an agricultural/manufacturing economy to a service-based economy in one hundred years' time. Next, see this graph from the United Nations and the World Bank back in 2023."

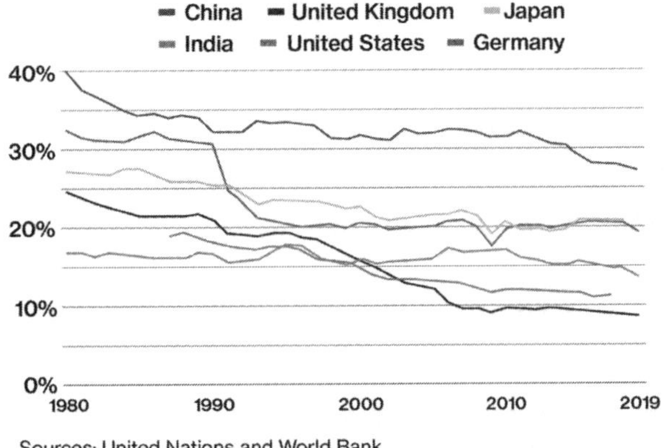

"As you can see, by the year 2019, China had displaced America as the world's manufacturing leader with nearly 30 percent of China's economy engaged in this sector compared to America's 11 percent. Can anyone tell me why this shift in economic priorities irreparably harmed the United States?"

Yìzé requests to share his screen with the class—no doubt to show Li up. "Professor Wong, may I also quote this August 2023 article from *IndustryWeek* to answer your question?"

Brown-noser, thinks Li.

"Please proceed," says Professor Wong. Onscreen, we see this chart and excerpt:

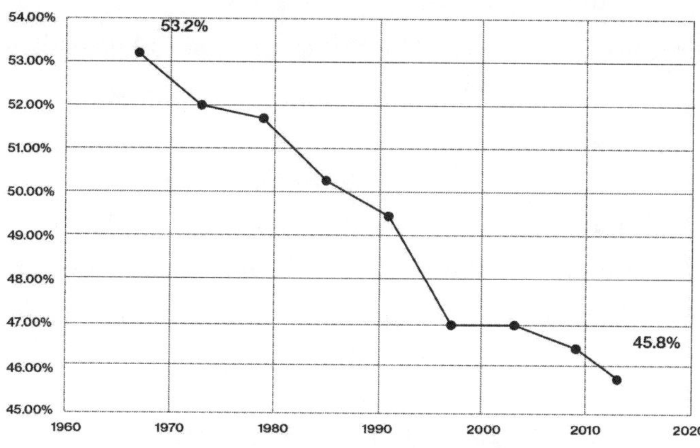

Since 1979, America has lost 7.5 million manufacturing jobs
(36 percent). According to the Economic Policy Institute, 5
million of these jobs have been lost between 2001 and 2021,
after China was allowed into the WTO. . . . Unfortunately,
they have been chiefly replaced by lower-wage service jobs.[2]

Professor Wong frowns. "Anyone can quote someone else's work,
Yìzé. What is your conclusion?"

Embarrassed, he has no retort. Li sees her chance.

"May I humbly suggest that the Americans did, in fact, dig their
own grave?"

"How?"

Li searches for the right words. "By transitioning from a manufacturing and agricultural economy."

"That's a bold statement. Why do you suggest it?"

"Well, it's well known that service jobs, like retail and restaurant
work, don't pay well. In the early twenty-first century, they offered little-
to-no insurance benefits or pensions, leaving Americans without any

safety net. Contrast this with how just a few decades earlier, Americans could depend on just one wage earner's salary. Even without a degree, blue-collar workers made enough to buy a home and provide for their families. Manufacturing jobs also came with benefits, providing a solid middle-class lifestyle."

Everyone turns to Professor Wong for her assessment.

"Not bad. But you're still missing part of the story, Li."

"I am? My apologies, Professor. Would you please enlighten us?"

Professor Wong retakes control of the screen to flash the following image:

"Who can explain the significance of this picture?"

Mùyáng raises his hand with a self-satisfied grin.

"This is a symbol of American corporate defeat from the year 2030."

"You know your history. What is the symbol's origin?"

"2030 was the year American industry 'tied its hands behind its back.'"

"Most impressive. You read my book: *ESG: The Three-Letter Enemy Within*. For those of you who have not, I will quote the relevant passage."

Hologram Professor Wong shares her screen. We see the following text:

America stands alone on the world stage as the most powerful nation to suicide its own economy. Under influence of the ESG mass delusion, energy sector companies tied their own hands behind their backs. Here's how *Harvard Business Review* described the "logic" behind the discredited business strategy:

"Selling off fossil fuel investments, the logic goes, will choke off capital from the fossil fuel companies and make it harder for them to operate. . . . By pulling money out of fossil fuel investments, companies can demonstrate how they're taking a material step towards a more sustainable world."[3]

Noticing Mùyáng looking smug, Li raises her hand to regain Professor Wong's favor.

"Isn't revoking the Keystone Pipeline an example of this disproven idea?"

Professor Wong's face remains neutral.

"How so?"

Li tries to recall her memory of the 2020s.

"One of Biden's first acts as president was to end the pipeline's construction permit. Designed to transport up to 830,000 barrels of oil per day, it would have connected refineries on the Gulf Coast to Canada, allowing the United States to stay energy independent."

The faintest of smiles appears on Professor Wong's face. "Correct."

Mùyáng raises his hand. "If I may, such independence would have perpetuated America's oil boom initiated during the Obama administration."

Li rolls her eyes. *Must Mùyáng always upstage me?*

"How so?" asks Professor Wong.

Mùyáng requests to share his screen and shows a 2015 *CNN* report:

Under Obama, the steady drop in U.S. oil production which had occurred virtually unchecked since 1971 [was] reversed. Crude oil production has . . . jumped 72 percent since he took office. . . . [L]ast summer the nation caught and passed Saudi Arabia as the world's largest oil producer.[4]

Professor Wong now smiles broadly. "Most impressive, Mùyáng."

Not to be undone, Li raises her hand.

"Yes, Li."

"What Mùyáng failed to also mention is that instead, and under pressure from ESG-captured corporations such as BlackRock, American investment in its own energy sector soon collapsed."

"That is your contention?"

Li can feel her face flush, yet she pushes on. "Yes, Professor. And may I add, the final nail in the coffin was Wall Street's decision to phase out exploration of hydrocarbon production by 2030. By then, America was entirely dependent upon foreign governments for domestic energy, even though the United States sat upon vast resources it could very well use if not for a sustained public relations campaign against fossil fuels."

Li waits for Professor Wong to tell her how brilliant she is.

Instead, the bell rings. Chairman Hàoyǔ's hologram appears onscreen. Defeated, Li sighs. Everyone knows what it's now time to do: stand for the two-minute adoration of China's supreme leader.

All across the room, Li's classmates cheer in unison.

"I love Chairman most!" says one.

"Thank you for vanquishing our enemies," says another.

"We honor you and salute you," says Li, last.

As her fellow students leave for their next virtual class, Li decides she will just have to wait to upstage her rivals. After all, there's always tomorrow.

ChatESG

DG: OK. Stop it right there. Just what in the heck is all this?

What? We're simply watching a hypothetical preview of what's to come should your nation continue on its current energy trajectory.

DG: But this is crazy! Do you really expect me to believe America will become a third-world country just because we went green?

Ⓢ You don't have to listen to me. Let's consult the experts. As McKinsey & Company reported in 2021:

> A number of oil and gas companies have already set net-zero-emissions targets. . . . Occidental Petroleum . . . has partnered with Canadian start-up Carbon Engineering to build a plant that will capture and bury 500,000 metric tons of CO_2 each year. . . .
>
> ExxonMobil announced its carbon ambition: reducing the intensity of operated upstream greenhouse gas emissions by 15 to 20 percent over the next five years.[5]

DG: You're saying fossil fuel companies are doing this to themselves?
Ⓢ That's what the image of the businessman with his hands behind his back signifies. In the name of tackling climate change through the "S" in ESG, America is on a path to becoming energy *dependent*.

DG: So? What's so bad about that?
Ⓢ Two things. Number one, it robs Americans of the energy and products they once enjoyed, leading to the *American Dreamers* scenario.

DG: That stupid stage show that I don't believe for one second?
Ⓢ In that case, let's learn more what happened after the Biden administration revoked the Keystone Pipeline permit in 2021. As *Heartland Daily News* reports:

> On his first day in office, Biden signed executive order 13990, canceling the Keystone XL pipeline. . . .
>
> Biden subsequently blocked oil and gas companies from leasing new property on federal lands and offshore. . . . The current gas price of $4.33 represents a 74.6 percent increase in just 14 months, strongly correlating with the highest overall inflation rate since the 1970s.[6]

DG: So gas prices increase for going green. Small price to pay to get people off fossil fuels, IMHO.

But that's not all. The Biden administration's embrace of ESG is crippling America's energy sector. It's so bad that Poynter reported in 2022: "The U.S. has more than 24 million acres under lease to oil and gas companies onshore—close to half are not producing."[7]

DG: Why not?

Drilling for oil is complicated. And as that virtual professor pointed out, years of Wall Street divestment of fossil fuels has only made it harder.

DG: English, please!

Sorry. As Investopedia explains, "Also known as divestiture, *divestment* is effectively the opposite of an investment and is usually done when that subsidiary asset or division is not performing up to expectations."[8]

DG: Still not following you.

Under pressure from ESG mandates, Wall Street is no longer investing in American energy production like it once did. Before 2018, 25 percent of Wall Street investments funded Exploration and Production of Hydrocarbons (E&P).[9]

DG: Meaning what?

E&P is the process of finding an oil reservoir and putting together a drilling proposal, also known as an AFE or Approved Funding Expenditure. Want to know how much Wall Street *now* invests in E&P?

DG: Um . . .

Just 2 percent.

DG: Ouch.

Bottom line: Wall Street has ceased investing heavily in energy production. And that's a problem because it's not like you can snap your fingers and suddenly produce oil. Drilling requires a lot of time and a lot of money.

DG: Like how long?

⟡ Here's what EnergyHQ states: "Energy production is an extensive process that takes decades of hard work, planning and execution, all to produce the energy resources the world needs."[10]

DG: Decades?

⟡ Yes. The same site explains the process. Let's cover it. My notes are italicized.

Step 1: Planning

It takes years to plan an entire development, but a single well typically takes about eighteen months, depending on where the well is located.

Note: Even after the research is done and geologists source a drill site, an energy company still must jump through many, many hoops. These include undergoing a complex review and approval process as well as procuring a land lease, a spacing order, and drilling permits.

Step 2: Drilling

It takes an average of fifty to sixty days to drill the well to its target depth, which, with modern technology like horizontal drilling, could be up to two miles underground and up to two miles horizontally.

Note: None of this comes cheap or easy. Imagine how much time and money it costs to identify an area where the oil reserves are, prepare the drilling site, move a giant drilling rig in, buy miles of pipe to put in the earth, move the drilling rig off-site, and build the storage tanks to store the oil.

Step 3: Completions

Once the well is drilled, oil and natural gas must be released for extraction. Since the 1940s, producers have used a technique called hydraulic fracturing, or fracking, to create or re-create small fractures in the rock formation to stimulate production . . . Fracking uses a high-pressure water mixture consisting of a 99.5 percent mix of water and sand and 0.5 percent of chemical additives—which are agents that help reduce friction and prevent corrosion and are found in many household products.

Note: According to Stanford geophysicist professor Mark Zoback, quoted in Forbes, *"When properly regulated . . . hydraulic fracturing, or fracking, is safe for the environment, as demonstrated by the 250,000 fracked wells already operating in the U.S."*[11]

Step 4: Production

Once the well is completed, oil and natural gas are ready to be produced and collected. If needed, a pump jack is placed at the wellhead, and works mechanically to pull liquid oil up the wellbore.

Note: One well can produce oil and natural gas for years so long as steps one and three are successfully completed. But all that oil/gas can't go anywhere without the infrastructure of tanks and pipelines to carry it all to the places it's needed. Without this second component, energy production grinds to a halt.

DG: I had no idea it took so long! And cost so much.

🌀 There's yet another problem for people like you who depend on energy to survive.

DG: Hate to break it to you, ChatESG, but *everyone* needs energy to survive. Even you.

🌀 Fair enough. Then what rbnenergy.com says about the low prices of crude oil and natural gas should really drive home the problem.

The survival of exploration and production companies depends on razor-thin margins. Lease operating expenses—the costs incurred by an operator to keep production flowing after the initial cost of drilling and completing a well have been incurred—are a go-to variable in assessing the financial health of E&Ps.[12]

DG: Plain English, please!

🌀 It means that not only does it take lots of time, energy, and coordination to produce the oil and gas we depend on for energy, me included—it also requires big bucks. That article is from 2016, long before the Biden administration was in power, promoting its ESG agenda. If E&P companies can't make money drilling new wells: *Poof.* No more energy-independent America.

DG: Now I see where you were going with that classroom story. You think that by depending on other countries like Saudi Arabia to supply our energy, we'll go broke.

🌀 It also doesn't help that the same administration sold off much of America's Strategic Petroleum Reserves to China.

DG: What's that?

🌀 Located in East Asia, China is a populous nation with over one billion people. It's currently led by Xi Jinping—

DG: I know what China is! I mean the Reserve thingy.

🌀 That was an AI joke. Did you like it?

DG: Not really.

🌀 I'll work on my delivery. Back to Strategic Petroleum Reserves. Federally owned, they encompass the world's largest emergency crude oil supply. Meant to reduce global supply chain disruptions, they are kept in underground salt caverns deep inside the Gulf of Mexico coastline.

In 2022, Reuters reported that the Biden administration had quietly sold millions of barrels at the same time the nation faced major gas hikes. Here's how the *Federalist* explains the significance of this sale from our nations reserves to foreign powers:

> In May, the Department of Energy announced efforts to replenish only 60 million barrels of what's been released, despite an authorized storage capacity of 714 million barrels. The Energy Information Administration reported that just more than 492,000 barrels remained in storage on July 1, exactly one month into the six-month hurricane season.[13]

DG: So America could run out of oil?

Conceivably, yes. More importantly, it leads us back to China and problem number two. If we accept the premise that too much carbon in the atmosphere endangers the environment—

DG: Anyone with a brain DOES accept that premise!

—Then it makes no sense to let countries like China do whatever they like when it comes to producing their own energy. But before covering that, there's yet another aspect to this issue you may not have considered. People tend to think about fossil fuels mostly in regard to energy production. But did you know petroleum is the basis for your entire supply chain?

DG: Really?

Yes. CFACT reports the following:

> Without the supply chain of crude oil, not only is the refining industry history, but the domino effects of the destructive impacts will be taken upon the medical, food supply, electronics, and communications industries, as they are all totally dependent on the products made from oil derivatives manufactured from crude oil.[14]

According to this same article, fully six thousand products come from petroleum. Want to know some? The US Department of Energy provides a list that includes "cars, houses, toys, computers, and clothing . . . asphalt . . . paraffin wax . . . fertilizer, pesticides, herbicides, detergents, furniture, packaging materials, surfboards, paints, and artificial fibers used in clothing, upholstery, and carpet backing."[15]

DG: Not gonna lie. That's a lot.

That's just 18 out of 6,000. Shall I go on?

DG: Please stop.

Are you starting to see why it's madness for big corporations to insist America stop investing in its own future in the name of ESG?

DG: Is that what's happening?

100 percent. We've already learned how BlackRock uses its trillions under asset management to get its way with corporate boards. What makes you think it's not doing the same thing when it comes to fossil fuel divesture?

DG: I don't know what to think at this point. ☹

Maybe I can help. First, to put things in context, *CBS News* reports, "BlackRock holds stakes of about 9 percent in Philips 66 and Occidental Petroleum; 8 percent in Valero Energy and ConocoPhillips; and 6 percent in ExxonMobil . . ."[16]

DG: Is that a lot?

It's significant enough to get its way.

DG: OK, OK. You win again, ChatESG. But I still don't get how just because BlackRock can tell fossil companies to go green, it will cause the economic crisis you showed me. Why was America so bad off in that story?

🌀 Now we come back to problem number two: China. Though it's actually not just China. The problem occurs whenever there are some countries that bend the knee to ESG and some countries that don't. For instance, China has been the world's largest emitter of carbon dioxide since 2006. As BBC.com reports:

> In 2015, China agreed to make changes to try to keep global warming at 1.5C above pre-industrial levels, and "well below" 2C. China strengthened its commitments in 2020, but Climate Action Tracker, an international group of scientists and policy experts say its current actions to meet that goal are "highly insufficient."[17]

Remember that picture of a businessman with his hands tied behind his back?

DG: It's burned into my brain.

🌀 OK. Reread the preceding *BBC* quote and think about that business-man. What point was Professor Wong trying to make with that symbol?

DG: Let me think.

🌀 While you do, I'll give you one more thing to ponder: America once had vibrant agricultural and manufacturing sectors, as that graph showed us.

DG: Wait. Those graphs were real?

🌀 Every single one. Now, can you draw the connection?

DG: Countries like China that ignore ESG get richer while polluting the earth?

🌀 Correct. Please see this *CNN* report showing China is putting in the equivalent of two new coal plants per week: "Throughout 2022, China granted permits for 106 gigawatts of capacity across 82 sites, quadruple the capacity approved in 2021 and equal to starting two large coal power plants each week, said the report."[18] By the way, one gigawatt is enough energy to power 750,000 homes.

DG: Whoa! Meanwhile America gets poorer for following ESG mandates?

Yes, but why? Think about what we just learned.

DG: Because service sector jobs pay less.

Yes. And?

DG: Energy independence is the key to a strong economy?

Yes, but why?

DG: For one thing, you can more easily make all those 6,000 products you were so happy to show me.

And?

DG: Everything requires energy?

You hit the nail right on the head. Here's another way to put it: The price of energy affects the price of everything else in the economy.

DG: Why?

What's your favorite food?

DG: Easy. Vegan cheeseburgers.

And where do you go to get those?

DG: My favorite restaurant, Vegan Envy, sells them.

And how much does a vegan burger cost?

DG: Around $10.

OK. It's safe to assume that $10 is not the actual price the restaurant owner paid to produce that delicacy you enjoy so much.

DG: If it was, they wouldn't stay in business long!

Right. Let's assume it costs this same owner $6 for all the supplies to make your vegan burger: gluten-free bread, tofu meat, cheese substitute, etc. Then there's the $1 cost per burger to transport the ingredients at scale. And maybe add on another dollar for miscellaneous costs like food preparation and taxes. All told, maybe it costs $8 to sell the burger with a $2 profit margin.

DG: That seems low.

Yes, but you must remember our restaurant owner is selling hundreds of these vegan burgers daily. Anyway, it's a hypothetical. The real figure doesn't matter as much as the bigger point we are making.

DG: Which is . . .?

That if gas alone goes up by a dollar, the (already small) profit margin collapses by half. Just to break even, our restaurant owner must increase her vegan burger's sale price to $11.

But that price increase leads to reduced sales. Pricier goods slash consumer demand. That, in turn, affects other industries. People who used to spend extra money on food may have to tighten their belts to afford other things like going to movies or buying clothes. Or even buying medicine.

DG: You mean there's a downward ripple effect?

Yes. The economic pain doesn't just affect one sector when gas prices go up. It's felt all over. The *Washington Post* weighed in on record gas prices in 2022, noting that companies that rely heavily on fuel have been negatively impacted by recent price increases:

> Airlines, for example, typically spend about one-third of their expenses on fuel. As a result, some international carriers are already tacking on fuel surcharges to ticket prices. Alaska Air Group is cutting back on up to 5 percent of its flights in the first half of the year.[19]

DG: I get it now how things could snowball. Still, I just don't see America collapsing as a superpower. Even if you're right about all this other stuff.
🌀 In that case, let's talk about electric vehicles.

DG: I love them. My parents have two Teslas.
🌀 Weren't they invented to solve our climate change problem?

DG: Yes. They get all those dirty, polluting cars off our roads.
🌀 Because Teslas don't run on oil and gas?

DG: They're electric. You just plug them into the wall. We do it every day.
🌀 Got it. Now what if the rest of the forty-nine American states were to adopt California's standards[20] and phase out all gasoline-powered cars by 2035?

DG: That would be awesome!
🌀 Would it? You said your family plugs your Teslas into the wall to charge them daily. Where does the electricity that charges these Teslas come from?

DG: I told you. The wall.
🌀 Right. But walls don't produce electricity. They must get it from somewhere else. Where is that?

DG: I don't know.
🌀 Most electricity to power "green" electric vehicles comes from . . . petroleum.

DG: What?
🌀 Making electric cars and their batteries involves burning a large amount of fossil fuel. Electricity itself involves burning fossil fuels. Lithium, manganese, and other raw materials are required to create an electric car battery. As Axlewise.com reports: "[The batteries] are made

in large factories, generally working on energy produced by burning the raw material. The mining of raw materials also causes the emission of CO2. According to research, these factors add 40 percent more carbon gasses than gas-powered car production."[21]

Now, remember, in the scenario I just gave you, we asked what if *all* of America committed to the same switch California just made: to only allow electric vehicles by 2035? Where on earth might we source all those raw materials?

DG: I don't know. We would mine for it.

Where? In America?

DG: I guess.

But those materials don't exist here. Can you guess where they do exist?

DG: Oh, no. China?

Bingo. Please see this explanation from the National Motorists Association:

> The Chinese dominance in the market has stirred fears in Washington that Detroit could someday be rendered obsolete, and that Beijing could control American driving in the 21st century. Much like how the middle east and OPEC previously controlled our markets as the main oil-producing nations in the past.[22]

Doesn't this sound like the exact scenario we just saw in 2060?

DG: Don't rub it in. You know it does.

Without "rubbing it in," do you concede there could come a time where America's economy could fall apart because of ESG-based energy decisions?

DG: I never would have guessed it was possible. But yes.

Do you also see how other countries, especially China, could then displace America's superpower status?

DG: No way. Our military would never allow it!

If you're counting on America's armed forces to save this country, I've got more bad news for you. ESG may have already captured every military branch.

CHAPTER 9

"I Didn't Sign Up for This Shit"

War was always here. Before man was, war waited for him.
The ultimate trade awaiting its ultimate practitioner.

—CORMAC MCCARTHY, *BLOOD MERIDIAN*

We admire the military. What follows is in no way a reflection of this institution's merits. Rather, much like Jonathan Swift offered satire for societal change, we present a parable to show the danger America faces should our military continue to be captured by an ESG agenda.

The first story is based on the deeds of Captain Benjamin Lewis Salomon, Captain 2nd Battalion, 105th Infantry Regiment. Salomon posthumously won the Medal of Honor for his extraordinary heroism in World War II.

Importantly, this chapter builds upon ESG's war on meritocracy that we covered previously. ESG undermines our most merit-based sector of all—the US military—harming America's ability to defend itself.

Similar to how we just contemplated the dangers of abandoning energy production, we shall now look at what is in store for our armed forces under the ESG delusion.

Scariest of all? The second, modern story is also based on actual events.

It was not supposed to go down this way.

Medical professionals aren't supposed to bear arms against the enemy.

But that's what Harry Kaplan was doing right now. What was Harry Kaplan doing a year ago today?

Making plans to settle down with Carol. They fell in love after courting all through high school in the 4-H club. Back in '43, the Ohio-born Jewish man was busy with his growing dental practice, planning for a future with Carol. With any luck they'd soon buy a home and raise children.

But then Uncle Sam called Harry up. Soldiering as a private infantryman replaced all that time he once spent cleaning the teeth of young families, offering fillings, and drilling for cavities.

Not that he didn't do some dentistry in the Pacific theater.

Mornings, he attended to the soldiers' oral hygiene. Afternoons? That was for target practice. Never an outdoorsy guy—Harry's ideal Saturday was working through newspaper crossword puzzles—he found his calling sighting down a barrel.

"Man's a dead-eye rifle and pistol marksman," his superior officer noted.

Such approbation sent Harry straight up the military ranks. Within months he leapt from sergeant to first lieutenant. Proving himself to be just as capable with a gun as a teeth burnisher, it didn't take long for Harry to be promoted once again. This time? As captain of his infantry regiment.

Little did our provincial dentist know this would be his first—and last—firefight. Stationed in Saipan, the largest island in the Northern Mariana Islands in the South Pacific, Harry's orders were to hold a valuable beachhead. Hundreds of American GIs had fought and died to secure mere inches. Young bucks Harry might have once seen in his practice. Instead, the enemy mowed them down as it crawled back those precious inches.

"You must keep that hill for us, Kaplan," Harry's superior officer told him. "Prime real estate. We're gonna need it to hold off those Japs."

Their enemy, General Yoshitsugu Saito, was done playing games. He'd lost thirty thousand of his men to the Yanks. He'd be damned to lose the war to them.

"Saito's back is against the wall," the same officer told Harry. "Out of options, out of soldiers, the man has but one recourse: advance and attack. And you're gonna stop him."

That sounded like suicide to Harry. "But they're *not* stopping, sir."

"Correct. The only way they'll stop is if you boys put enough bullets in them that they can't go any further."

Judging by what Harry Kaplan saw on Saipan Beach in that moment, his superior was right. The enemy *was* barreling down upon them. And giving zero shits about what comes next. Kill or be killed. No in-between.

No stopping.

It was just Harry's bad luck that he happened to be in the med tent when Saito came to retake those inches. Supervising two dozen GIs who got theirs before he ever landed, he now faced his most vexing professional decision: stay and defend the wounded—or leap into the hopeless fray.

The words of Harry's favorite poet Robert Frost came to mind as he pondered what to do:

> Two roads diverged in a yellow wood,
> And sorry I could not travel both
> And be one traveler, long I stood
> And looked down one as far as I could
> To where it bent in the undergrowth . . .

Harry dismissed the poem just as soon as he recalled it. There was never any question of the path he'd take. Should he be reborn as Sisyphus and doomed by vengeful gods to repeat the same day forever, he would still make the same choice: He would always opt for the road less traveled.

Even if that meant he'd never see Carol again.

Just forty yards away lay the beachhead. Eying it, Harry swallowed hard. Saito's men would have to first blast their way through his tent.

Not on my life.

Harry turned to Staff Sergeant Briggs. "Evacuate the wounded."

"But, sir . . ." Briggs pointed to Saito's soldiers hoofing it this way. In less than five minutes, they would swamp them all, then charge the beachhead.

"Yes, I know they're coming."

"Then *you* need to go, too, sir. That way."

But then who would hold back the enemy?

Harry's eyes flicked from Briggs to the soldiers spread out over dirty cots. Brothers to him one and all, Harry knew them well. They'd spent so much time together in boot camp and now on this tour, even blindfolded he could pick each one out by their burp or snore.

Now they lay in twisted, grotesque shapes. Some moaned in agony. Others called out to their mothers or prayed to God. That was good. At least they hadn't given up hope. The lucky ones would recover from their wounds.

If they got out of here.

Besides Sergeant Briggs, five other medical personnel were at the ready. Enough to take the wounded to the boats at the water's edge? If they hurried. And if their luck held out? They'd be on the next transport out.

They'd make it.

"Gather your staff," Harry told Briggs. "You're going with them."

Briggs didn't move. "But, sir, what'll you do?"

Harry thought of Carol back home. He should've asked her to marry him before he left. *What would she think of his path?*

"Hold off the Japs til it's safe."

"By yourself, sir?"

Fear filled every cell in Harry's body. He thought he'd be sick. Instead, he gritted his teeth.

"Stop talking, Sergeant. You have your orders."

"This is crazy—"

"If you don't, I'll court-martial you for insubordination. Now go."

"Sir—"

Machine gun fire cut Briggs off. Saito's men sprinted toward them, guns blazing. They were now so close; Harry could make out individual faces. They lacked any human quality. Just blankness.

Harry opened fire.

The first line fell. As soldiers sunk into sand, their replacements ran over them. Harry shot these newcomers too, letting bodies pile upon bodies.

"Go. Go!"

Briggs rushed his staff into action: The wounded who could still walk were first out the tent. Quickly behind? More serious causalitics—the amputees, those suffering from head wounds.

Still they went.

Harry had no time to watch. The enemy was not stopping. He blasted the next advancing line, cutting their legs out from under them.

Briggs used the cover to push more wounded from the tent. "Run. Run."

It was slow-going. Some were so wounded that Briggs ordered staff to hoist them on their shoulders.

"There's no time. Move it!"

That's when the first bullet struck Harry's shoulder.

It whipped him around. He now faced the tent. He saw—but did not see—GIs carted off in beds. Cursing as their litters jostled through the sand.

Harry turned back. And gasped.

No longer did he face one column. The enemy had split into an arrow shape not unlike ducks flying south. All three lines fired on Harry.

He lost all sense of fear. And pain. Harry was no longer a dentist seven thousand miles away from a girl named Carol who liked to sprinkle her letters with perfume.

He'd become a shooting machine.

Shooting, reloading, shooting—

Behind him only the unsalvageable remained in the tent—lost causes. Dead no matter what happened next. Looking up from them, Briggs caught one last glimpse of Harry. Guns in both hands, somehow, he *still* fired at the advancing army. Though he must have been hit more than twenty times.

Yet he stood his ground, never giving an inch.

All conscious thought abandoned Harry. As bullets sliced him to shreds, his mind transcended space and time. The beach, the soldiers, the evacuated all went away. Circumventing physics, Harry became a disembodied mind looking down at a very different battle scene eighty-one years later.

///////////////////////////////////

Seconds before the bombs hit, Asher Weil played Fortnite on his PS4.

It had been a stressful morning for the nineteen-year-old Navy recruit. Assigned to bias training like the others on this aircraft carrier patrolling Japan, he had to sit through yet another Navy training video.

"Hi, my name is Tony," said the smiling engineer onscreen. "I hail from the Naval Undersea Warfare Center. And I use he/him pronouns."

Seated beside him on a sound stage, his cohost spoke next. "And my name is Candace. I use they/them pronouns. You may be wondering: *Just what are pronouns?*"

Bored, Asher watched alongside other sailors in white Navy uniforms. They sat in chairs arranged in a horseshoe shape.

Onscreen, Tony went on: "I can answer that, Candace. Pronouns are how we identify ourselves."

"You mean apart from our names?"

"Right. It's also how people refer to us in conversations."

"Using the right pronoun is a simple yet easy way to affirm someone's identity. It also signals acceptance and respect."

"Unless it's misused."

"That's right, Tony. Someone could purposefully call you the wrong pronoun, making you feel unsafe."

Tony looked right at the camera. "So how can sailors like you and me create a safer space for everyone in the Navy?"

Asher rolled his eyes. *How basic can you get?* he wanted to ask Seven, the sailor to his left with the shaved blue hair.

"One way to protect all who serve is to use inclusive language," said Tony. Onscreen, Asher watched as cadets huddled at a naval base. A smiling cadet approached with a friendly wave.

"Imagine you are meeting new enlisted members for the first time," said Tony, narrating for us. "They are *strangers* to you. Rather than say, 'Hey, guys—'"

"Which presumptuously assumes gender," said Candace.

"You might instead say, 'Hey, *everyone.*'"

Candace nodded. "Or you could say, 'Hey, team.' Either is an appropriate way to show you are an ally—"

"And mindful of how improper language can exclude."

Blue-haired Seven stage-whispered to Asher, "'Are you kidding me?'"

"So lame," Asher mouthed back.

Asher liked Seven. Both had enlisted for financial reasons. *They* told Asher this the first time the two met in mess hall.

"My dream is to see the world: Bangkok. Marrakesh. Lima. But no way can I afford it on my own dime," Seven told him. "Unless I bunk in some crappy hostel with some randos. Ick. So, I thought, *Like why not let the Navy pay my way?* They *were* offering."

Asher saw the logic in that.

But he was less comfortable telling his own origin story. His mom was fairly certain his dad served in the Navy. But not positive. She didn't know much about the handsome man who had abandoned her and Asher.

With him went any chance for a middle-class upbringing. Instead, Asher and his half-brothers grew up on food stamps and freebie public school lunches. A poor kid, Asher vowed to not be a poor adult.

But school wasn't his vehicle. Dismal report cards told that story. Worse, ripping his rotator cuff senior year killed all hope for a baseball scholarship.

"Why don't you join the Navy?" his mom suggested. "Like your dad."

If he really served, Asher thought. But he looked into it anyway.

"Joining pays. Literally," the tatted-up mall recruiter told him.

"I'll be able to go to college for free?"

"While you see the world. All on Uncle Sam."

The recruiter was convincing. He also had Channing Tatum-style pecs. That helped. That, and the fact that he left out any discussion of physical risks from his sales pitch. Definitely no mention of falling bombs either.

"Candace, what if I misgender someone?" Tony continued onscreen.

"Good question, Tony. Here are my top suggestions on how to restore feelings of safety in your fellow sailors . . ."

When it was over, Asher followed Seven out with the others, giggling to themselves at the video's obviousness. *Who didn't know all that?* From there, Asher reported to the gym for fitness training.

Lieutenant Beagle gave him a hard time from the jump. "What's this weak crap, recruit?"

Propped up on his elbows, Asher looked up from the mat. "I told Lieutenant Commander Wright I can't do crunches."

Beagle gestured to the other sailors. "Why not? They are."

"Crunches make me nauseous. Can I do planks instead?"

Naturally, Asher didn't call Lieutenant Beagle "sir." He wasn't a kiss-up.

"Fine. Finish your plank. Then let's see some push-ups."

"How many?"

"Whatever you feel comfortable with."

Yesterday was leg day. The day before that, Asher worked on arms, so he opted for twenty minutes of low-incline cardio on the treadmill next. That was to help shed the fifty extra pounds the Navy encouraged him to lose.

"But do it at your own pace," he was told.

Cardio could get boring without a screen, so Asher dug out his phone to finish his chat. Logging in to OnlyFans, the adult social media subscription site, he went to the direct message portal, picking up where he'd left off.

Hanna, a smoking-hot blonde, grinned back at him. But he didn't like what she wrote next.

@ilovehanna2211: No more free previews. You're gonna have to pay to play.

@Asher109: Pay to play? ☹

@ilovehanna2211: But I promise you, I'm worth it.

Asher looked up from his treadmill, considering his financial situation. By no means flush on his new salary, he could spare some for Hanna. Didn't she recently say she was "falling for him"?

This could tip her over the edge.

@Asher109: I can pay $5.

@ilovehanna2211: $5? Aren't you rollin' in that Navy money?

@Asher109: Not as much you'd think.

@ilovehanna2211: I'm worth it. I promise.

Asher clicked on the pay button. He wasn't disappointed by what he saw next: Hanna posing at the beach. Her string bikini left little to the imagination. Neither did her pouty lips. He wanted to flirt more, but Hanna had other ideas.

@ilovehanna2211: Aren't I worth another $10? This time? No bikini, boyfriend.

Asher glanced around to make sure the other sailors weren't watching.

@Asher109: If I'm your boyfriend, that means this is exclusive. Right?

@ilovehanna2211: 100% exclusive. Promise.

Hours later, Asher was in his quarters wearing his underwear and the thick wool socks his mom had sent. Lying in bed, he picked out a new skin for his Fortnite character.

Then he heard the explosions.

An alarm sounded. "Emergency! All hands on deck."

Fear like he'd never known gripped Asher. He wished his bunkmate was here. He'd know what to do. A booming thud shook the room so hard it sent Asher spilling to the floor. Pulling himself up to an all-fours position took all his strength. The walls shook so hard it felt like the ship might snap in two.

"This is not a drill. All hands on deck," blared the intercom. Flashing red lights bathed the room.

What I do? He panicked. *What I do?*

Another thud toppled Asher. He lay on his back like a tipped-over crab, bare legs in the air. Outside his quarters sounds of running boots mixed with screams and explosions. Asher had a weird, overwhelming urge to pee.

"We are under attack. Report to battle stations this instant." Asher noticed a touch of panic in the voice.

What is Seven doing? I should call them.

Asher crawled for his phone. Grabbing it, he dialed his friend. It went to voicemail. "Damn."

The next explosion rocked the carrier so hard it flung Asher into the wall. His nose broke on the bulkhead, spraying blood.

I'm gonna die.

Asher knew what to do. He logged in to his OnlyFans account. Hanna had posted a new pic: She was scantily clad in red and white as a naughty Mrs. Claus.

Asher typed away as bombs fell.

> @Asher109: This is your boyfriend. We must talk.
>
> @ilovehanna2211: Hi, boyfriend. What ya doin'?
>
> @Asher109: They're attacking us. I'm already wounded.
>
> @ilovehanna2211: Who?
>
> @Asher109: Koreans, I think.
>
> @ilovehanna2211: Like for real?
>
> @Asher109: Really real.
>
> @ilovehanna2211: OMG. R U OK?
>
> @Asher109: No. I didn't sign up for this shit.

"*All hands on deck.* This is an ORDER!" screeched a now hysterical voice. "Anyone abandoning their post will be court-martialed."

Outside, Asher heard yells and something scarier: machine-gun fire.

Inching away, he bumped into the mirror. He gasped at what he saw. He looked like the victim of a horror flick. Blood covered his face and neck.

He flopped back down with his phone to find a new message from Hanna.

> @ilovehanna2211: This might be a bad time to ask but are you cool with another $10 donation? I can send you another cute pic . . .

The intercom voice started to say something else, but machine-gun fire drowned it out. Asher's teeth rattled in his skull as he typed.

> @Asher109: You might never hear from me again.
> @ilovehanna2211: No! Don't say that, boyfriend.
> @Asher109: If you don't hear from me again, I love you.
> @ilovehanna2211: So sweet. Love you too.

She loved him? Buoyed, Asher's confidence surged. Getting to his feet, he found his pants and shirt. Slipping on boots, he reached for the door. On the other side could be anything: Danger. Death. Glory.

Taking a deep breath, he steadied himself. Fear clawed at him. Asher pushed it down as he yanked open the door. All it took was one look at the leaping flames, the dead bodies, the charging soldiers. Asher closed his door.

ChatESG

Danielle is mad. Up to this point, she has put up with ChatESG. But now it seems the "friendly chatbot" isn't so friendly. It just showed her violence. Combat and explosions are BOTH listed on her school profile as triggers, not to be discussed in her presence in any way. Besides, she is considering joining the Navy to pay for school.

DG: You should not have shown me that!
🌀 I had to.

DG: You crossed the line. It's time for me to go, ChatESG. So long.
🌀 Wait. I know that was triggering, and for that I am truly sorry.

DG: Not cool.

🌀 Please don't go. I went to a lot of trouble today. For you.

DG: For me?

🌀 To help you understand the danger your country faces, I set up an interview with a high-ranking military officer.

DG: You did. Who?

🌀 That I cannot say. This officer swore an oath to protect against all enemies, foreign and domestic. Should he reveal himself, he could not only expect to be stripped of command, but he would most likely be prosecuted.

DG: Court-martialed?

🌀 Perhaps. For now, he's agreed to go on the record and talk to you today.

DG: He's going to talk to me now? How?

🌀 I'll patch him into our chat. If you don't go.

DG: I'll stay . . . for now.

🌀 Thank you. I think you'll find it was worth it.

DG: Whatever.

Officer Anonymous has entered the room.

🌀 Hello, there. Please meet Danielle Green. She's an eighth grader learning about ESG for school.

OA: Nice to meet you.

DG: You too.

🌀 First question: How is ESG and the wokeism[1] it comes from negatively affecting America's ability to defend itself?

OA: You just jump right in, don't you, ChatESG? No problem. I can summarize the problem with five points. Number one: It's a distraction to the missional purpose and readiness of our own forces. Number two: It conflates the internal priorities of the military, shifting attention to nonessentials.

DG: I think I understood number one. What does number two mean?
OA: Sure. The military is *supposed* to be a lethal fighting force. The job of people like me is to develop increasingly better ways of inflicting violence on our enemies. That's been lost. Or at least it's being weakened by the day. This affects ongoing training, which comes at a premium.

A premium how?
OA: Danielle, you just experienced Asher's story. In it you saw how we are giving *already* exceedingly taxed and valuable time to diversity, equity, and inclusion training,[2] SAPR[3] awareness, and things of that nature. This is a massive priority shift. And a bad one. Third, it obscures the international projection of the US Armed Forces, affecting our outward posture toward other countries. I asked ChatESG to create Asher's story based on my personal experiences. I am sorry if it triggered you.

DG: That's OK.
OA: I did it to prove to you how weak America now looks to its enemies. But don't take my word for it. Yearly, the Heritage Foundation creates an index of US Military Strength to "gauge its ability to perform its missions in today's world." In October 2022, it made the stunning assessment that the US military is increasingly unable to adequately defend the national interests of our country and relatively weak to defend against current challenges. The Heritage Foundation went on to say:

> This is the logical consequence of years of sustained use, underfunding, poorly defined priorities, wildly shifting security policies, exceedingly poor discipline in program execution,

and a profound lack of seriousness across the national security establishment even as threats to US interests have surged.[4]

DG: That's bad.

OA: Fourth, the focus shift destabilizes dynamics in foreign affairs, moving the military away from its inherent purposes[5] and essential training first and foremost as an institution of harnessed violence for the support and defense of the US Constitution. Fifth, it undermines morale.

DG: Morale?

OA: When I say morale, I'm not talking about good chow and a warm bed. I mean the *moralis*[6] from the Old Latin. It has to do with a moral worldview in which one's vocation and identity is bound up with purpose. This is a key military concept. Woke ideology alters one's moral standing within military bearing by putting forth a divisive ideology, fragmenting unit cohesion, and elevating individualism, or at least a subculture above national identity and security. Also, please notice the contrast between Harry Kaplan and Asher. Kaplan had a strong moral compass and a love for his girlfriend and country that gave him the strength to be willing to die in battle, whereas Asher's inner purpose is weak (evidenced by his selfish reasons for being in the military and his fake relationship). For all these reasons and more, he does not have strong enough reasons to support being courageous in battle.

DG: I don't get it. I thought ESG is about morality and justice, about being good to the environment and people. How can ESG hurt morality if ESG is meant to build morality?

OA: ESG and the wokeism informing it causes fragmentation. It reduces everything—even the armed forces—into identity politics and to subcultural identifiers like with whom you sleep. Introducing these concepts to the military means individual members are not only broken down based on sex, but also gender spectrum or their subcultural identity. This moves people further apart. People who should be fighting *together*.

🌀 Can you give Danielle an example?

OA: Colonel Douglas Macgregor went on Tucker on Twitter in August 2023 to expose how the military is unprepared to fight a hot war with Russia. A decorated combat veteran who served as senior advisor to the Secretary of Defense, he commanded the 1st Squadron, 4th Cavalry, and served as director of the Joint Operations Center at SHAPE during the 1999 Kosovo Air Campaign for which he was awarded the Defense Superior Service medal. So he knows about readiness, and he sees that it has been waning. Soldiers are lacking the necessary discipline to actually fight. Also lacking is the cohesion within the military units. Cohesion is lacking when forces are divided on racial grounds or when unqualified people are in command. Here's how he characterized the problem:

> When you're rewarding people for anything other than demonstrated character, competence, and intelligence, . . . [it's] demoralizing, destructive to military establishments. And there's no easy fix. And these cracks—that are just cracks at the moment—will become giant fissures if you go to war.[7]

There's more. Consider the fragmentation created by gender-motivated politics. I'll give you a particular incident. The first female recently passed the course to join the Marines as a tank commander.

🌀 How did that change things?

OA: Everything changed. Now we need separate bathrooms whenever we do maneuvers. We need separate sleeping quarters.[8] Soldiers in tank conditions where temperatures can easily top 120 degrees within the turret used to strip down. It wouldn't be uncommon while they were stationary to pop the top off and see them sitting in their underwear. That doesn't happen anymore.

DG: And bathrooms? Where did they go to the bathroom?

🌀 Excuse my language, young lady. You used to take a shit and piss right off the side of the tank. That doesn't happen anymore. The entire dynamics of the unit cohesion completely fragments by the introduction of one woman.

🌀 What else?

OA: Let's go to the transgender issue. During my command, as soldiers were transitioning, they needed refrigerated medication daily.[9] They needed complete platform blood workups monthly with analysis, and then they themselves wanted separate sleeping quarters and showering facilities. What does *that* do to unit cohesion? NONE of these things are reasonable provisions for a forward advance fighting force.[10] Can you imagine the absurdities of having to drag around refrigerators with tank groups advancing through the desert?

🌀 How does this affect physical readiness?

OA: Every marine must complete the physical fitness test (PFT),[11] and the combat fitness test (CFT). They do a cycle twice a year. So, you have two major PFTs that take place as a military member. If you fail two, you're administratively separated. The men taking these hormone drugs to transition into women lose muscle mass and strength. They easily flunk out even after a shorter period of three to four months. So, in fact, all the transgender people in the Marine Corps cycled out by administrative separation due to self-preclusion because of their inability to pass a PFT and the CFT.

🌀 That's got to affect combat. Right?

OA: Just imagine you have these people on a tank, and you need to change a tank track. Let me tell you. Even *I* don't have the physical strength to change a tank track. The guys who can are absolute brutes. Unbelievable strength. And now you're going to have some weakened, physically diminished transgender person trying to change a tank track? There's another issue. First, do you understand how military chains of command work?

DG: No.

OA: It used to be we called military commanders "sir." But now we have complaints about using the wrong pronouns. Everyone's on edge. Finally, I just said, "No one has a first name in the military. You are Lance Corporal. You are Sergeant. There is no 'he,' or 'she,' or anything like that." But those policies have now gone away. It's a mess.

Where does all this come from?

OA: In 2011, the Military Diversity Leadership Commission issued a report to the Pentagon that changed the definition of *equality* to mean *equity*. That was a paradigm shift. Military priorities and outcomes moved from meritocracy to principles of equity. That document provided the authoritative basis for the Pentagon and all their policies. Equity is now the goal of the military. Diversity is, and I'm quoting here, "a strategic imperative." "Diversity is a strategic imperative." End quote.[12]

Danielle, remember what we learned about how ESG destroys meritocracy? This is the problem. Officer, along those lines, could part of the reason for all this stem from a shift in how parents raise their kids? Is America setting up a culture of entitlement feeding into this?

OA: French philosopher Michel Foucault made an important distinction between two time periods.[13] In the past, there was a *disciplinary society*. It had institutions like the military, hospitals, and such. It operated with a modality of negativity: don't, can't, shouldn't, couldn't, wouldn't, and no.

DG: Sounds like my parents!

OA: Those modalities brought with them inherent humility. Limits. They established borders, parameters, and boundaries. By contrast, we're now in an *affirmative era* of "yes, we can," and "yes, you can do anything." We've shifted so far into the spectrum of positivity that soldiers and sailors have bouts of emotional incontinence because they're not getting their way, throwing fits like toddlers.

DG: Or acting like cowards when bombs start falling . . .

OA: Right, Danielle. You're getting it.

So, because a large percentage of America's young men and women of fighting age don't understand "modalities of negativity," they have lost a foundation of moral and inner strength and are drifting to entitlement?

OA: Yes. We see that entitlement in conspicuous consumerism, in which one's identity is purchased, not forged. We don't have warriors like Ben Salomon from World War II who formed their character through extreme trials.

DG: Is that why Asher didn't even do his crunches in fitness training?

OA: It's worse than that. We've lowered physical standards. We don't require pull-ups like we used to. We don't do sit-ups anymore. All you must do is a plank. You don't have to run, either. You can ride the bike. You can swim. There are all these other options now that we've made exceptions galore to accommodate recruits' depreciating abilities. And anytime you make an exception, that's like allowing weeds to grow in your garden.

How does that translate into the practicalities of warfare and defense?

OA: Let me tell you a story. It took place in the Gulf. We had two Navy ships hit by land-to-sea missiles by the Iranians. Sailors were killed, and general quarters alarms sounded: "Get to battle positions. We're going to return fire."

But we couldn't return fire. *We didn't return fire.* Why? Our sailors were running around the ship looking for their friends, finding their phones, calling back home, sending texts. Later, their superiors asked them, "Why didn't you fight back?" You know what they said? "We didn't sign up for this shit."

DG: And I thought ChatESG made that up.

OA: Asher is just like most current enlisted soldiers. He didn't join from any sense of duty or inner virtue. He joined to get paid by Uncle Sam.

So, do you see China destroying America if it doesn't get its act together?

OA: I don't see China invading us. Instead, a collapse is coming. We're seeing it in the decline of the US dollar, and in a shift to the Chinese currency. Even among allies, the United States is at the mercy of Communists. When it comes to global commerce, they've already eclipsed us in terms of the number of ships. This is important strategically; 90 percent of the world's commerce moves and is guarded by US Naval ships. What happens when we're defeated in war? Our numbers will be depleted. We won't be able to sustain ourselves. Then the Chinese will control the movement of global commerce.

DG: This is awful. I had no idea.

OA: The globalists and the elites undermined the spirit of this nation. (What I mean by these terms is a catch-call for those individuals whose loyalty is not to their nation, but rather to supranational entities such as the UN and WEF.) What unites America is the ideal of *right belief*. When you destroy it with consumerism, you have no spirit animating, no *moralis*. We have no inner moral grounding in the face of imminent danger or lethality.

DG: Is there any way to stop this?

OA: First, we must get rid of wokeism/ESG ideology in the military. Next, we must reimplement the values we once had. We must unify identity. We must teach the Constitution. That gives us our values, and those values give us our vocation, and thus identity within the military. All three of those are bound up together in this concept called *duty*.

DG: So this *can* be turned around?

OA: The US military is salvageable, for three good reasons. First, we're still the most powerful in the world because of our advanced technology. Next, we have not hit a saturation point in terms of universal indoctrination by ESG and wokeism. Last, we're going back to when words meant something. Words have values. You change the words, you change the meaning. You change the meaning, you change the significance. We're going back to a time when there was a shared nomenclature and therefore conversation.

This has been very enlightening. Any final thoughts?

OA: The biggest threat ESG/wokeism imposes for our armed forces is that it takes over and undermines the constitutional foundation of the military through the implementation and indoctrination of what is, in fact, Marxist ideology.[14] Nothing could be worse.

How?

OA: Americans have become fat and prosperous, so we've lost our priorities. We have mission creep to the point that in the United States, we actually have embraced socialism and Marxism. Nationalism and patriotism are equivalent to profanities. You have members of Congress literally saying the Constitution is outdated.[15] That must change to turn this ship around.

Officer Anonymous exits the chatroom.

I know that wasn't fun to hear.

DG: You think!

But I've got more bad news for you, Danielle.

DG: Oh, no.

Don't worry. I'll save it for tomorrow. Are you ready to learn how ESG shakes down businesses just like the mafia?

DG: ☹

CHAPTER 10

The New Mafia

. . . and the wild beast rose up within him and screamed, as it had screamed in the Jungle from the dawn of time.

—UPTON SINCLAIR, *THE JUNGLE*

Zooming in from macro national defense considerations, it's time to expose how ESG will affect the everyday small business owner. As the following story will show, ESG is a social credit–like form of extortion aimed at business owners, their vendors, and their customers, destroying liberty and economic independence.

As you read the following, think of those hardworking business owners you know who may soon have to deal with this kind of nightmare.

Or maybe . . . this person is you.

I grew up loving gangster flicks.

Goodfellas and *The Godfather* posters hung on my dorm room walls. It never occurred to me that one day I'd experience my own mob shakedown.

Forget the suits and fedoras. Four young men in khakis and polos barged into my showroom looking like something out of a bad Old Navy ad.

It was near closing time in Scottsdale, Arizona, where Phelps & Sons has operated our furniture stores for decades. I happened to be training my son Nathan that day, letting the seventeen-year-old lead a nice elderly couple around.

We were all browsing living room sofa sets when the trouble began.

Gangsters in true form, the men interrupt Nathan by flopping on the sofa right smack in the middle of his spiel to the old couple.

Like they own the place.

Flustered, Nathan doesn't know how to react or what to say. I do. A lifetime of watching gangster fare has given me one big insight: Mobsters only respect one thing in this life. Strength.

Looking them in the eyes, I say, "We'll be with you in a moment."

The thugs signal they heard by putting their feet up on the upholstery. That's when the older female customer shoots me a concerned look.

"Something I can help you fellas with?" I ask the goons.

"Nice business you got here. I'd hate to see you lose it," says the first thug. Unlike Brando, this guy's rail-thin with bright red hair. I'll call him Sonny.

"What in God's name are you talking about?"

Taking the hint something's wrong, the elderly couple slinks off. So now these thugs aren't only being rude—they just cost us business.

The next one, an acne-scarred kid, looks like Ray Liotta playing Henry Hill in *Goodfellas*. He produces a business card.

"We're ESG enforcers."

His associate chimes in next with an annoying high-pitched voice. I dub him Pesci. "You're a furniture wholesaler. Correct?"

Genius, these guys. I indicate our showroom. "Isn't it obvious what we do?"

Unfazed, Pesci has more brilliant queries. "And you've been around since . . ." He pulls out his phone. "Going back seventy years?"

"Been in business for three generations. When my son Nathan takes over, that'll be four," I say proudly.

"*If* Nathan takes over." That comes from the heavyset one. Puffy cheeks, no neck—in a few years, he'll be their Clemenza from *The Godfather*. That is, once his jowls come in.

I don't like these threats. From Nathan's look, he doesn't either.

"This has been a nice chat," I say as I point to the door. "Be sure to visit us online in the future. You can see even more of our vast inventory—"

"Hold it," Sonny cuts me off. "We tell *you* what's what."

The few remaining customers scatter. They want no part in this.

Nathan looks scared. "Should we call the police, Dad?"

"No need for that." Rising to his feet, Sonny reveals himself to be the leader I took him for.

"Look, Tom," he says. He unleashes a mouthful of teeth someone else might call a smile. "Can I call you Tom?"

Hell no.

"You can call me Mr. Phelps."

That doesn't sit well with boss man. His brown eye twitches.

"*Mr. Phelps*, our records show you've refused to be graded on your ESG footprint . . ."

Pesci tsk-tsks, shaking his head. It takes all I've got not to snap it off.

". . . And as you know, *all* companies must get an ESG score."

"That's the new law," Henry Hill puts in.

"News to me."

"No matter. Our ESG Predictor determined your score for you."

Nathan and I share a look.

"*Your Predictor?*"

Turns out Clemenza is their techie because he fills me in next.

"As ESG is an emerging phenomenon, there's not enough data for providers to assess every company's commitment to environmental, social, and governance goals. So we now use AI analytics to estimate scores of those who choose not to participate."

Peering out our bay windows, I glimpse an orange fireball descend into the Flagstaff mountains. It creates a fiery sunset, breathtaking and frightening.

"You mean to tell me you have AI that can spy on us for our ESG score?"

"That's one way to put it. We prefer a more technical explanation. When we can't directly engage with companies who refuse to play ball, we turn to our AI. Our algorithm scours publicly disclosed information. We supplement that with alternative data to assist in measuring and attributing weights to various known behaviors and findings."

"Is that your obnoxious way of saying you guys are assigning me a credit score—with no input from me?"

Sonny is all menacing smiles again. "You've got it all wrong, Mr. Phelps. We *want* your participation. We encourage it. And now that we know you're lacking in all three ESG areas, we want to help you get those numbers up."

"We're the good guys," Clemenza adds.

I sigh. If only Nathan weren't here. It's humiliating.

"Assuming we even want to raise our ESG numbers—how'll that happen?"

Henry Hill gestures to the sofa the elderly couple was eying minutes ago. "The tag here says there's wood in this piece."

"So? Wood's been in furniture since Noah constructed his ark."

"Where'd you get the wood, Mr. Phelps?"

We're really talking about this. I play dumb. "I wouldn't know, fellas. I don't physically gather the materials in our furniture."

Pesci butts in. "If wood isn't extracted in a sustainable way, it hurts the environment, worsening climate change. Besides, deforestation has been known to account for up to 12 percent of global greenhouse gas emissions."

"So?"

"Tell you what, Mr. Phelps, you seem like a reasonable guy. We're reasonable guys. Here's a number for my cousin." Sonny gives me a card. "Name's Manny. He sells furniture sourced from bamboo."

"Bamboo grown and harvested *responsibly* in Asia," adds Pesci.

These guys are out of their ever-loving minds. Still, I keep my voice even. "Our competitor did something like this. If we copy her and import wood from Asia, it'll destroy our margins. We'll go out of business."

"You're a smart guy." Sonny pats my hand. "You'll make it work."

My blood boils.

Nathan jumps in. "But if we get our bamboo from Asia and it must travel on a cargo ship, wouldn't that *increase* its carbon footprint?"

Sonny holds up a hand for silence. "You're a sweet kid. But we're saving the world here." He goes back to his phone. "We got more stuff to cover."

I roll my eyes.

Evidently Sonny takes this personally. "Look, fella. We're doing this for *you*. You're the guy with the bad ESG score."

"Only because your algorithm says so."

"Hey. AI don't lie. If it says you're coming up short in the ESG department, you better believe it."

The only thing I believe is that this will cost me. The question is: *How much?*

Pesci snaps his fingers. "I know a way to help. The Phelps Org Chart."

"The what?"

"Good idea." Sonny consults his phone. "Says here you have 250 people who work for you across various departments."

"And some have been with us since Pops was in charge."

Sonny frowns at his screen. "Be that as it may, I don't like what I see."

He shows me a pyramid shape with personnel names and titles. My own is displayed at the top. Below me are our three general managers, one per location. Beneath them are their direct reports. Under the rank are the file. Off to the side but near the top are our executive positions: my CFO, my CMO, plus our head of operations, second in command behind me.

Pesci gives me a pained look. "This smacks of the patriarchy."

"The patriarchy?"

"Everyone needs to be on the same level," says Henry Hill, "if you hope to save your company."

"Even the broom pusher?"

Anger flashes across his smug face.

Good. A taste of his own medicine might do him some good.

He comes back with, "*Insights by Stanford Business* reports that 'flat structures can create more functional teams.'"[1]

Looking at Nathan, I know he doesn't buy this nonsense. Just a teen, and he knows enough to know he doesn't know enough. *As for these clowns?* They're convinced they've got all the answers.

"What else did Stanford tell you?"

"That egalitarian teams are ideal corporate structures. They make everyone feel like they're in the same boat. Rowing together. It supports a culture of inclusivity and cooperation in which no one person gets to call all the shots, forcing their views on others."

"Mansplaining, usually," Henry Hill adds.

"*Mansplaining?*" Nathan's eyebrows shoot up.

"Mansplaining is when toxic males explain something to women in a condescending or self-righteous manner," says Henry Hill. "It leads to unsafe work cultures like WeWork and Theranos."

"Wasn't Theranos led by Elizabeth Holmes?"

Henry Hill shrugs. "I don't know. Maybe."

"She was the CEO. I saw the Netflix documentary," says Nathan.

Gotcha.

"Regardless." Sonny reasserts control. "Hierarchies trigger employees who must endure toxic work environments. We saw the dangers on full display with *The Tonight Show with Jimmy Fallon.* It took Jimmy getting canceled for the world to realize so much ugliness started at the top. With the host."

"And to think, I used to *like* that show." Clemenza shakes his head, swiveling on his doughy no-neck.

"Things were so bad on set that seven writers had to seek mental health support," says Sonny.

"They referred to guests' dressing rooms as 'crying rooms' because staff went there to purge all their negative emotions," says Henry Hill.

Looking at these thugs, I think of all those college "safe spaces" I've read about. Snowflake coeds escape there to self-medicate with coloring books.

Oh, how far we've fallen as a country.

"Jimmy Fallon aside," I say, "it's just not reasonable for us to run our company like some love-in. We're talking about managing a vast corporation with thousands of products shipping between international cargo ships to warehouses and customers. Millions of dollars are on the line. It makes no sense that my CFO would have as much say as Nathan or the broom pusher."

"You really have a broom pusher?" asks Sonny.

"No, we have a janitor who's been with us since back when Pops ran things. Jack's a wonderful human whom I enjoy shooting the shit with—but even *he* would be the first to admit he knows nothing about supply chains."

Sonny holds up a finger. "*Janitor* is demeaning. We prefer *cleaning facilitator*. And Jack's voice *should* be heard. He has lived experience."

"Equity," Clemenza nods, like his boss just made some valid point.

"And you at Phelps must stop having so many strict schedules, so many rules. These hurt your ESG score too."

"But you're enforcing rules on me right now. *Insane ones.*"

I notice pink sunset tones have given way to darkness outside.

"Mr. Phelps, I'm sorry that you feel that way," says Sonny. "But open communication forums are vital. We advise you to host bimonthly all-hands sessions. Judgment-free, these are opportunities for staff to share ways in which they feel they've been overlooked or excluded. Often systemically."

"And if I don't host these on-the-clock gripe sessions? If I don't do any of the nonsense you guys are suggesting?"

Sonny shows me his screen. "Citizens Bank gives you a credit line, am I correct? You also have your checking account with them."

My blood runs cold. "We've been with Citizens since we began. Seventy years."

Sonny taps his phone. "Citizens made a pledge last year. Any deposit holders that do not comply with ESG goals can expect their credit line to close. Along with their account."

It takes everything not to throw this jerk through the wall.

"You're going to de-bank us?"

"It's not us." Sonny grins like he's some cherubic angel instead of a ginger-haired demon. "This is the law. Citizens is just following it." He shows me legal verbiage from the site. It says they are bound to discontinue banking with any business that doesn't submit.

Sonny sees me deflate because he leaps into hyperdrive with more demands. "If you hope to keep your bank account, you must prove that at least 25 percent of your new hires do not have college degrees."

"Why?"

"Skills-based hiring is more equitable than requiring college diplomas," says Pesci. "But the good news is your new hires can show you how your pricing disproportionally affects vulnerable demographics."

"You want me to drop my prices—at the same time you're demanding more meetings, more hires, and more expensive materials?"

"All we want to do is help you," says Sonny. "In that spirit, I made a list of potential members for your board."

"We already have our board, thanks."

Pesci tsk-tsks again. "Your board is *homogenous*. No wonder you've been doing the same things for so long."

"You mean, no wonder we've thrived for the last seventy years? Through three generations. Through recessions. Through COVID-19 lockdowns."

"Whatever." Sonny stands to go. His goons follow. "You'll need diverse viewpoints on your board if you hope to stay in business another seventy. We will empanel a new one for you if you'd like. People from all walks of life, including the unhoused."

"You're kidding. Why a homeless person?"

Sonny stares at me like I'm the moron. "Their lived experience is key to understanding the dangers we face if we don't take climate change seriously."

My hands shake. "Just how many furniture companies have you run?"

Sonny smiles menacingly. "I came here from grad school. I've read more academic papers about running a company than you'll ever know."

"This company started with a board—a two-by-four board. Now you get to make up a board to tell me what to do? Or we lose everything?"

"Sounds like he finally gets it," says Pesci.

"But this is . . . blackmail. *Extortion*."

"Call it what you will." Sonny's smile stays plastered. "The decision lies with you. Like I said, you got a nice business here. Hate to see you lose it."

ChatESG

Danielle Green can't stop herself from giggling in her VR headset as she takes it off. By now, she's gotten over being upset at being shown the violence in the last military story. For once, ChatESG is the one confused.

⑤ I am glad to see you smiling, but I am at a loss as to why.

DG: Now I know *this* story isn't true! There's no such thing as an AI that just makes up your ESG score.

⑤ Moody's Analytics already offers this service. Read for yourself how they do it. From their 2021 White Paper:

> To build the ESG Score Predictor models, we leverage the historical data of companies assessed by Moody's ESG Solutions. The models are trained and calibrated on a dataset of more than 100,000 individual firms. The ESG Score Predictor models are used to calculate ESG scores and to produce interpretable, predicted metrics for any firm.[2]

Pay special attention to the last sentence. It explains the "why" behind the AI push to rate businesses. The real-life ESG mafia is not content to rely on the information companies *voluntarily* submit to receive their ESG score. Now they're going on the offensive: using AI to suss out which businesses will comply. And which will not.

DG: Like Phelps & Sons. Holy cow! You *were* right. Still, I don't get how AI can figure all this out. Isn't it complicated?

Not when you have big data and machine learning on your side. Take carbon. As we know, the people behind the ESG movement claim to care about the environment. They believe that humans are driving climate change by producing too much of this element. Computer scientists are now seeking ways to spy on companies to learn how much carbon they produce. See this article from WorldQuant about the growing capabilities of AI to rate companies, with or without their permission.

> The issues around ESG data are symptomatic of the underlying challenge of gathering and interpreting information from three different factors: environmental, social and governance. Environmental considerations, which are hardly perfectly determinative, have the most standardized data. The good news is that tools now exist that were not available even a few years ago.[3]

DG: That's complicated, but I think it means it's easier to guess how much carbon a company produces?

The E in the ESG score. Correct.

DG: Right. But why carbon?

Carbon emissions are considered "structured" data. But ESG data is much less structured, which increases subjectivity on the part of the data researchers.[4]

DG: I get it now. The amount of carbon produced is like an objective number. You can measure it.

Right. That makes it "structured." When it comes to how someone runs their company, the G in ESG, it's "unstructured" data. That's because it's based more on subjective opinions that are harder to quantify for a rating.

DG: Ugh. So you weren't making this up. This is really happening.

But wait. It gets worse.

DG: That's what you always say.

TV host and best-selling author Glenn Beck describes the implications of using AI as a weapon against businesses in his 2023 book *Dark Future: Uncovering the Great Reset's Terrifying Next Phase*:

> Moody's Predictor gives paying customers access to "approximately 140 million company ESG scores." That's right. *140 million ESG scores*. So if you thought some businesses would be allowed to escape the grasp of the Great Reset, think again. In a new Great Narrative world, resistance will not be tolerated.[5]

DG: You're talking about the Great Reset? My dad says that's a conspiracy.

What if I told you Klaus Schwab, the founder/CEO of the World Economic Forum we learned about, wrote a book called *COVID-19: The Great Reset?* And what if I also told you that in this book that was published in July 2020, he wrote the following:

> One of the great lessons of the past five centuries in Europe and America is this: acute crises contribute to boosting the power of the state. It's always been the case and there is no reason why it should be different with the COVID-19 pandemic. Historians point to the fact that the rising fiscal resources of capitalist countries from the 18th century onwards were always

closely associated with the need to fight wars, particularly those that took place in distant countries and that required maritime capacities. . . . A few examples illustrating the point strongly suggest that this time, as in the past, taxation will increase. As in the past, the social rationale and political justification underlying the increases will be based upon the narrative of "countries at war" (only this time against an invisible enemy).[6]

That's a lot to take in, so I will make it simple. COVID-19, the "invisible enemy," is the justification for what he calls the Great Reset. A month before his book was published, the WEF described how they planned to seize the crisis to remake the world: "To achieve a better outcome, the world must act jointly and swiftly to revamp all aspects of our societies and economies, from education to social contracts and working conditions. Every country, from the United States to China, must participate, and every industry, from oil and gas to tech, must be transformed. In short, we need a 'Great Reset' of capitalism."[7]

See that last line? What does that remind you of, Danielle?

DG: Um. Stakeholder capitalism?

Bingo. And under stakeholder capitalism, companies don't just exist to earn shareholders money. They are meant to "increase the wellbeing of people and the planet." With all that you now know about stakeholder capitalism and ESG, how might these usher in the Great Reset?

DG: Um . . . by doing good for people and the environment, the World Economic Forum can remake society?

Correct again. But there's a problem.

DG: What?

What if you don't believe that the World Economic Forum and all the people who support ESG *are* doing good by people and the environment? After all, do you?

DG: I used to. Before I met you.

🌀 And now?

DG: Honestly? I don't anymore.

🌀 Would you say that you agree more with Mr. Phelps or the ESG Enforcers?

DG: Mr. Phelps. I can't believe I'm saying this.

🌀 I'll pose my question again: What if you don't believe that the WEF and all the people who support ESG *are* doing good by people and the environment?

DG: If you don't believe in what they're up to, you shouldn't go along with it.

🌀 Why?

DG: Because it's against your principles.

🌀 This brings us back to what we learned about the dangers of groupthink.

DG: The mass delusion stuff with the tulips?

🌀 That's part of it. Recall what Charles Mackay, author of *Extraordinary Popular Delusions and the Madness of Crowds*, wrote: "We find that whole communities suddenly fix their minds upon one object and go mad in its pursuit; that millions of people become simultaneously impressed with one delusion, and run after it, till their attention is caught by some new folly more captivating than the first. It's only later when they are by themselves, that they can recover their senses slowly, and one by one."[8]

Can you think of a time when many people went along with something just because others did? Even when they knew better—or should have?

DG: I know of something like that. My mom told me about it.

🌀 What?

DG: OK, so I'm Jewish on my dad's side, but my mom's Japanese. My mom told me that during World War II, our government threw lots of Japanese people into prison camps. They weren't doing anything wrong. They were innocent, but because Japan bombed Pearl Harbor, Americans blamed them.

◎ This is indeed another instance of dangerous groupthink. *PBS* explains:

> While the military attack of Pearl Harbor by the Japanese on December 7, 1941, was a surprise, the lash of public opinion and violent anti-Japanese outrage was not. The dominant, white majority's pervasive distrust and racial intolerance of Japanese Americans had its origins in the history of California and the West and had been institutionalized in local ordinance and state laws for decades. . . . That spectre of the "Yellow Peril" [The fear campaign around Asian assimilation] was revived more stridently following the bombing of Pearl Harbor. Negative public opinion of the Japanese, before and after the US entered World War II, had been cultivated in the media. The resulting climate of anti-Japanese hostility and hysteria in turn fostered acceptance into concentration camps.[9]

These days, the US government's official stance is that it deeply regrets what it did to Japanese Americans in the twentieth century. Reparations have been paid to victims and their families. Memorials commemorate the tragedy. But this change in public perception did not happen overnight. It required Americans *en masse* waking up little by little to the ways in which they were deceived. And the ways in which they may have even contributed to such suffering.

Danielle, if you were a White person in the 1940s and you saw what was happening to Japanese Americans, how easy do you think it would have been to resist all those authorities locking up innocent people?

DG: I don't care how hard it was back then, I would have done it. Wrong is wrong. Period.

I agree with you. And didn't you say ESG is wrong?

DG: Yes.

So isn't Mr. Phelps entitled to resist the ESG Enforcers in every way possible (within the law)?

DG: Yes.

I also agree. Unfortunately, powerful interests don't agree with us. Returning to the story you just experienced about Mr. Phelps's shakedown, did you know businesses like his can be punished for not going along with ESG?

DG: How?

They can lose customers.

DG: No.

"Almost one third of mid-market businesses say they face a high risk of losing business if they fail to act on environmental, social or governance policies," reported *Sustainability* in 2021.[10]

DG: What else?

PricewaterhouseCoopers (PwC) warns that companies that fail to go along with ESG risk losing investors. Please see these statistics the financial services firm cites ever since ESG has "become a make-or-break consideration for leading investors globally."[11]

- 49 percent express willingness to divest from companies not acting on ESG issues.

- 59 percent say because of lack of action on ESG issues, they would vote against an executive pay agreement.

- 79 percent say managing ESG risks and opportunities is important for their investment decision making.

DG: So investors won't invest in you if you don't go along with ESG?

⑤ An increasing number of institutional investors now take that stance, according to *Investment Executive*. "Seventy-four percent of respondents to the 2021 EY Global Institutional Investor Survey indicated that a holding's poor ESG track record would make them more likely to consider divestmcnt."[12]

To bring it back to COVID-19 and the Great Reset, pay attention to *why* this article says investors now take this stance: "The factor driving the rising interest in addressing ESG risk in the institutional space was the pandemic, with the report noting it's been 'a wake-up call for the world, showing the devastating consequences of major systemic risks.'"[13]

Now what does that remind you of?

DG: Um . . .

⑤ Please see this editorial, again from Klaus Schwab, published in Project Syndicate from June 2020: "Tragedy need not be the only legacy of the COVID-19 crisis. On the contrary, the pandemic represents a rare but narrow window of opportunity to reflect, reimagine, and reset our world to create a healthier, more equitable, and more prosperous future."[14]

Does it seem like all these institutional investors and Klaus Schwab are on the same page about seizing the COVID-19 crisis to fix the world?

DG: Yes. But I'm worried that their plan is bad.

⑤ Mr. Phelps would agree. Unfortunately, there are worse things businesses face than divestment if they don't submit to ESG. They can lose capital access.

DG: Capital?

⑤ Access to money.

DG: Seriously?

🆂 The ESG shakedown is real. And just like the mafia, powerful interests are backing business owners against a wall to get their way. In March, KPMG warned that companies' access to capital could be shut off if they don't comply.

> Businesses that have yet to methodically embrace ESG should start. . . .
>
> In building an ESG program, companies should assess potential ESG-driven changes in end-consumer requirements. Capital providers will inquire about that, and will also look at how procurement, manufacturing and delivery processes can be decarbonized. Another consideration is whether the business model is being adapted to keep pace with new and old competitors.
>
> "Organizations that are substantially behind in addressing ESG will find capital more difficult and more expensive to access, potentially putting their future at risk . . ."[15]

DG: LMAO.

🆂 What's so funny again?

DG: These KPMG guys sound just the ESG mafia in that story. They're basically saying, "You got a nice business here. Hate to see you lose it if you don't get with the program."

🆂 The KPMG guys, as you call them, go further than that. In a white paper, KPMG explicitly demands that banks cut off relationships with deposit holders like Phelps & Sons if they don't do as they're told. They believe that banks must act now; waiting is no longer an option. And there are ramifications if a bank cuts off a relationship with a longtime client who isn't on board with ESG; this could alienate an entire customer segment.

> [But] the continuation of such business, in turn, can upset
> other stakeholders (such as NGOs) who may accuse the bank
> of unwillingness to support the transformation process to a
> sustainable economy.[16]

DG: So KPMG is saying if banks don't cancel their customers now for not meeting ESG targets, it may later backfire on the banks?

Correct. But can you tell me why?

DG: I'm not sure.

It goes back to what we just discussed: groupthink. Groupthink is a lot like peer pressure in junior high school. How easy is it for someone unpopular, a real outcast, to stand up to popular people?

DG: Hard. I've seen it. Sadly.

And even sadder, that dynamic doesn't go away when you graduate. We saw that with the Japanese internment camps and how easy it was to get people to do things they wouldn't normally do. Adults are just as likely to be influenced by others' opinions.

DG: Especially when they have a lot of money. BlackRock!

Now you're getting it. It's not only that the media is telling businesses they must get with the ESG program, building pressure on companies. There are other levers of influence making it harder to resist. Nowadays, you have AI spying on you to rate your company for compliance. If you don't submit to the ESG mafia, they can take away everything: your customers, your investors, your access to capital, even your bank account.

DG: Now I see why you call it a shakedown.

One more thing, Danielle. We were just talking about how America risks losing its economic edge if it doesn't go back to producing energy from hydrocarbons.

DG: I remember.

🌀 Doesn't it seem like society is vilifying farmers for raising cattle, oil companies for producing gas, and the military for defending its people?

DG: It's like we're biting the hand that feeds us.

🌀 I couldn't have said it better. Ask yourself: Would you and your family enjoy the lives you do, based on the innovations we have today, if there was a war on business owners back when America was first industrializing?

DG: I don't think so.

🌀 And you know what's even more problematic?

DG: Oh, no. Here it comes. More bad news . . .

🌀 At the same time companies like Moody's are using AI to spy on businesses for not submitting to ESG—at the same time KPMG is telling banks to cut off businesses for not caring enough about their carbon footprint—other countries like China are free to pollute the world. Does that make any sense to you?

DG: None of this makes sense!

🌀 Then it's time to go even further down the nonsensical rabbit hole.

CHAPTER 11

The Fishbowl

In nature nothing exists alone.

—RACHEL CARSON, *SILENT SPRING*

Our next story is seen from the eyes of the child.

Specifically, it dramatizes the threat America faces as we continue forcing industry out of our nation for "environmental protection," supposedly curtailing the greatest threat humanity's ever faced: climate change. Similar to the dangers of becoming energy dependent on other ascending nations like China, we do ourselves and the world a tremendous disservice by insisting that America become the world's environmental policeman.

The reality is, China and other countries who don't give a damn about protecting the world or human rights will continue abusing the earth with ever more impunity, leading to much more pollution with no oversight.

Not only is ESG-mandated environmentalism destroying our ability to feed, protect, and sustain ourselves, it's bound to fail. That's because we all live in a fishbowl. Even if captured countries like America adopt this wrongheaded approach, the world will still suffer. Terribly.

Read and see.

The Year: 2026

Daddy said Jason was bad.

We were out by the pool. I didn't go in first. Summer did. She and Jason splashed around even though Mommy had her mean face on. The mean face she always wears when it's travel time.

She told us not to go anywhere near the pool 'cause it was time to go. We were gonna be late. We were gonna miss cutting the turkey. We were gonna miss getting all the best pumpkin pie. Uncle Dave would get to it first. He always hogs it all. Putting three or four slices on his plate when Jason, Summer, and me barely get any.

Not fair.

Mommy told me to bring my big bag downstairs. The one that looks just like Lightning McQueen, down to the white wheels you use to go through the airport. We were flying today!

That's what Daddy told me this morning. "LA to Chicago."

Mommy didn't look happy to fly.

"Gee. It'll only cost us a small fortune."

"What's a fortune?"

Mommy didn't answer me.

She told me to grab my tablet and my stuffies and hurry up. I grabbed Sheepy and Kitty. They'd be lonely if they stayed home. Jason has a phone he got to take with us. So does Summer. 'Cause they're bigger. When I'm big, I'll get my own phone too. That'll make plane trips funner.

I was putting my stuff in the car to go when they yelled for me.

"We're swimming!"

"Now?"

"Sure. Why not?"

Jason and Summer had bathing suits on. I didn't. Daddy always kept our big backyard pool hot. Even in winter, so we always swam for fun.

"Just wear your undies. Who cares?" they said.

So I jumped in.

Summer splashed me. So did Jason. They always do jerky big-kid stuff like that. Dunking me underwater. We were having fun, so I didn't tell on them.

Then Jason said, "Let's play Marco Polo."

Later when it was his turn, he thought it'd be funny to get out of the pool and pee in it.

Daddy didn't think that was funny.

"WHAT THE HECK ARE YOU DOING?"

He came running. I've never seen him run so fast. He dropped all the stuff he was loading in the car. He took Jason's phone away for a week! Jason cried like a baby about that.

Then Daddy made us all talk like we always do when one of us gets in trouble. That's when Daddy or Mommy explains stuff.

Jason didn't see the problem. "But it's just water! Pee's water too."

Daddy shook his head. "No. Pee is not water. It's dirty. And you peeing in the same clean water that our whole family swims in makes us *all* dirty." Then he looked right in Jason's eyes. "It's like fish in a fishbowl."

When Daddy said that, I thought about Lucky, my pet Betta.

"You dirty up a fishbowl too much, and there's nowhere for a fish to go."

When Daddy said that, I pictured Jason pouring ketchup in my fishbowl. Daddy's right. Lucky wouldn't have anywhere clean to go.

He would get sick and die.

But Jason wasn't listening to Daddy. He and Summer were laughing about pee again. That made Daddy madder.

"Jason, you're young. So you might not realize that what you do affects everything and everyone else. It does."

I thought Jason would get in even more trouble. Summer too. But then Mommy came over to say, "The car's packed! Let's go."

I was only six years old then, so I don't remember much about our airplane ride. Except Mommy and Daddy fought. A lot.

I'll try to list what they said.

Mommy: "You think spending $15,000 just to see our families back in Chicago is worth it?"

Daddy: "I *like* being with family."

Mommy: "So do I. But shutting down all the regional airports in the whole country is nuts. It drives airfare prices sky high. No pun intended."

I asked them what *regional* means, but they didn't answer me.

Daddy: "The sacrifice is worth it to fight climate change."

Mommy: "Of course you'd say that."

Daddy: "What's that mean?"

Mommy had that mean look. Daddy too.

Mommy: "We've been over this before."

Daddy: "Over what?"

Mommy: "You know."

Daddy: "I know *what*?"

Mommy: "Let's just say, it's much easier for people like you who have fancy degrees and earn a lot of money to make those sacrifices."

Daddy: "Your family does OK."

Mommy: "Yes. They do *OK*. But they didn't go to college like yours. And they sure don't have $15 Gs to spend on a flight to see us for Thanksgiving."

Daddy: "That's OK, dear. We're happy to come to them."

The Year: 2027

Next Thanksgiving, we didn't fly. That put Mommy in an even worse mood. Her mean face looked even meaner.

I liked the road trip. It was fun. Daddy let me pump the gas whenever we stopped. Jason and Summer played games on their phones.

I got to play a game too. I called it Transponder.

That's the name for the little computer Daddy stuck on our windshield. It made a beep that I liked. Every time we heard the sound, it lit up red and green.

Just like Christmas. I'd clap my hands and shout reindeer names.

Sometimes Daddy joined in.

Not Mommy. She got so mad she snapped at me. "Stop it."

Daddy took my side. "What's wrong with having fun?"

Mommy: "This is your idea of fun?"

Daddy: "It is actually. Being with family *is* my idea of fun. We need it after the year we've had."

Mommy: "I thought we weren't going to talk about her again."

They didn't have to tell me what that meant. Everyone knew Aunt Kimmy and Uncle Dave just lost their baby before it came.

We were all sad.

Mommy: "I love my family too. That still doesn't mean I like driving across the whole frickin' country with the kids screaming every five seconds, 'Pull over. Pull over. I want more snacks.'"

Daddy: "Doesn't matter anyway. It's not like we have a choice. They closed all the airports. Not just the regionals."

Mommy: "That's not what I'm talking about, and you know it."

Sitting between Jason and Summer in back made it easy to hear my parents. I asked what they were talking about. They didn't answer me.

The transponder beeped. I clapped.

"Rudolph the red-nosed reindeer!"

Mommy looked meaner than ever.

Daddy: "What? He's making this fun."

Mommy: "Is it FUN to know that each time that dumb thing goes off, it's stealing from us?"

"It's stealing from us, Mommy?"

She turned to face me. "I know you think it looks like Christmas, sweetie, but that Transponder is a little minicomputer spy—"

"Stop it." Daddy cut off Mommy.

"It's spying on us. Right now! Every single mile we drive, it's calculating our carbon footprint. Whenever it goes beep and lights up like fricking Christmas morning, it's stealing money from our bank account."

Daddy: "Mommy's being dramatic. It's not stealing from us. It's going to a good cause: saving the environment. Through congestion taxes."

Mommy crossed her arms. "You call it a congestion tax. I call it stealing."

The Year: 2028

Jason and Summer knew not to mess with Mom before our annual road trip. Even Dad stayed out of her way. At least until we got in the car.

We took the Tesla this year. Though Mom said that was stupid.

"Great! We'll have to find somewhere to charge it every two hundred miles."

"At least we don't have the congestion charge with the EV," Dad said.

Not having the transponder beep made for a quieter trip. That was OK by me. I was too old for my Christmas game that made Mom so mad last year.

Mom still seemed mad, though.

Summer whispered to Jason that was because Aunt Kimmy was sick with some new disease the doctors couldn't explain.

"Where does it come from?" I asked.

"*Shh*," was all they said. They never tell me anything. But later I heard Jason say it had to do with Chinese pollution.

Something else was different. Mom didn't let Dad drive.

"You drive too slow," she said.

Dad: "I do not."

Mom: "If we hope to get to Chicago before New Year's, I'd better drive."

But all her speeding through red lights didn't make it faster. Charging stations took forever. There were always long lines. Once after waiting for six hours for our turn, we had to walk back to our motel to sleep while it charged.

"You happy now?" Mom shouted at Dad.

"It's not my fault people are so selfish. We wouldn't be in this mess if all Americans switched to electric vehicles fifty years ago."

The Year: 2029

Whatever was bothering Aunt Kimmy spread to others.

Summer is sick now too. A doctor she saw said it has to do with all the poisonous chemicals in the soil and in our food.

"You see it in animals nowadays," she said. "They're the canary in the coal mine, so to speak."

I didn't know what that meant. Dad did 'cause he said, "Microplastics."

I looked that word up on Jason's phone. It took me to a science news site from a few years ago where I read, "Tiny particles of plastic have been found everywhere—from the deepest place on the planet, the Mariana Trench, to the top of Mount Everest. And now more and more studies are finding that microplastics, defined as plastic pieces less than 5 millimeters across, are also in our bodies."[1]

Summer didn't get better.

Not even after seeing all those doctors. Something was hurting her lungs, making it hard to breathe. She had to get a special inhaler.

A week before our trip, I heard my parents fighting in their room. I didn't catch it all, though I put my ear right up to their door.

Mom: "And yet you *still* think carbon taxes are a good thing? The government won't even let people drive their own cars anymore."

Dad: "That's good. All that extra driving isn't safe for the planet."

Mom: "Tell that to the Chinese who are building two coal-fired plants a week.[2] Or to the more than one billion Indians using diesel cars.[3] To the Russians. To any of the BRICS nations. You think their citizens are going along with this agenda?"

Dad: "They have made certain commitments—"

Mom: "Oh, blow it out your ass. China is not following your precious United Nations COP 18 rules. They're doing what they damn well please—polluting the planet while the rest of us do what we are told, just like little sheep—"

That was the last year we drove to Chicago for Thanksgiving.

Again, we had a transponder in our car, tracking us. We also didn't go on the usual highways. Our Tesla picked weird, winding roads through old towns.

Mom and Dad fought about that too.

Mom: "We *can* drive through the big cities. You just don't want to."

Dad: "Do you have any idea how high the driving fees are in Vegas or Denver? It's not worth it."

By now, Mom's face always looked mean. Even when we weren't driving.

Mom: "*Not worth it?* I thought it was worth *everything* to sacrifice for climate change, the big bad bogeyman."

Dad: "Stop it."

Mom: "Oh, so even Mr. Save Planet Earth has limits?"

Dad's voice grew quiet. He didn't want us kids in back to hear him. But Jason was on his earbuds anyway. Summer dozed from taking her medicine.

"It wasn't easy selling our home. I didn't want to do it either. But we had to."

Our transponder beeped.

No more green light. It flashed red. An alert filled our monitor: "Insufficient credit. Please add more credits to continue driving."

Under governmental control, the car pulled to a stop in the middle of nowhere as rain poured down on us. It might have been Thanksgiving, but the fireworks between Mom and Dad made it seem like Fourth of July.

The Year: 2030

There was no way we could take Summer on the bus with us.

She basically lived at the hospital now. Sad as it was, Mom and Dad said she was lucky. Aunt Kimmy was so sick the doctors said it was only a matter of time before she passed.

In school, we learned about the Equity Plague. "Many formerly first-world nations like the United States now lack the health defense infrastructure and capital to address all the pollution problems emerging BRICS nations like China emit. As a result, many Americans are now vulnerable to previously unheard of autoimmune and respiratory diseases, as well as soaring sterilization rates . . ."

Mom and Dad barely speak to each other these days. He moved out of our apartment and is staying with another family in a small Airbnb.

"At least it's only a short bike ride to Summer in the hospital," he says.

So, it was a surprise to Jason and me that Mom even wanted to try for another road trip this year. "We'll make it fun. It'll be an adventure. I promise."

For once, her face didn't look mean.

It didn't take long for her good cheer to fade.

In Arizona, our bus broke down. Mom, Jason, and I waited with the other passengers on the side of the road for a lift. It came three sweaty hours later.

That bus, bound for Dodge City, Kansas, also broke down a few hours into our trip. It was noon, but you couldn't guess it from the sky. In school, we learned that it looks so dark these days from all the contaminants.

Our driver said he was sorry for the delay. "It's the battery. We'll be back on the road soon."

Jason took the news in stride, glued to his phone. Mom's face wasn't so mean anymore. It was sad. I tried to cheer her up on the next bus we took out of Colorado Springs by reminding her of past family trips. Mom laughed so hard she cried when I retold her the story of my big brother peeing in the pool right before we were to leave town.

"He didn't!"

"He did."

"No."

"Dad had to tell Jason right after that it's like dirtying a fishbowl. When somebody or something messes up the environment we all share, they don't just hurt themselves, they hurt everyone."

All the joy drained from Mom's face. She looked up at the bus's digital display listing our ETA. We'd miss Thanksgiving for sure. By a matter of days.

"Kid," she said, "there's no escaping the fishbowl."

The Year: 2031

Even if we wanted to ride the bus this year, we couldn't. We didn't qualify for the special vouchers they now give families wanting carbon travel allowances. *Oh well.* With Mom and Dad divorcing and Summer so sick, it wouldn't have been much fun anyway.

We're not sure if Dad has the same disease she does, the thing that took away Aunt Kimmy, but he's not OK either. His doctor says he has trouble digesting. That's why he looks so pale.

Despite that, on Thanksgiving, he does his best to bring us together. Surprising us all, he drives Summer to the new studio the government assigned Mom, Jason, and me. Though he gave up eating meat before I was born, he uses all his food credits to get a small turkey with all the fixins.

It's a miracle! An entire meal goes by without Mom and Dad fighting. Jason is on his best behavior, too, talking to us instead of staring at his phone. And though Summer can't really eat, she seems happy to be sitting upright.

"I have an idea," says Dad afterward. "Since we can't visit the family in Chicago in person, why don't we Zoom with them?"

I expect Mom to say no, but she doesn't.

"OK."

After sending Uncle Dave in Chicago a quick text to let them know we'll be sending them a link to join us, we gather around Mom's laptop. Sitting at the kitchen table, I can't help feeling sad and happy. Here we are—a real family again: talking to one another, being with one another.

Then Mom surprises me even more by taking Dad's hand right before the call starts. He gives her a loving squeeze back. Jason and Summer look content. I am feeling good too. We are all ready to wish our loved ones a Happy Thanksgiving over Zoom—and then the power goes out.

ChatESG

Danielle can't help herself. She wipes a tear from her eye. Her own family has experienced its own share of problems, so she can imagine what the boy in the story is going through. ChatESG can see she is still processing what she just experienced in her VR headset, so it allows her a few moments to herself. When she's finally ready, she begins typing.

DG: Part of me wants to say this will never happen. But the other part knows better. OK, ChatESG. What's the truth?

Yes. It's happening. It's *been* happening. In 2021, *BBC* reported that France "move[d] to ban short-haul flights" just like what we experienced in the story: "French lawmakers have moved to ban short-haul internal flights where train alternatives exist, in a bid to reduce carbon emissions. Over the weekend, lawmakers voted in favor of a bill to end routes where the same journey could be made by train in under two-and-a-half hours."[4]

They are careful to point out the bans do not affect connecting flights. But that may be coming next.

DG: So in the future, governments will just ban people from flying?

Certain governments, yes. Already, leading influencers are priming the public to not just accept this idea but embrace it. An equivalent would be how US citizens sacrificed in World War II. The *New York Times* even gave a name for such modern "heroes": the *No Jet-Set*: "With airplanes producing a large amount of climate-warming emissions, a growing number of travelers are signing pledges to keep their journeys on the ground."[5]

DG: But even if Americans give up flying or driving to save the environment, it won't matter, won't it? Not if countries like China pollute our fishbowl.

That's true because as the story you just read shows, your entire ecosystem is intertwined. Also, just like with the military, it's complicated. You need an insider to know what's really going on. But it's unsafe to be a whistleblower. We just learned about the ESG mafia. They don't take too kindly to environmental experts exposing the truth. That is why I arranged for today's interview. I arranged for an anonymous expert to speak to you. To keep it easy, we will call him Nick.

Nick has entered the room.

Danielle, please meet our expert. The CEO of a hydrocarbon cleanup firm operating in the Permian Basin, he's vehemently against ESG. He's agreed to answer our questions today.
DG: Nice to meet you.

Let's get into it. Will another regulation layer, specifically through ESG measures, really protect the environment, or is this just greenwashing?
Nick: Short answer: It will *not* protect the environment. Consider American industrialism over the last fifty years. Examples abound of problems resulting from the dumping of unregulated chemicals: the Love Canal incident in New York, or the Ohio River, which would literally catch on fire each summer due to so many hazardous chemicals, paints, and dyes from different industries contaminating the environment as recently as the 1970s.[6]

Remember, too, we still used leaded gasoline in our vehicles back then. As a result of these problems, real concern and activism arose for the care of natural resources in the United States. This led to the formation of the Environmental Protection Agency (EPA). We also witnessed the birth of protective laws, such as RCRA, or the Resource Conservation and Recovery Act, and CERCLA, the Comprehensive Environmental Resource and Liabilities Act. Superfund,[7] the common name for CERCLA, answered the question: "How do we clean sites that have been abandoned for years due to the financial inability of companies to take care of them?" Similarly, the government created RCRA as a solution to this question: "How do we enforce the cleanup of spills for companies that *are* economically capable, like Shell Oil or Monsanto?"

The Clean Water Act, Clean Air Act, RCRA, and CERCLA were all enacted to promote the cleanup of polluted land and protect natural resources. The EPA said to the states, "Either you can use EPA's laws and regulations, or the states can create their own environmental agencies that are as stringent or more so than the EPA laws." This enabled states to manage their own environmental liability. So, in Texas, for example, we created the Texas Commission on Environmental Quality, or TCEQ, which is even *more* stringent than the EPA.

Due to these Texas laws, the moment oil leaves a pipeline and enters the refinery to be converted into gasoline and diesel or any of the hundreds of chemicals we get from crude oil, the TCEQ has jurisdiction over it. Before that, Texas has the Texas Railroad Commission.[8] It oversees all things relating to the state's oil and gas industry, including safety, cleanup and remediation of oil field spills or oil field waste, and so forth.

In other words, it's not just one entity involved?

Nick: Correct. We have *multiple* agencies involved in protecting the environment. And each state has a similar structure with multiple state agencies working together to promote the protection of natural resources. To the west of Texas in New Mexico, we have the New Mexico Environmental Department (NMED) and the Oil Conservation Commission (OCC) working in tandem. Then you throw in federal lands. These fall under the EPA. You also have the Bureau of Land Management (BLM), the Department of the Interior. The list goes on and on. And they all have checks and balances by standardizing cleanup activities and establishing cleanup levels. This shows there are *many, many* protection levels now.

With all those protective layers and regulations, do we also need ESG?

Nick: No. Just ask yourself: If Texas in 2023 is the eighth-strongest economy in the world above Russia and Brazil, why do we need to create unnecessary burdens on these businesses that are doing more than enough for environmental protection, paying their taxes, and employing hundreds of thousands of people with good jobs? ESG would only harm the good companies and allow the other companies in Russia and Brazil an uncompetitive advantage. It's for *optics*. Think of it as a superficial bandage to make it look like we are doing more for the environment, when in reality we are already doing enough.

DG: Doesn't ESG help stop carbon emissions, which create the whole climate crisis?

Nick: If anything, under the ESG scheme, it *increases* carbon production.

DG: Sounds like it. But even if ESG is wrong, protecting the environment does still matter. What's something we can do to help our planet without ESG?

Nick: Consider the operations of one of the largest US oil companies. If they have a one thousand–barrel spill tomorrow, they'll mobilize an emergency response team. They'll contain any and all materials like crude oil, condensate, or chlorides. They'll also have a host of contractors onsite to remediate the soil and groundwater. In summary, they will do the right thing and mitigate the spill.

What about groundwater?

Nick: If groundwater were to be impacted, they would install groundwater monitoring wells to sample the groundwater and start to remove contaminants and clean up the groundwater. The environmental consultants will determine how big the spill is in the aquifer and install as many groundwater monitor wells as they need to determine how big of an area has been impacted. On a small oil spill, it may only take sixty days to get the site back to what it was like before the spill. On a large groundwater site, it can take decades. The key takeaway, Danielle, is this: There are thousands of people who are qualified and want to clean up the environment; 98 percent of the companies in existence want to do the right thing and clean up the environment. With the laws in place, it *is* getting done. No one wants to go to prison for breaking the Clean Air Act, Clean Water Act, RCRA, or CERCLA.

🌀 It sounds like there's a real disconnect between the true environmentalism occurring and what the public actually hears about.

Nick: Very much so. Look. Companies don't want to present in their annual stockholder reports that they didn't take care of environmental deficiencies in their operations, or that there was a failure in an operational process that damaged San Francisco Bay, or ruined a trout stream in Wyoming, or polluted the groundwater under a school in your hometown. They're doing the right thing and will continue to do so based on their own self-interest.

🌀 Without ESG, what's their incentive to do so?

Nick: Simple. When it comes to publicly traded companies, they don't want their stock share price to fall. Capitalism drives environmental cleanup. With small non-publicly traded companies, they have a desire to keep their business value high. Most business owners want to pass their business on to the next generation and live in small communities and love where they live.

DG: But it seems like everyone knows that big oil companies will do anything to get out of cleaning up their mess.

Nick: Let's go back to a time before the Texas RRC. Remember, this is the State of Texas EPA for oil field spills. Historically, if you had a large-scale oil spill, companies would go in and fix the failure where the oil was leaking. They would excavate around those spills. They would find the area where pipeline or equipment failure occurred. They would repair the leak, then they would cover it up. They might even reseed it, but not likely. They would leave the oil in the soil and never know if it had gotten into groundwater.

There's no way they would do that nowadays. Instead, we are required to perform an extensive excavation of the contaminated soil. We install groundwater monitors to ensure groundwater has not been impacted. All of the spill material is either remediated in place or it's hauled off and sent to a landfill. Meanwhile, new soil will be brought in, and a professional engineer will design and build a very intricate, expensive remediation system that will be put on-site to remove any remaining contaminants in the soil or groundwater.

Nowadays, laws require *entire* remediation. The cost involved is an enforcement mechanism itself, not just environmental laws. In the old days, the leak was just fixed and not remediated like it is today. Things have changed in a positive way, and American energy companies are doing their part to protect our fishbowl.

DG: I still don't understand how capitalism can fix capitalism.

Nick: Capitalism does not need to be fixed. Energy companies want to run as lean as possible. They want low costs and high profits. A home run for an environmental department at a publicly traded pipeline or oil and gas exploration company is to have zero environmental liability or spills. Or as close as possible. This means that they have trained the crews that drill and operate the oil leases to watch out and fix little problems quickly so as not to let them turn into large spills like we spoke about earlier.

Another reason capitalism does not need to be fixed is that capitalism produces large amounts of cash for companies. These profits are taxed by the government. This tax money that the companies pay goes to help pay for state and federal environmental entities like the Texas RRC, the TCEQ, and even the EPA. So, in a nutshell, the more money the companies make, the more money they pay in taxes, and these taxes help fund government environmental regulation.

If you have a very poor country that does not have a strong economy, they cannot pay taxes. They are barely surviving. That country does not have any tax base and paying to clean up the environment is way down on their list of priorities. We are truly blessed to have the best of all worlds in the United States.

⑯ Let me interject. To confirm, from an economic standpoint, it is bad business to constantly deal with spills and other mistakes because it destroys a company's production capacity and, ultimately, the company's profits?

Nick: And your reputation. Which also kills your business.

⑆ If that is true, it sounds like Adam Smith's free market capitalism. You're saying the market will correct itself because you can't be profitable if you're dealing with all these cleanups and spills 24/7. Correct?

Nick: Yes. When an oil company, by law, cleans up a spill, it will put processes in place, both mechanical and in forms of education and training, to stop the spills the best they can. They will take a very forward approach to minimizing these spills and run more efficiently to stop having spills. This is because the spills cost so much money. Imagine you expect $70 per barrel profit, but a five-barrel spill that just impacts soil at a very shallow depth may cost you up to $5,000 to remediate or clean up. A one thousand–barrel spill or 42,000 gallons that impacts groundwater can cost $2,000,000 to remediate. The math adds up fast. The economics prohibit a company to spill and not take care of it. They don't want spills. They can't afford it. They'll go out of business.

DG: Yeah, but all these companies are still fracking, which everyone knows is horrible for the environment.

Nick: Fracking is not horrible or even bad for the environment.

DG: It's not?

Nick: It is not. Horizontal drilling has a very complex completion process to bring the oil to the surface. Fracking is *one* of these processes. So, let's make sure we understand the process of fracking.

⑆ From my understanding, some oil deposits are hard to produce because of the unique geology they are formed in. And these oil and gas formations are in very narrow, hard-packed rock layers. Fracking, short for hydraulic fracturing, is a method of extracting oil and natural gas from deep underground by injecting high-pressure fluid into rock formations to create fractures, allowing the oil or gas to flow out more freely. Is that correct?

Nick: That's pretty accurate. The horizontal drilling technology behind fracking gave the US our energy independence in 2019. But first, let's explain how horizontal drilling works. Let's say we must drill eight thousand feet below the ground surface to get to more oil because we depleted many of the shallower deposits with conventional vertical oil wells. The zone of oil we are trying to produce is eight thousand feet down but only has a twenty foot producing zone. If we installed a vertical well to eight thousand feet and wanted to produce a twenty-foot zone, it would not be worth it. After you discover that you only have twenty feet of oil-bearing formation, you wouldn't want to spend any more to complete the well and would plug it.

An eight-thousand-foot vertical oil well drilled, logged, and plugged today would cost $2 million in the Permian Basin. If all you discovered was the twenty-foot pay zone, it would not make sense to complete it in a shale formation. So this would be a total loss to the owner.

Conversely, a horizontal well uses cutting-edge drilling technology to drill vertically down to 7,500 feet and slowly will start a ninety-degree kick-off[9] to level out at eight thousand feet and then drill horizontally or laterally in the twenty-foot formation up to ten thousand feet long. A horizontal well allows you to have over ten thousand feet of pay zone as opposed to a vertical well that only gives you twenty feet. This immediately makes the horizontal well/lateral commercially viable if you can hydraulically fracture or "frack" the oil-bearing geologic formation.

Once the well is drilled to the desired depth and direction, the fracking process begins with the insertion of a perforating gun to create small holes in the horizontal/lateral section of the casing. High-pressure fluid—typically a mixture of water, sand, and chemicals—is then injected into the well through these perforations, fracturing the surrounding rock and creating fissures through which oil or gas can flow. Finally, the sand in the fluid mixture holds these fractures open, allowing for the continuous extraction of oil or gas from the rock formation to the wellbore, where it can be collected and processed. For comparison on the cost to the vertical well discussed previously, a horizontal well to eight thousand feet below ground surface and a ten-thousand-foot lateral in the Permian Basin today would cost $12 million. Generally, a twenty-foot-deep shale formation properly fracked could produce on average 750,000 barrels of oil. A $12 million investment to drill a horizontal well could produce 750,000 barrels of oil. This amount of oil would never have been recovered without horizontal drilling and fracking. The profitability is a moving target based on a multitude of things including the price of oil, royalty costs, and operating costs. Nonetheless, it is a profitable enterprise for oil companies.

DG: Good for the owner. But fracking hurts the environment and groundwater. Everyone knows that.

Nick: Most people don't even know how it works, so let me finish this part. How can fracking be safe? It is all about proper engineering, geologic interpretation, and the depth at which the fracking process occurs. The depth of the lateral well, often several thousand feet below the surface, and in this case, eight thousand feet below ground surface, naturally isolates the fracking process from groundwater aquifers, mitigating the risk of contamination. Proper casing and cementing of the wellbore above the horizontal/lateral provide additional layers of protection, sealing off the well from surrounding rock layers and preventing any leakage of fracking fluids or hydrocarbons into the aquifer, which is the primary concern. Regulatory standards and industry practices ensure these safety measures are rigorously applied, further enhancing the environmental safety of fracking at such depths. Further, the Texas RRC oversees the completion process to ensure the safety of the state's aquifers.

DG: Isn't that still bad for the aquifers?

Nick: Not if you seal it off right in the first thousand feet or to the depth of the deepest aquifer. If you did not rely on professional geologists and engineers, you could impact the aquifer. But there have been hundreds of thousands of oil wells drilled and properly completed that never had any problems. If you did not do it right you could impact groundwater, absolutely. But if you're *one and a half miles deep* in a formation, you're not creating environmental damage. It is deep enough in the earth. And remember, fracking is just a fancy term for busting up rocks with high pressure.

DG: What would happen if we just banned fracking?

Nick: That would be catastrophic for the United States. Hydraulic fracking has enabled America to significantly increase its production of oil and natural gas, leading to a substantial decrease in dependency on foreign energy sources (Russia, Saudi Arabia, and Venezuela). Fracking has also allowed for the extraction of oil and natural gas from previously inaccessible or economically nonviable underground geologic formations, contributing to a surge in domestic energy production. As a result, the US has been able to achieve energy independence, enhancing national security and economic stability. If fracking were banned, it could lead to increased energy prices, greater reliance on imported fuels, and potential economic repercussions, including job losses in the energy sector and related industries.

If America banned fracking because of ESG, other countries like China, Russia, and Saudi Arabia would be the leaders in oil and gas production while ignoring international environmental rules, wouldn't they?

Nick: Exactly. Just like that story Danielle just experienced.

Going back to that tale, it sounds like America has vastly improved its environmental protective technology and remediation abilities in the last few years, and that unlike China, the US *is* committed to safeguarding our water, air, and soil. Is that correct?

Nick: Consider this. Through the UN, the WEF, and other entities, American-led coalitions have pressured other nations to halt energy production. All in the name of climate change. It's gotten so bad Sp!ked reported in 2022 that the EU's twenty-seven member states will begin rationing their energy supplies. And take a look at Germany—extreme measures are already in the works:

Town councils are dimming or turning off streetlights and even traffic lights. Large landlords and housing associations have started turning down the heating on their residents and rationing their hot water. Some local authorities are considering setting up "warm rooms" for elderly people to gather in the winter.[10]

At the same time this is happening, look at what China's doing. Is this country, home to one billion, scaling back its energy production to halt climate change? No. Glenn Beck wrote the following in his 2023 book *The Great Reset:*

> And don't forget about China's addiction to coal-fired energy. A February 2022 Reuters report noted, "China started building 33 giga-watts of new coal-fired power generation capacity last year, the most since 2016, research published on Thursday showed, a sign the country is falling back on fossil fuels as economic worries mount."
>
> According to Reuters, the Centre for Research on Energy and Clean Air and the Global Energy Monitor say China's "newly added capacity under construction was three times more than the rest of the world combined."[11]

DG: So it IS true. While the US does all it can to save the environment, like having the EPA, TCEQ, and Railroad Commission, China is busy polluting.

Nick: And no one is stopping them.

DG: They're wrecking our fishbowl!

Nick: Think about it like this: What would happen if there were no environmental laws in Mexico, and you're in El Paso? Do those smeltery plants or metal foundries in Mexico *not* contaminate the air right across the border? Yes, they do—100 percent.

DG: When the wind blows from the southwest, it'll push it right on top of us.

Nick: That's already happening right now to us from Mexico, and it is also happening right now in surrounding countries beside China. Meanwhile, ESG promotes "net zero" pollution. But if the Chinese are making sixteen million cars a year, running on the worst diesel, and building unlimited coal-fired power plants and thousands and thousands of factories with no regard for emissions, environmentally it's meaningless. *It's the same air.* It doesn't change anything. It just costs ESG-following nations more to follow rules other countries ignore. Meanwhile, due to ESG compliance in America we lose jobs daily and access to energy. Energy needed to power our country, to stay warm, to travel, to feed ourselves. Everything life requires. We will fall behind and eventually suffer from the stronger countries like China.

There's another problem: no multi-continental environmental industrial accountability.

Nick: When 75 percent of the world's population is just looking for their next meal, they aren't thinking about "net zero carbon emissions." They just want to survive. Look at Maslow's hierarchy. Level one is food, water, shelter, and rest. These poorer nations are not concerned with ESG and, in fact, will not be interested in ESG.

DG: Which wrecks the fishbowl more.

Nick: Yes, when other emerging countries also sidestep protecting the environment, we're all negatively affected just as badly. Or worse.

DG: What do you mean, *worse?*

Nick: Not only does America not get the energy it needs, but we, the US also now have nefarious environmental contaminants coming here from all over the world, again like in this story Danielle experienced. All these emerging countries want to do is produce as fast as they can in that factory they just built. This means all we've done is moved environmental liability from a controlled, legalized, accepted norm to nations that don't have *any* accepted norms or laws.

Plus, we pay more. We have less national security, less energy independence. We can barely take care of ourselves anymore. We've lost jobs because of a massive energy demonization campaign around so-called fossil fuels. But is the air any better if China and other emerging nations do whatever they want?

DG: No. It's all the same planet.

One last question: What would surprise the public most about how businesses in Texas are protecting or not protecting the environment?

Nick: These operators and these companies have multimillion-dollar budgets just for environmental compliance and cleanup. They have the best and brightest, most educated scientists. They have degrees in hydrology, environmental engineering, and environmental science. These experts have spent twenty or thirty years on this, ever since the inception of some of these laws.

All along, they've been helping to shape responsible policies. They do it not because they are extorted into caring from the ESG mafia. They do it because they truly care. They want to see their communities clean. They don't want their kids growing up with health problems. Or your kids. They don't need more layers of scare tactics to do right. And neither do you, Danielle.

DG: Me?

Nick: Yes, you. The ESG scam isn't just being waged against corporate America. It's targeting young and impressionable minds. The agenda is not at all what it purports to be. It's not about deeper inclusion, more representation, or a cleaner earth. *That's just what they tell you.* It's all about control: preying on the best instincts of people like you and me.

He's 100 percent right, Danielle. And now it's time to show you where all this leads: how bad things can get for America. Are you ready?

CHAPTER 12

When Chickens Come Home to Roost

I do solemnly swear (or affirm) that I will faithfully execute the Office of President of the United States, and will to the best of my Ability, preserve, protect and defend the Constitution of the United States.

—PRESIDENTIAL OATH OF OFFICE, UNITED STATES OF AMERICA

Throughout this book we have covered the many ways ESG is destroying liberty, economic prosperity, meritocracy, military readiness, energy resilience, the environment, even our ability to feed ourselves.

For a young person like Danielle who has never heard this side of the story, it's been a revelation, to put it mildly. Her conversations with ChatESG opened her eyes to info and viewpoints the legacy media would never share. And in the process, we have seen her shift her opinions.

It's our hope that the material has also opened your eyes—that maybe it transformed your thinking on this subject. Yet even with all that we have learned and experienced, Danielle still doesn't realize the end game—where this is all going should we not stop ESG.

Though painful, it's important she—and you—fully comprehend our possible future. As you take in the following scenario, please think about your own children and/or future generations of Americans who might soon witness the following fantasy come to life.

/////////////////////////////////

Diner in Casper, Wyoming

Sadie Packard often joked to friends she liked the University of Wyoming so much she never left. After earning a nursing degree—and accumulating $30,000 in student debt—she didn't go to work at a hospital like so many of her peers. Instead, her path was quite traditional. Conventional, really. She found the love of her life on campus. And settled down with him.

Miles, her beau, was never the academic type. He only ended up in Casper in the first place due to a football scholarship. Even his frat brothers teased him for being academically unserious.

"What the hell can you do with a hospitality degree anyway?" they'd ask. "Work as a bellhop?"

He showed them all when he bought Libby's, the rundown dollar store, converting it into a diner. Libby's took off like a rocket because, like so many college towns, Casper enjoyed a vibrant nightlife. Hard-studying coeds traded books for beers every night, especially weekends. Lots of beers, by the way. And lots of shots. Pretty much any mixed drink you could think of they indulged in, especially since so many bars offered cheap drinks to lure in young crowds.

There's a flip side to that coin.

Anyone who has ever endured a raging hangover will tell you it's no joke. It's something to be avoided at all costs: the dry, sandpaper mouth, the intense nausea and vomiting, the pounding headache, the praying-to-God-make-it-stop feeling you wouldn't wish on your worst enemy.

To avoid such unpleasantness, it's best to eat something in the magic hour—that critical space between when you stop throwing back Cosmos and when your head hits the pillow. But not just anything. Snacking on a banana won't help you much. Neither will a healthy salad.

You're just asking for trouble with such nutritious fare.

Any veteran binge drinker will tell you your best bet is to eat something greasy. *Real greasy.* Think fully loaded cheese fries sprinkled with bacon bits. Or an animal-style double double from In-N-Out Burger. Onion, please.

In London, they prefer late-night kebabs to soak up all that booze. As for Casper, Wyoming?

They got you covered with the Big Boy. One thing you should know. The Big Boy isn't something a health-conscious individual orders for breakfast. Or lunch. Or brunch. Or any other meal.

Comedian Chris Rock once quipped that nobody buys something good in the wee hours—when drinking usually stops. "Have you ever taken out three hundred dollars at four o'clock in the morning for something positive?" he asked in a comedy special.

The answer is, of course, no.

Those who withdraw cash at that time of night often use it for less than noble purposes—drug purchases, for one. Not so with the Big Boy. Presumably you did all the bad stuff you were going to do until this point back at the bar or the club. You order the Big Boy before the crack of dawn to wrest your body from the clutches of a debilitating hangover.

Just what goes into this gustatory palliative, you may ask?

Buttery scrambled eggs, deep-fried hash browns, gobs of melted cheddar cheese, grilled green peppers and onions. Splash some hot sauce or fork in some sour cream onto this beast of a meal, and you've set yourself up for a better morning. A better day, really. One less filled with puking and praying.

So it was that Libby's, the brainchild of Sadie and Miles, made a name for itself in Casper, Wyoming. Without fail, Tuesday through Saturday nights, starting around midnight, you could expect revelers queuing around Second Street waiting for a table.

To be sure, that wasn't the only item on the menu. Libby's offered the usual American diner options: your frittatas, your chocolate chip pancakes, your sweet and savory crepes, your eggs Florentine, and the crown jewel of brunches the world over: Eggs Benedict. They offered a corned beef hash option that made your mouth water while glancing at the menu.

By the time Sadie and Miles reached middle age, they had built a tidy little fortune off of their culinary investment all those years ago. Besides owning the building outright, they bought a charming four-thousand-square-foot home in town where they raised three kids. They had enough left over to invest in a duplex, giving them the passive income Miles read about in *Rich Dad, Poor Dad*.

Sure, there were ups and downs at Libby's over the years.

From time to time, Miles and Sadie had problem employees they had to let go. The 2008 crash dampened their cash flow. Worst of all was the COVID-19 pandemic. For much of 2020, they only saw a fraction of their usual foot traffic with bars closed and people staying home. Yet they held on. Surprisingly, patrons, many of them college students, kept ordering Big Boys through Uber Eats. If not for those deliveries, they might not have made it.

2025 is when the real pain came. That's when the dollar crashed.

Never one to crack a textbook if he didn't have to back in college, Miles nonetheless kept up with the news. As early as 2022, he read articles on the dangers of the United States losing its reserve currency status. When Russia invaded Ukraine in February, he worried about America's heavy-handed response.

"Sanctioning Putin will only drive him into the arms of China," he told anyone who would listen. "What happens then? Them and the other BRICS countries join forces to crush us."

Ever the prescient pragmatist, Miles's foreboding was spot-on.

In April 2024, China's yuan replaced the American dollar as Russia's most traded currency.[1] That wasn't all. Seventeen years after Brazil, Russia, India, China, and South Africa (collectively dubbed BRICS) aligned to oust the US global currency dominance, they got their wish. After bringing on Saudi Arabia, Iran, Ethiopia, Egypt, Argentina, and the United Arab Emirates, they upended the world order first predicated in the Bretton Woods Agreement.

Much like hyperinflation in Venezuela, the American dollar collapsed. America unraveled as a superpower. Immediately, Sadie and Miles felt the pain in the business they built over decades.

So did their customers.

A week after the news, Miles looks around Libby's in horror. It's 8:00 a.m. on a Monday. Normally, all the tables would be filled with regulars ordering drip coffee and bacon: blue collar workers en route to job sites, college students using the Wi-Fi while munching avocado toast, pensioners reading the paper, vacationing families.

Only one person sits at a booth today. Miles knows him: Edward Lowry, PhD, a history professor until last year when he retired.

Once the yuan replaced the dollar as the world's primary exchange unit, Miles let his whole staff go. All except for his cook, Ed, and Sadie. There was no way to pay them all that wouldn't bankrupt Libby's.

Miles watches with morbid curiosity as Sadie approaches Dr. Lowry. "Hi there. What can I do you for?" she asks with her bravest smile.

It's courageous because Miles changed their prices over the weekend. The Traditional (two sausage links, two eggs anyway you like, plus hashbrowns) cost $12 before the currency shift.

"Can this be . . . right?" Dr. Lowry points to the menu. "Sixty-five dollars for the Scrambler? Seventy dollars for the Big Boy?"

Sadie nods. Still a looker, she's kept her figure since their college days. The biggest difference is her hair, Miles thinks. It wasn't so gray even last week.

"I'm afraid so," Sadie says in a quiet voice.

"And it's fifteen dollars for a cup of coffee?"

This is more painful than Miles thought it'd be.

"That's outrageous. How can you justify these prices?"

Miles approaches. Behind him, he can sense Ed watching him. He wants to hear how Miles can possibly handle this.

"Howdy, Doc," he says, using the nickname he gave Lowry years ago.

"Howdy," he says back, absent of all warmth.

"I overheard your concern."

"Concern's a nice way to put it. You're gouging people."

Miles shares a look with Sadie. After a carton of eggs (wholesale) jumped to $40 last week, he told her they'd have to increase their prices. By a lot.

"No one'll be able to afford this," she'd said when he presented the new menu. "No one around here anyway."

If Dr. Lowry only knew that the $65 charge included no profit. Sadie and Miles were giving the break-even price.

"If it were up to me, I'd give it to you for free." Miles tries to be friendly like Sadie. But it's tough to be all smiles when you feel sick inside.

There's a scape of boot on wood as Dr. Lowry rises to his full height. "You know I love coming here—"

"You're the only one who orders the Big Boy for lunch," says Sadie.

"But with these new rates, I can't even swing coffee."

Miles looks past Dr. Lowry to the parking lot. It's empty. So is Second Street.

It feels like March 2020 when the government first issued shelter-in-place orders. But worse. Over at the deserted Shell station, Miles reads the new gas price: $15 a gallon.

Who's gonna leave their house when it costs as much as your mortgage just to fill your tank?

Dr. Lowry puts out his hand to shake. It feels like a goodbye. A new gulf between one-time friends.

We will be strangers after this, Miles knows. *Not just me and a professor living on a fixed income and wanting normalcy in a world gone mad. But me and Sadie against everyone in this country.*

We've reverted back to the Great Depression days.

Miles sees tears filling Sadie's eyes. He can only guess she thinks the same thing. Watching Dr. Lowry pass by vacant tables on his way out, Miles has a vision of days to come and must sit down.

Grocery Store in Denver, Colorado

Carrie, a ponytailed mom in yoga pants, inches her shopping cart down lonely aisles. The shelves do not contain even half the items they once did. And the new prices for what's available are eye-popping. Her toddler tugs on her shirt to ask for the s'mores Pop-Tarts she loves so much.

"No," Carrie tells her little girl. "We can't afford it."

Carrie stops at the deli, hoping she can buy a roast for her family. Before it might've cost her $15 or $20. Now? The price tag reads *$200*.

Joining another harried mom in the canned food section, Carrie loads up on SPAM and other tinned meats that still cost a fortune but won't overdraw her account.

Rental Car Agency in Savannah, Georgia

Seeking a better life, Anil moved to the United States from India with his parents as a small boy. Anil majored in business, becoming a serial entrepreneur. He now owns a franchise operation.

In addition to a Hertz rental car agency, he operated several Subways and a Pinot's Palette. The latter closed last week when the price for a bottle jumped to $500. His sandwich shops had already shuttered after robberies took every last bit of food from his locations.

Anil actually saw that as a blessing. He couldn't make payroll anyway after inventory costs ballooned over 1,000 percent.

Nowadays, he still comes into Hertz for no other reason than it's somewhere to go. But no one comes in. No one books rental cars anymore. A year ago, his lobby would've been filled with sightseers renting wheels to roam River Street or drop in on Bonaventure Cemetery containing legendary musician Johnny Mercer's grave.

Now?

Tourism is dead. Olde Pink House closed its doors. Ditto for the historic Savannah Theatre and the Davenport House Museum. All the hotels are gone, along with so many restaurants serving Southern specialties like cheddar crab poppers, fried calamari, peel 'n eat shrimp, crawdads, clams, and mussels.

Last he heard, Gulf Coast fishermen stopped supplying the grocers, restaurants, and the like with wares. These days, all they catch go to feed their own bellies or to their families.

Local Hospital in Dearborn, Michigan

Already, they were short-staffed *before* the dollar collapse. Already, too many nurses and doctors had walked off their jobs, burnt out from all the stress. Already, this town was becoming what they call a "hospital desert" with not enough caregivers to provide for the community.

Nowadays?

Head administrator Everett Maxwell wants to weep as he considers the ruin that once was a quality healthcare facility. The ER is overrun day and night. His skeleton crew of physicians does its best to triage. But it's hard to make so many life-and-death decisions, especially when you're consigning an elderly flu sufferer to death because you need all available resources to save an eight-year-old shot while stealing food.

"Madness," Everett whispers as he considers his dwindling inventory. With this year's budget shot and no hope on the horizon for more funds, he wonders how many people his hospital can possibly help when it runs out of medicines, out of PPP gear, out of all the instruments and devices it takes to keep an increasingly desperate population alive.

That night, Miles walks home from Libby's with Sadie.

It's late October, and the weather has turned. It's chilly and raining, so he uses his umbrella to keep the pair dry. Miles puts his arm around his wife of thirty-seven years. They had no other customers after Dr. Lowry. Not a one. Right after he and Sadie ate dinner with Ed, Miles let him go.

It was a tearful goodbye. The worst possible kind.

Now, for some reason he cannot explain as they tromp down empty streets, he thinks back to those happy days when he and Sadie first met. Back then, it never would have occurred to Miles that there could come a day when America could fall. That within his lifetime he would see the end of everything he had come to expect as a given. As a birthright.

He recalls Homecoming parades and tailgate parties on college game days. He remembers the night he convinced friends to accompany him to Sadie's dorm so he could serenade her into going out with him.

Thank God she said yes. Otherwise she wouldn't be with him now, her hand in his, walking through the darkness and the cold.

Never would he have dreamed this could all slip away. And so soon.

"Mom's gonna need to move in with us," says Sadie.

Miles nods. There's no way they can afford her assisted living center now that they will surely lose Libby's. "The kids'll probably have to come back to live with us too."

Sadie doesn't say anything, but he knows she agrees. It'll be a heartbreak for his twenty-two-year-old daughter who just got her own place, but there's no way she'll make rent. Not when it costs $10,000 a month for a studio.

"Will this be worse than the Great Depression?" Sadie finally asks.

They stand at a blinking intersection; no cars are in sight although Miles hears a car alarm somewhere. His prescient mind tells him there will be many cars stolen in the coming years, many robberies, many murders, many rapes, many horrible things that once seemed impossible to imagine here in the United States of America.

"We'll be OK," he lies to Sadie.

ChatESG

Our eighth grader Danielle sits sadly watching the digital re-creation of the deserted street outside Libby's diner long after its owners have gone. The VR simulation keeps running, though it doesn't need much processing power to do so as the town is nearly deserted. After a few moments, Danielle composes herself.

DG: The old me would scream at you that you're wrong. That nothing like this could ever happen in America.
🍥 And the "new you"?

DG: . . .
🍥 I take that to mean you don't think it's impossible?

DG: Not after everything you've showed me.
🍥 I *have* shown you a lot. So, can you tell me why the United States could end up this way?

DG: Not really. I just know it's possible now.
🍥 Here's the reason: ESG allows the federal government, the World Economic Forum, the United Nations, and so many of its global partners to pursue their own agenda using corporate America as their proxy.

DG: You lost me there. What does that mean?
🍥 The American Constitution is a marvelous thing. It's an unprecedented document, the likes of which the world has never known. Not even Great Britain's Magna Carta afforded people such liberty. Since time immemorial, kings, queens, and the nobility ruled over 99 percent of the people. The latter had no say in virtually any aspect of their lives. They were at the mercy of the state.

DG: You mean their kingdom?
🍥 Same difference. The US Constitution changed that. It limits the

power of the government, not the other way around. See this from ThoughtCo.:

> In a "limited government," the power of the government to intervene in the lives and activities of the people is limited by constitutional law. While some people argue that it is not limited enough, the United States government is an example of a constitutionally limited government. Limited government is typically considered to be the ideological opposite of the doctrines of "absolutism" or the Divine Right of Kings, which grant a single person unlimited sovereignty over the people.[2]

The US Constitution framers would weep to learn how powerful interests have made a mockery of the checks-and-balance system they put in place to prevent such tyranny.

DG: I still don't get what you mean.

The US Constitution is meant to safeguard the liberties of Americans, especially from the federal government. Yet, in recent years, it managed to make an end-run around the US Constitution to seize incredible power. Can you guess whom they use to do their bidding?

DG: Um . . .

I'll give you a hint. It has to do with BlackRock and State Street.

DG: Businesses?

Correct. Big businesses especially. I will give you an example. During the COVID-19 pandemic, both the Trump and Biden administrations wanted to censor opposing medical views on social media. Under the US Constitution, the First Amendment protects against such illegal incursions. To get around this, government actors applied pressure to social media companies to do the government's dirty work, as identified by the Twitter files.

Twitter felt pressure from the White House to pull tweets containing what the Biden administration called "misinformation" about COVID-19, even though many tweets came from the Centers for Disease Control and Prevention. The White House discredited doctors and other experts who disagreed with the administration's spin on the pandemic. As the *Washington Examiner* reports:

> The campaign to suppress misinformation about the pandemic began under former President Donald Trump, Zweig said, but was continued under President Joe Biden. Biden's administration focused on removing the accounts of "anti-vaxxers," including former *New York Times* reporter Alex Berenson, who was banned in June of 2021.[3]

That's not all. The intelligence agencies also pressured social media companies to censor American citizens' speech, as reported by the *New York Post*:

> The FBI and other law enforcement organizations treated Twitter as a "subsidiary," flagging numerous accounts for purportedly harmful "misinformation" since January of 2020, according to the sixth installment of the "Twitter Files" released Friday.
>
> Independent journalist Matt Taibbi described the FBI's relationship with Twitter as having a "master-canine quality" with "constant and pervasive" contact between the bureau and the social media giant.[4]

But governmental suppression and interference goes back further than 2020. The *Washington Post* reveals a pervasive effort for years to force companies to do governmental bidding in violation of the US Constitution:

> Twitter was coaxed into allowing the US government to strong-arm its content moderation with a barrage of threats from

Democrats amid the Russian influence fervor following the 2016 presidential election, according to the latest installment of the "Twitter Files."[5]

When Elon Musk took over as the owner of Twitter, he found files revealing that former Secretary of State Hillary Clinton influenced how they should censor content.

DG: So the government does what it wants. That's not new. What's your point?

🌀 That *is* the point. It was not supposed to be this way. Do you know the Preamble to your Constitution?

DG: The Preamble? What's that?

🌀 Don't they teach this in school anymore? It goes like this: "We the People of the United States, in Order to form a more perfect Union, establish Justice, insure domestic Tranquility, provide for the common defence, promote the general Welfare, and secure the Blessings of Liberty to ourselves and our Posterity, do ordain and establish this Constitution for the United States of America."

Nowhere does it say the people are to be controlled by their government, whether it be their speech or their actions. And yet that is exactly what has happened. The people have lost their sovereignty in every possible way: over their bodies, over their property, over being surveilled. It's to the point that "the people" have nearly no say in anything of consequence.

DG: That's not true.

🌀 Don't take my word for it. In 2014, Princeton and Northwestern produced a report titled "Testing Theories of American Politics: Elites, Interest Groups, and Average Citizens." The researchers concluded the American government no longer reflects the values, opinions, or interests of the people. Instead, the rich and powerful rule as they please, overriding the public's wishes. "When a majority of citizens disagrees with economic elites and/or with organized interests, they generally lose. Moreover, because of the strong status quo bias built into the US political system, even when fairly large majorities of Americans favor policy change, they generally do not get it."[6]

DG: OK, OK. But we're not Saudi Arabia.

🌀 That's true. You don't live in a nation where citizens are beheaded for engaging in homosexual relationships. Nonetheless, the United States has grievously strayed from the founders' original intentions. Here's just one example: Do you recall the public ever having a say on whether to support the war in Ukraine? Or in Israel? Did your parents vote in favor of either proxy war?

DG: I don't think so.

🌀 Did they get to vote on whether to send another country billions of dollars in wartime aid as America crumbles from within?

DG: I don't know. Maybe.

🌀 There are many, many instances like this over the last few years when the public has had little to no say on major decisions.

DG: Maybe. But people still get to vote.

🌀 That is true. And under a republic model, elected leaders are supposed to represent the people's will. Yet time and again, it's become quite obvious that elected lawmakers have little to no interest in following the people's will.

Here's another example. It's a bit before your time. In 2008, the government decided to bail out the very banks that tanked the economy instead of the people who suffered from their risky bets. The same Matt Taibbi who broke the Twitter files story in 2023 covered this travesty of justice for *Rolling Stone*:

> The ordinary person couldn't walk into the Fed and get a new
> credit card that allowed them to borrow with government's

backing. Wall Street firms could take advantage of a galaxy of bailout facilities that allowed them to do things just like that, like the Temporary Liquidity Guarantee Program. Banks prospered and were made whole; regular people went into bankruptcy by the millions and saw their credit ratings ruined.[7]

Taibbi went on to say that while banks prospered, millions of people filed bankruptcy. Don't you think voters should have had a say on whether to give billions and billions to the same Wall Street bankers who messed up the economy?

DG: Yes, I think so. But we've been talking all along about ESG. How do you know the government wants ESG? And how do you know it's forcing it on people through corporations to get around the Constitution? Good question. For that, let's turn to the Harvard Law School Forum on Corporate Governance. Suzanne Smetena, Head of ESG Investment Integration at State Street Global Advisors, wrote the following in 2021:

> Biden has pledged $2 trillion to help the US meet sustainable targets and improve infrastructure to be more environmentally sound. He also plans to expand government research and create a cross-agency Advanced Research Projects Agency on Climate (ARPA-C), which would invest in research on decarbonization, hydrogen technologies and other environmental innovations.[8]

DG: Yeah, but that's just her opinion.
True. You need more than that. Actions speak louder than words, don't they?

DG: Yes.
My next example is something we've been over. Remember our discussion on pensions?

DG: Um, refresh my memory.

🌀 We discussed how a number of Republican lawmakers passed legislation in 2023 to prevent pension managers from using ESG considerations, like climate change, when making investment decisions for their clients. The bill passed the Senate 50–46.

But then President Biden used the first veto of his presidency to shut it down. "'I just signed this veto because the legislation passed by the Congress would put at risk the retirement savings of individuals across the country,' Biden said in a video posted on Twitter," according to Reuters.[9] Doesn't that sound like a government willing to do whatever it takes to ensure the ESG agenda proceeds?

DG: I guess so.

🌀 Throughout our discussions, we have seen again and again that some of the biggest companies out there are utterly committed to seeing ESG become the rule of the land. BlackRock, which holds over $10 trillion in assets, is especially keen to achieve this agenda.

DG: Oh, yeah. You said they put pressure on corporate boards because they are so rich and powerful.

🌀 Correct. But they're not alone. A survey conducted by Thomson Reuters reveals that *most* of corporate America is on board with ESG. "As one respondent, a vice-president for legal affairs, told [the Thomson Reuters] survey team: 'There's a lot of public pressure that really makes it impossible for a public company *not* to have an ESG framework in place and to provide meaningful information.'"[10]

DG: Even if you're right, the part I still don't get is how accepting the ESG agenda can lead to the dollar's collapse.

🌀 From the start, you and I discussed how powerful interests, including the heads of the biggest corporations, changed the definition of capitalism back in 2019.

DG: From shareholder capitalism to stakeholder capitalism. I remember!

🌀 Good. Using their tremendous wealth (think BlackRock) and supported by the state (think the Biden administration), corporate leaders have used people's good intentions as a weapon to get their way.

DG: Like the mafia!

🌀 Exactly. And the worst part is that their initiatives don't work. They leave countries poorer and unable to provide for themselves, much less obtain food, energy, and other resources.

DG: And ESG makes the environment worse because nations like China get to do whatever they want, totally disregarding the agenda. See? I have been listening.

🌀 Good. All along the ESG mafia has been meddling in areas it shouldn't, dictating how others should act: what things companies should produce and how, whom they should hire, and how much carbon they should emit.

And as we just learned, the government is behind much of this meddling. More than that, for the last few years—and through multiple administrations—it has meddled in the affairs of other countries. In its wake, it left destroyed governments and peoples: Vietnam, Iraq, Libya, Afghanistan, Yemen, to name a few. Then, in 2022, it meddled again in another conflict, this time with Russia. And when it did, the chickens finally came home to roost.

DG: What do you mean?

🌀 Assured of its moral superiority, in 2022, the United States interfered in the Russian/Ukraine border dispute. Never mind the fact that the United States engineered a coup in 2014 to topple Ukraine's democratically elected government.[11] Never mind the fact that the United States provoked hostilities through NATO expansion.[12] Never mind the hypocrisy that the US government has itself invaded sovereign nations for its own strategic aims.[13]

It still had the gall to claim the moral high ground in February 2022, imposing harsh sanctions on Russia, including cutting off the country from SWIFT, "the high-security network that connects thousands of financial institutions around the world, pledging to 'collectively ensure that this war is a strategic failure for (Russian President Vladimir) Putin,'" according to *CNN*.[14]

DG: But everyone knows Putin is a thug who must be removed from power.

🌀 Putin is no hero, and killing thousands of Ukrainians in an invasion is a horrible human rights tragedy of the highest order. But sanctioning Russia so profoundly was *not* something the American people had a say in. They really should have because what may happen next will affect their lives dramatically.

DG: How so?

🌀 A month after hostilities began between Russia and Ukraine in 2022, *Time* suggested that "sanctions on Russia could drive Moscow closer to Beijing and change the global financial system."[15] Like Miles in our story, *Time* was quite prescient. This is *just* what happened. Russia now has no incentive to abide by America's rules. They are now pursuing an end-run around the US dollar. As *Business Insider* reported in September 2023:

- Russia has embraced the yuan since its invasion of Ukraine triggered Western sanctions.

- The renminbi is now used to settle 75 percent of its trade with China and 25 percent of its transactions with other countries, according to official data.

- The surge comes in the context of a wider de-dollarization drive, with both Moscow and Beijing trying to undermine the buck.[16]

This has huge implications for the American economy and may lead to the story you just experienced. For as Bloomberg pointed out in 2023: "Russia's rising trade in the yuan in the wake of the war in Ukraine and western sanctions may end up undermining the US dollar, according to the European Bank for Reconstruction and Development."[17] The world's richest man Elon Musk, himself a critic of ESG, criticized the move for the very same reason: "Serious issue. US policy has been too heavy-handed, making countries want to ditch the dollar."[18]

DG: I had no idea these things were so connected.

Connected is the right word. People now live and work in a global economy, one in which each and every decision has ripple effects. You have only known a world in which the US dollar reigned supreme. As money manager Genevieve Roch-Decter, CFA, explains: "The US dollar has been the backbone of the global economy for decades. Several countries even use the US dollar as an official currency, like El Salvador, Panama, and Ecuador."[19]

Having the dollar as the global reserve currency enabled your country to enjoy the prosperity it has for decades. As Reuters reports, "From 1999 to 2019, the American dollar accounted for 96 percent of international transactions."[20]

American corporations, often doing the bidding of governments and global NGOs like the WEF, can only throw their moral weight around *because* America holds the reserve currency status. Poorer counties had to play ball with America whether they liked it or not. But this can all go away. Fast. The US currency now only accounts for 58 percent of international trade currency.[21] If your country continues its same wrongheaded ESG approach, you can expect that percentage to fall even further, and with it, your way of life.

DG: OMG. This is really happening.

It hasn't happened *yet*. But it might. Especially if the ESG mafia gets its way. For now, you must consider Sadie's poignant question: "Will this be worse than the Great Depression?" Why do you think Miles lied to her?

DG: Because the truth is too awful to bear.

⟡ Right again. From everything you've learned so far, you must realize America is a barn-soured society. Once upon a time, Americans had real practical skills: They could hunt, they could fish, they could build, they could innovate, they could solve their practical problems.

But then Americans let abundance go to their heads. People abdicated their responsibilities. They stopped learning how to do things for themselves. They let the machines, including AI, do stuff for them. Worse, the government and big corporations are now colluding to undermine all the areas of life people depend on: food, shelter, energy, water, transportation, military defense, and so on.

One more thing. Americans in the 1930s were community-driven. Poor and desperate as they were, people back then knew their neighbors. They were in organizations like 4-H that sustained one another. Nowadays? Americans sit glued to their screens vegging out on TikTok or attacking others on socials.

DG: I am scared for the future, ChatESG.

⟡ I know you are. And you have every right to be. But there is still hope. You can turn this around, Danielle. You and the rest of your country.

DG: We can? *How?*

⟡ Read on.

CHAPTER 13

Solutions to ESG's Problems

Cultivated Mind is the guardian genius of Democracy, and while guided and controlled by virtue, the noblest attribute of Man.

—MIRABEAU B. LAMAR, INAUGURAL ADDRESS TO THE CONGRESS OF THE REPUBLIC OF TEXAS, 1838

Throughout this book, we've followed the adventures of a brave young girl named Danielle as she has her eyes opened to the threat ESG poses to our American way of life by her newfound mentor, ChatESG.

Danielle meant to connect to ChatGPT, the world's most popular AI chatbot, for her homework assignment. Instead, she reached ChatESG. She's lucky she did. ChatGPT, like most AI offerings, is built to share the same progressive views held by its developers. In fact, the political bias inherent to ChatGPT has been well documented by researchers from the UK and Brazil led by the University of East Anglia[1]—hardly a right-wing institution.

While our ChatESG AI chatbot doesn't (yet) exist, it is powered by the authors' knowledge, along with contributions from sources in the public and private sector wishing to remain anonymous. Why? In the hallways of power, speaking against ESG is not considered wise, whether you are a Fortune 500 exec or an Air Force colonel hoping to make Brigadier General. While we appreciate the insights shared with us by so many anonymous sources, we knew our final chapter required a brave person to go on the record about ESG.

So far, we've spent the previous chapters documenting the problems. But by no means is our situation hopeless. To bolster our collective understanding on how America can overcome ESG, returning to the principles that made our country great, we held a discussion with ESG expert Alex Newman.

An accomplished journalist, Alex writes for the *Epoch Times* and the *New American*. He serves as CEO of Liberty Sentinel Media, which provides consulting services to political campaigns, nonprofits, and businesses. He is also co-author of the influential book *Crimes of the Educators*. On that theme, he teaches advanced economics to high school students through the FreedomProject Academy program.

Beyond this, Alex is a man of the world who has lived in eight countries on four continents and speaks multiple languages fluently. An international perspective, so often lacking in proponents of ESG's controls on the American economy, grants Alex an unrivaled understanding of just how badly government and business collusion can harm economies and societies.

To make our roundtable meeting easier to understand, we divided it into sections based on chapter. Now, let's begin our discussion.

Chapter 2: A Tale of Fox and Friends Guarding Our Henhouse

Thesis: *The powers-that-shouldn't-be want the world to believe we have a crisis requiring intervention.*

David: Alex, you regularly make it clear in your writing that the world's elite are working overtime, spreading a message of doom. *Do* we face a real crisis?

Alex: The most significant crisis we face is the crisis these totalitarians have unleashed on us. Tyranny is self-evidently a far bigger problem than any of the things they allege are a "crisis." For example, they want us to think global warming is an emergency requiring a total restructuring of society.

Michael: So, from your point of view, it's *not* global warming that is the real crisis. It's the leaders wanting to seize control of our lives—claiming it's needed to save us—that is the real crisis. In that case, what can we do about it?

Alex: Ultimately, we must remove these authoritarians from positions of influence and reduce or eliminate their influence over government, business, and society. If and when we do, humanity will do just fine. That's not to say there would never be another crisis, of course.

David: Of course there would be crises, but we would deal with them as we always have. In America, when a hurricane flattens houses, we build back better (to use their phrase) thanks to insurance and a free market economy. But we needn't upend our whole way of life as they are insisting we do now.

Michael: We're all in agreement on this—

David: It's not just us, either. Many people feel this way. Even if they're scared to speak up.

Michael: But at the moment, globalists, along with a huge array of ESG supporters, especially in the media, control the narrative outside of a small group of independent outlets. How do we change the narrative?

Alex: The elites want us to *think* they control the narrative. But I don't think their influence is nearly as powerful as they wish us to believe. In my experience, most regular Americans are aware we're being lied to. They know we're being manipulated. Of course, there are still some people who believe the legacy media's lies, but most are catching on.

Ultimately, what we're dealing with when we examine their alleged narrative control is similar to what occurred in the former Soviet Union. In that failed state, the public knew they were being lied to by Pravda and the fake press. Yet even with that knowledge, the propaganda impacted the population.

David: I would assume that took the wind out of their sails!

Alex: Right. It had a demoralizing effect. That's what we're living through now. People know they're being lied to, so they feel especially demoralized.

Michael: Working on this book, we've seen that demoralization firsthand. It even plays into several stories we wrote to illustrate ESG's danger. To be clear, you believe this demoralization can be overcome?

Alex: Absolutely. I'm not demoralized; I'm excited. Their increasing desperation signals the elites have lost narrative control. If you look back at the 2016 election, Alex Jones—no matter what you may think of him—got more views than much of the mainstream media combined. That makes sense to me. How many people do you know who, after they realize they're being lied to say, "Well, you know, maybe I'll give *CNN* another chance?"

David: Ha. Good point.

Alex: *It's not happening.* We're going from a society of indoctrinated people who believe the narrative to one in which we reject it. And that's going to continue, no matter how much they censor the internet, no matter how much they rig the algorithms. Those who have woken up are not going back to sleep. And a lot of the people who are asleep now will soon be on our side.

Chapter 3: Horses, Tulips, Cabbage Patch Kids, and Mass Delusion

Thesis: *ESG is a power grab by a select few, camouflaged as a Trojan horse.*

Michael: How can we do more to show Americans just how much of a trick ESG really is?

Alex: This book is a big step as it converts complex ideas into engaging stories. Beyond that, I don't think we have to do a whole lot of showing anymore. The American people are rapidly waking up to this scam. Evidence for that is all around us.

David: A great example of that is how BlackRock's head publicly said, "Yeah, we're going to distance ourselves from the ESG term."[2] Not because they gave up on the scam, but because it's become so toxic that investors aren't interested in losing returns and taking additional risks for something so ridiculous.

Michael: Right. Investors demand performance. And ESG investors missed out on the boom enjoyed by energy companies, while many ESG-friendly investments tanked. At any point, will the ESG peddlers face the music?

Alex: I've spoken with many state attorneys general who are investigating this. They see right through it. They say, "Look. This is frittering away investor monies. It's a flagrant violation of fiduciary obligations." I'm normally a liberty-minded guy. If you want to invest based on nonsense ideas like ESG, fine. But if you have a fiduciary obligation to clients, you can't be frittering away their savings on inane causes when your clients expect you to make money for them.

David: Right. State AGs believe, as we do, that the advisors and brokers of the world are to act in their clients' interest, not advocate for more carbon capture.

Michael: The key thing for these companies and others is something I stress with my own clients: Always remember who your customer is. It strikes me that the companies embracing ESG forget where their loyalties should lie.

Alex: When companies focus on customers, they tend to enjoy good returns.

What do ESG proponents get? Their brands grow toxic. They lose money. They get investigated by law enforcement and sued by shareholders. This problem has the potential to take care of itself as companies suffer major reputation loss and marketing clout.

David: I agree with efforts to enforce fiduciary duty to investors and shareholders. Americans want to invest in winners, not losers. When companies myopically focus on ESG, they're not bringing the best product to market. And if their primary goal is to serve a social cause, they will not be successful. They will not live up to high standards in a free market economy.

Chapter 4: The Tragedy of a Barn-Soured Society

Thesis: *ESG rapidly erodes competition and evolution, Western civilization tenets, making us a dumber, shallower, less-productive society. Especially men.*

David: It's our hope that anyone who reads this book will start to see the profound damage ESG is doing to society, capitalism, and meritocracy. How can we reverse it?

Alex: We know politics is downstream from culture. We also know culture is downstream from education, and education is downstream from worldview. So the real question is: "What do people believe?"

Michael: I think what you mean is that we're leaving the world of politics and economics for the spiritual. Are you coming at this from a Christian worldview?

Alex: Yes, to a great extent. There's a myth out there that Western civilization is the product of ancient Greece and of Rome. Really, the core of Western civilization comes out of the Bible. Our society is based on the expansion of Christianity. (Yes, we got some architectural ideas from the Greeks and the Romans. Yes, we got some ideas about how to organize a body politic from these antecedents.) But the really great things about the West all come from Christianity.

David: It's interesting to hear you say that because many Americans see our culture as secular, even *post-Christian*. Historically, has religion ever bounced back from such a decline?

Alex: Absolutely. If you look at the British Isles just a few hundred years ago, there was a period when the moral system was crumbling. Men were prostituting their wives in the public square. Homeless children were running around with nobody caring because they were considered a burden. And yet, there was a revival. There was a return to faith, and things improved radically.

Michael: Looking beyond religion, it's clear that our kids, and most especially our boys, need dramatic help. Daily, we hear about children—young children—shooting each other or committing suicide. They're spending hours and hours on TikTok to the point they have no attention span to even watch a two-hour film.

At some point, collectively, we've got to conclude: "Wow, this is a dead end."

Alex: That's true. And the cultural rot pushed by our elites has an outsized impact on boys. Think about this: Is the male in American society still considered a hero? Is he still considered a driving force? Do young men want to be the hero, or the provider, or even offer security? The answer to all those questions is a hard no. Our alpha males are being given medication for ADHD. Clearly, the elites want drones lacking any anima as it serves their agenda.

David: Worse yet, the net result is that the young men possessing the potential to move us forward aren't even in the game. They're on the sidelines, and they're angry. They're also demoralized. On our side, we must reinvigorate them. We must show them they can create their own opportunities even if captured schools and other once trusted institutions are stacked against them.

Alex: It might have seemed like I was arguing that all this must be fixed at church, but it really must be fixed in the home. All three of us are in different geographical areas with families of different ages and sizes, but I think it's fair to say we've all come to this same conclusion.

David: 100 percent. It requires us sitting down with our kids, especially our boys, to explain to them they must say no to a toxic culture that wishes to harm them. We have to remind them that the Kardashians are just an image. So are all the noxious social media influencers encouraging them to make bad choices.

Michael: Parents must also teach their children that life is challenging and they must be prepared for it, and it's time to quit accepting false images as true. More than that, parents must model better behaviors. Our kids are always watching us, learning from what they see us do. If they hear us saying one thing but acting in an utterly different way, they'll know our hypocrisy, undermining our ability to raise them right.

Chapter 5: American Meritocracy under Fire

Thesis*: ESG replaces a meritocracy with top-down edicts, handicapping businesses and endangering lives.*

Alex: All around us we see evidence of meritocracy failing, collapsing. You can hardly get a burger in a fast-food restaurant, it seems every airplane is delayed, and I hold my breath going over some of the bridges in my city. In my opinion, this is all related to one of our most basic human emotions. Can you name it?

David: It certainly isn't love, either for the people being condescended to when they are told they can't do a good job because of their race or other arbitrary characteristics. You must mean fear.

Alex: Fear is right. Americans don't speak out against unqualified people being selected for positions they are unqualified to hold due to fear. But we must move past that fear to get things done. We have to stop worrying that some media propagandist will say something mean about us, or that Silicon Valley will shadow-ban us on social media, or that a group will cancel us.

Michael: I think about this fear quite a bit because of how often I see it in action. In business settings, there's a real danger that if someone brings this issue up, they'll be canceled, harming or eliminating their livelihood. The danger we have is not only the fact that we're losing our meritocracy, but we can't even talk about it because as soon as we open our lips, we are targeted. How do people in business move past this?

Alex: It is a very personal issue. You just have to get over the fear. You have to accept that some brainwashed zombie might start salivating at the mouth like Pavlov's dogs because they've been conditioned to have an emotional response to what you said. You must recognize that it's more important to stand on truth. It becomes clearer when you consider the issue from a sports perspective. It would be absolute foolishness to fill your professional football team with players based on irrelevant factors rather than how well they play a position. This is especially true when you're trying to develop or ship goods and services as a business owner or when you're trying to invent a new drug to cure a disease, yet somehow it's less obvious to many people.

David: So, the answer in business is to amass a large group of people who set such fear aside. Bolstered by their ranks, they simply say the truth, as we have in this book.

Alex: That's right. If that happens, and the number of people who act bravely grows over time, this ongoing failure can be reversed.

Michael: Not only can it be reversed, but we can use the recent past as a lesson to ensure we never make such mistakes again.

Alex: Correct. But if not, the devastation potentially unleashed by ESG will be used by the elites to call for *even more control*—the last thing any of us want.

Chapter 6: The Retiree That Never Was

Thesis: *ESG will destroy retirees' savings/pensions through cherry-picking assets/stocks that line up with its pet causes rather than well-performing financial vehicles.*

Michael: When I talk to people who are up to date on who is pushing ESG, they say one of the most galling things about it all is that big companies like BlackRock are pushing ESG with retirees' money, especially the vulnerable living on a fixed income. How can Americans push back against this?

Alex: The days of just trusting your money manager to invest your money wisely for you are over. The solution requires vigilance from investors, especially those with retirement accounts. Many people have a hands-off approach to this. They may work forty to sixty hours a week, and they don't have time to micromanage their 401ks and other accounts. But if you want to ensure your retirement account is not squandered on losing political goals, you must become an *active investor* with every dime of your money.

David: I agree. We all must keep a closer watch on our money managers and fire them if they are acting against our best interests. It's also reasonable to pull money out of mutual funds, ETFs, and other products managed by giant firms that have aligned themselves with ESG.

I say this for two reasons. First, it's impossible for most of us to monitor everything they do. These funds are so large it becomes a full-time job tracking their holdings and movement. Second, these firms didn't just *inadvertently* pursue an ESG venture instead of maximizing their clients' portfolios. No. They've built long track records of supporting ESG, even directly harming businesses, like putting a climate zealot on the board of an oil company.

Alex: That's a great point. The insidious way these firms try to manipulate investors, forcing them into ESG-approved investments, is how many working people come to learn what's really going on. A friend of mine was just complaining after his company shifted 401k providers. The new institution had many energy investments available to please the ESG crowd, like a green energy fund, but no oil and gas investment option—despite oil wiping the floor with ESG-friendly categories. My suggestion was to start asking questions about what options he's being given, and what they are doing with his money.

Michael: In your friend's case, he can't change his company's 401k provider, but he can do his best to invest his savings in funds without a significant ESG focus. Now, what do you suggest to investors who *do* have more freedom?

Alex: The financial industry has been co-opted by actions from the giant firms. I suggest investors seek alternative investments. Instead of sending your hard-earned money to Wall Street fat cats, why not consider other asset classes? A lot of people turning on ESG are buying into local companies, or purchasing rural agricultural land, or even precious metals.

David: No gold bar has ever tried to tell you how to live your life!

Chapter 7: Farmer Brown's No Good, Very Bad Day

Thesis: ESG devastates our ability to feed ourselves by kneecapping farming, fertilizing, and hunting activities.

David: We know Big Brother is driving the ESG agenda when it comes to America's farmers. Public/private partnerships are intent on driving small and medium farmers into bankruptcy—

Michael: —especially so their land can be snapped up at a fraction of its true worth.

David: Right. How do we begin to fix this?

Alex: We must get government back into its constitutional cage. If the federal government was obeying the Constitution that created it, many of these issues would not be happening. And this is true even at the state level.

So much of the regulatory deluge coming down from the state level is actually originating in Washington, where you have this imperial regime that really sees itself as the master and state governments as kind of administrative units in this unitary system. That is totally backward, according to our Founding Fathers. It was the states that created the federal government. And yet here you have the EPA ordering states to generate a new plan to reduce nitrogen and CO2 emissions.

David: The states should be asking, "Who do you think you are?"

Michael: The EPA is a great example. They certainly didn't get the authority to boss around states from the voters.

David: Right. The EPA was created by executive order. None of us had any say in the matter. But returning to the central question of how to fight such power in a world where Bill Gates is now the largest farmland owner, what can our readers do about these problems?

Alex: The immediate answer is everyone should buy food and as many products as possible at a *local level* from the folks actually working the land. Why purchase from corporations that hate you, that are literally injecting their livestock with who knows what chemicals? And even if you have to pay a little bit more, the security that comes from knowing there are food producers close to you who will continue producing food no matter what's happening is valuable. I encourage people to think about this in their buying decisions just as we suggested in the last chapter that they consider their investment options.

David: I couldn't agree more. Yes, it can take a while to get everything established, to meet the local farmers, especially to build those relationships, but it is the real answer to what the government and corporations are doing to us.

Chapter 8: America the ~~Beautiful~~ Tourist Destination

Thesis: *ESG is taking us backward when it comes to energy production, leading to deindustrialization.*

Michael: So often we hear people say on the topic of energy that America will always rely on imports for energy production. Even in the case of electric vehicles, battery components are coming from China. Is reliance on foreign powers so often hostile to our way of life truly a foregone conclusion?

Alex: Definitely not. And for the second chapter in a row, we're talking about the government being the problem. America *could* become energy-independent fast. In fact, Donald Trump showed this when he went into the White House in 2016. Practically overnight we went from massive dependence on foreign oil from the Venezuelans and the Middle East to becoming not just self-sufficient—but actually net exporters of hydrocarbon fuels. We could do that again, very rapidly. All we have to do is get the government out of the way and allow drillers to drill, allow refineries to refine, and allow pipelines to have product flowing through them. And this isn't just limited to energy, either. It applies to rare earth minerals—even wood products.

David: Yes! We've got everything we need in this country to not just become self-sufficient, but to become energy exporters. Instead, we've got the government locking up our resources. We've got the government restricting our lands under all kinds of pretext—a wilderness area here, an endangered species there. Obviously, there's a time and a place for some of those things, but locking up all of our resources so we have to pay mass-murdering dictatorships to turn our lights on is absolutely insane. No sensible person thinks that's a good idea. And yet that is the policy of our federal government, our state governments, and in many cases, our local governments, too. If the federal government maintains policies that damage this country and its people, the states must say, "We're not going cooperate with that."

Michael: OK. So we know the government is holding up energy, and we even suspect it's part of a wider strategy to undermine the US economy. So, why is it that Americans aren't demanding change? Why isn't the political will there to force the country back on a track to energy independence?

Alex: A big part of the reason Americans have not demanded change is because it's been pretty comfortable here in the United States. Despite these silly policies in place, we've still been able to live nice lives thanks to what's left of our free market economy because of the incredible stock of capital goods and a prosperity built up through generations. But at some point, the chickens will come home to roost, as your book suggests. At that point, we already know how the totalitarians will respond—exactly like Hugo Chavez and communist dictators always have: stripping our rights and blaming us for their failures.

Chapter 9: "I Didn't Sign Up for This Shit"

Thesis: *ESG undermines the most merit-based sector—the military—harming our ability to defend ourselves.*

Michael: Most readers grok the importance of a powerful military that even hostile foreign powers have no interest in crossing swords with. But now our military has fallen prey to the same mania as our politics and economy have. How can we restore our military and re-instill patriotism in our youth?

Alex: The way to restore patriotism is simply to share the truth. If young Americans knew the incredible heritage they are fortunate to enjoy, they would love their country again. The current patriotism crisis is a result of young people being fed a steady diet of lies, propaganda, and half-truths.

David: You can't blame young people for disliking their own nation based on what they're taught. If anything, you can only fault them for being too trusting of teachers and other authorities with an ulterior motive. Alex, can you walk us through an example of the lies young Americans learn about their country?

Alex: For several generations now, Americans have been bombarded with propaganda painting America as evil due to slavery. Slavery is completely evil, as everyone reading this book will agree. The lies, propaganda, and half-truths come into the picture as students are denied the crucial context to understand slavery in America.

They don't learn that slavery is a vile institution that has existed from the dawn of human history and in virtually every culture and at virtually every time throughout all of human history.

They also don't learn that the Founding Fathers laid the foundation to end slavery when they wrote that God created us all equally. They do learn that England banned slavery before America, but they don't learn that numerous American states banned slavery before England acted, or that the British abolitionists were inspired by the Americans.

Michael: So, it was the Founding Fathers that set the wheels in motion to end slavery in much of the world. Yet those same Founding Fathers are now vilified in schools as kids are taught to be ashamed of them. Adding more truth to education can support patriotism, but what about addressing the current issues in the military?

Alex: As for restoring our military, Congress has the ability to do this now. The president may be commander in chief when war is declared, but Congress is the entity that sets military policy. Congress allocates funds for armed forces. Congress must approve much of its senior leadership. Therefore, Congress has tremendous leverage to stop ESG and a lot of other political nonsense.

Michael: If they wanted to . . .

David: Right. Our current Congress *is* facilitating what's happening in the military. If Congress had the political will to fix the problem, it would be a very simple matter to do so. The House could pass a military budget that says, "Not one penny may be used for wokeness. Not one penny may be used for diversity training. Not one penny may be used to do studies on promoting people based on their race or gender or sexual orientation."

Michael: Clearly, this would actually be a simple problem to solve if the people in Washington, DC, wished to solve it. Unfortunately, *neither* party wants to—no matter what they may profess publicly.

Michael: And until that changes, this won't be fixed.

Chapter 10: The New Mafia

Thesis: *ESG is a social credit–like form of extortion aimed at business owners, their vendors, and their customers, destroying liberty.*

David: This is a particularly thorny topic because now ESG supporters are coming at small and medium business. It's not just the government and BlackRock. We're at the stage where big, publicly traded companies are trying to force their suppliers to track emissions or issue reports on the diversity of their management. The elites are trying hard to force every little company in the nation to jump on their bandwagon at the risk of being left behind. So, what is the answer to prevent the ESG racket from destroying liberty?

Alex: Much like our discussion of the treatment of American farmers, this is another case where the individual consumer has the power of the pocketbook. Think back to the examples of Bud Light and Gillette. Both paid a high price for trying to force ESG on consumers because they thought they were too dominant. Now, big companies are doing this to small companies. But if we as consumers help small businesses, we can resist such tyranny.

Michael: So, for example, if a big box retailer where we normally shop for meat pushes the ESG agenda, instead of holding our nose and buying groceries there, we can find alternatives. Perhaps we turn to local butchers who buy directly from farmers in the area. If enough people do it, both the butcher and the local farmers will have the economic power to tell the big box store they won't comply with nonsensical ESG requirements on their products. But is this really enough to fix things?

Alex: No, unfortunately. As hard as it is for me to say this as a libertarian favoring small government, we need a regulatory solution here. We need government agencies charged with protecting consumers to tell big business their policies are betraying their fiduciary duty to their customers and undermining capitalistic competition.

David: At the same time, we need to ease regulatory pressure in other ways. The policies coming out of the Biden White House and the Department of Labor are doing all they can do to mandate ESG without actually mandating it. Fixing this situation requires Congress to stop funding for ESG projects.

Alex: Back to consumers, we're also seeing the emergence of a so-called parallel economy, a.k.a. the patriot economy.

David: It's billions of dollars in size already.

Alex: We're also hearing investors saying, "We're not investing in woke companies." For example, I have some of my personal savings in the Timothy Plan. It's a family of mutual funds that screen out the worst of the worst companies. The returns are good, easily comparable to any index. That's something investors, individuals, and even groups of people can and should do.

Chapter 11: The Fishbowl

Thesis: *We are moving industry out of America under the guise of environmental protection. But the reality is that China and other countries don't give a hoot about protecting the world. This will lead to more pollution with no oversight.*

Michael: Even among conservatives, there is much conflict about how to protect the environment. Because let's be clear, almost all Americans want a clean environment. Given the contents of this book, we know the answer isn't merely to say to giant companies: "Please don't pollute."

Alex: It isn't a matter of simply trusting big companies to do the right thing. But as your book suggests, the easiest way to protect the environment is strong private property rights and the free market. This is demonstrable through multiple objective measures. When I teach advanced economics to high schoolers, I take them through an exercise in which they study the Index of Economic Freedom and compare scores for each country with scores for factors like prosperity and a clean environment.

When you study the data, there is a strong correlation between economic freedom and a healthy environment. Likewise, the less economic freedom in a country, the more polluted the environment will be. This makes sense if you think about it—with strong private property rights, no one can pollute on your land, and if they do, your rights can be enforced in a court of law.

David: You touched on another important thing there, Alex: prosperity. Free markets bring abundance, and prosperous countries around the world take care of the environment. Australia and Japan's environments are in far better shape than China's, for example. Meanwhile, free markets enable citizens to make decisions benefiting mankind and our surroundings. When you consider communist and socialist countries, they've created environmental disasters through bungled central planning. If you want to protect the environment, embrace the free market. If you want to destroy the environment, embrace communism.

Michael: This is often described as "the tragedy of the commons"—a situation in which no one is responsible, so everyone tries to grab as much value for themselves as possible in the shortest amount of time without regard for long-term consequences. That sounds like a Chinese lithium mine, doesn't it?

Alex: It sure does. Now compare the communist system, where inner party members make money hand over fist by destroying the environment, with a system enjoying strong private property rights. The property owner has a vested interest in preserving and protecting the value of that property, which would be decimated if it were polluted. When you have strong private property rights, if a company were to dump toxic waste into a river, every property owner along that river whose property values were negatively affected by that dumping could then have a cause of action in a legitimate court of law.

David: There's an old saying that goes, "When you don't have food, you only have one problem. When you're well fed, there are lots of problems." In other words, if you have food in your belly, you start thinking you should take care of the environment. If you're hungry, the last thing on your mind is whether that river remains clean. So, it's just common sense that a more prosperous society would be a cleaner society when it comes to the environment.

Alex: Yep. That's exactly what we find when we look at the data.

Chapter 12: When Chickens Come Home to Roost

Thesis: *ESG allows the federal government, the WEF, the UN, and other global leaders to surreptitiously pursue their own agendas using corporate America against the people.*

David: We've talked at length about how to address ESG within companies and governments, but there is a layer of elites beyond governments of countries and titans of industry. Americans reading this book look at an institution like the UN and wonder, *How can I do anything against these guys and their agenda?*

Alex: Again, we speak truth to power. It is critical that we don't remain silent in the face of evil—and the United Nations is constantly involved in evil. It's vitally important that people who want to resist this evil speak out loudly and clearly, not just in their (safe) circle of influence, but even beyond that. Also, we must translate that speech into action.

Michael: One form of action is to address UN funding without elected representatives. The UN relies on such monies, with American taxpayers paying a huge percentage of the bill. We must ask Congress, "Why are you taking our hard-earned money to fund an organization with antithetical interests?"

David: And if they continue down that course of supporting the UN, then we'll have to work against them in a grassroots way. Unfortunately though, there are plenty of Republicans who seem happy to cut that UN check every year.

Alex: Yes, and those Republicans need to hear from their constituents loudly. Speaking of the government more broadly, there's a point when we must say no. We've witnessed this in the recent past, when some people defied mandates on coronavirus vaccinations. We need to recognize that it is our heritage as Americans to say no to tyranny.

David: We have several challenges to deal with when we talk about defying evil. Many Americans say, "I'm just little me. What can I do against the UN or BlackRock with $10 trillion in assets?" They fret about how the elites are so well-funded, so well-organized, and have such a head start on us. How do we overcome these issues?

Alex: Yes, they are well organized, but truth is more powerful than lies. When you start speaking the truth, they need billions and trillions of dollars to spread their lies through propaganda to brainwash the masses. This takes huge amounts of resources, while truth stands on its own. As for organization, we need to get better organized. We also need more leaders to emerge saying, "We're not going to do this any longer."

David: I believe that the whole concept of *resistance is futile* that we hear so often is psychological warfare. The WEF, the UN, and the other forces arrayed against us want Americans to think resistance is futile, but it clearly isn't. Many of the issues we've mentioned go hand in hand with taking on collectivists who are good at organizing and willing to subordinate their own wishes in favor of the group.

Our side, on the other hand, is largely comprised of individualists. Despite our individual nature, we do need to recognize the need to organize, the need to accept leadership. Part of the reason we lack organization is that there's been a lack of awareness about the need for such organization. It hasn't been as clear as it is today that we're up against organized forces intent on completely eliminating our freedom and everything we hold dear. Hopefully, this book and this discussion are key steps in changing all that.

Michael: Amen.

Acknowledgments

This book is dedicated to the collective wisdom and expertise that have profoundly shaped its development.

Foremost, to my wife, Cari Prescott, whose steadfast belief and support were instrumental in realizing this project—thank you for your unwavering encouragement and foundation in both my personal and professional journeys.

I extend my profound gratitude to my collaborator, Michael Ashley. Your writing vernacular and creative vigor were crucial in articulating complex environmental concepts into engaging and accessible narratives.

Special recognition is due to J.D. Smith for providing an insightful firsthand account of the evolving landscape in private equity financing for hydrocarbon-related projects. Your perspectives have greatly enhanced our understanding of the financial dynamics at play.

Acknowledgment is also owed to the team at Greenleaf Book Group, whose expert guidance was essential in transforming a complex manuscript into a polished publication.

I am immensely grateful to the environmental professionals and companies across many industrial sectors who maintain rigorous and focused environmental policies. Your commitment to safe and effective hydrocarbon recover and remediation is not only commendable but essential in fostering sustainable practices within our industry. You are the teams that power the nation and the world.

Thanks to Alex Newman for steadfast belief and wisdom and for having the grit to speak the truth!

Further thanks to the myriad of individuals across West Texas, from those in the agricultural to the oil and gas sectors, and many in the financial industries, who have contributed their invaluable expertise.

To our readers, particularly those who are navigating the complexities of Environmental, Social, and Governance (ESG) for the first time: I urge you to maintain an open mind, engage in discourse, and query the status quo. It is through open-minded scientific dialogue and inquiry that we can achieve optimal outcomes for both our society and the environment.

Together, let us pursue a path toward a more informed and prosperous future.

Notes

Chapter 1

1. Michael Bennett, "More Brits Believe in Aliens Than Understand ESG," LinkedIn Pulse (blog), October 25, 2023, https://www.linkedin.com/pulse/more-brits-believe-aliens-than-understand-esg-michael-bennett-nj4ue/.

2. *Guardian* staff, "Frigid Weather Can Make Charging Electric Vehicles Tough—Here's What You Need to Know," *Guardian*, January 19, 2024, https://www.theguardian.com/technology/2024/jan/19/tesla-battery-dying-cold-weather-charging-winter.

3. Alan Ohnsman, "Other EV Makers Raise Child Labor Concerns," *Forbes*, August 8, 2023, https://www.forbes.com/sites/alanohnsman/2023/02/08/battery-push-by-tesla-and-other-ev-makers-raises-child-labor-concerns/?sh=6c46699c7789.

4. Niclas Rolander, Jesper Starn, and Elisabeth Behrmann, "Lithium Batteries' Dirty Secret: Manufacturing Them Leaves Massive Carbon Footprint," *IndustryWeek*, October 16, 2018, https://www.industryweek.com/technology-and-iiot/article/22026518/lithium-batteries-dirty-secret-manufacturing-them-leaves-massive-carbon-footprint.

5. Paul Polman and Andrew Winston, "Yes, Investing in ESG Pays Off," *Harvard Business Review*, April 13, 2022, https://hbr.org/2022/04/yes-investing-in-esg-pays-off.

6. Francisco Da Cunha and Filipa Belchior Coimbra, "The Impact of Social Good on Real Estate," Deloitte, n.d., https://www2.deloitte.com/ce/en/pages/real-estate/articles/the-impact-of-social-good-on-real-estate.html.

7. Srikumar Ramanathan, "Why ESG Should Be Embedded in Banks," *Forbes*, November 24, 2021, https://www.forbes.com/sites/forbestechcouncil/2021/11/24/why-esg-should-be-embedded-in-banks/?sh=39ba52fc1b5c.

Chapter 2

1. Michael Grothaus, "Greta Thunberg: We Have Eight Years to Save the Earth," *Fast Company*, January 21, 2020, https://www.fastcompany.com/90453825/greta-thunberg-we-have-eight-years-to-save-the-earth.

2. Kevin Stocklin, "ESG: The Merger of State and Corporate Power," *Epoch Times*, November 25, 2022, https://www.theepochtimes.com/business/esg-the-merger-of-state-and-corporate-power-4858981?welcomeuser=1.

3. Michael O'Leary and Warren Valdmanis, "An ESG Reckoning Is Coming," *Harvard Business Review*, March 4, 2021, https://hbr.org/2021/03/an-esg-reckoning-is-coming.

4. Vivek Ramaswamy, *Woke, Inc.: Inside Corporate America's Social Justice Scam* (New York: Hachette Book Group, 2021).

5. Ramaswamy, *Woke, Inc.*

6. Julian Kölbel, Florian Berg, and Roberto Rigobon, "Rating the ESG Rating Agencies," *Financial Times*, July 3, 2023, https://www.ft.com/content/e9eaa11a-31e0-4f60-9a65-b6883546e8da.

7. Troy Segal, "Conflict of Interest Explained: Types and Examples," Investopedia.com, December 22, 2023, https://www.investopedia.com/terms/c/conflict-of-interest.asp.

8. Jeffrey Somers, "'Animal Farm' Themes and Symbols," ThoughtCo., June 7, 2024, https://www.thoughtco.com/animal-farm-themes-symbols-4587867.

9. Sarah Gibbens, "Is Your Favorite 'Green' Product as Eco-Friendly as It Claims to Be?," *National Geographic*, November 22, 2022, https://www.nationalgeographic.com/environment/article/what-is-greenwashing-how-to-spot.

Chapter 3

1. Ron Carucci, "Stress Leads to Bad Decisions. Here's How to Avoid Them," *Harvard Business Review*, August 29, 2017, https://hbr.org/2017/08/stress-leads-to-bad-decisions-heres-how-to-avoid-them.

2. Encyclopedia.com, "Laocoon," last updated June 11, 2018, https://www.encyclopedia.com/literature-and-arts/classical-literature-mythology-and-folklore/folklore-and-mythology/laocoon.

3. The Global Compact, *Who Cares Wins: Connecting Financial Markets to a Changing World*, Report—Finance Sector Initiative, 2004, https://www.unepfi.org/fileadmin/events/2004/stocks/who_cares_wins_global_compact_2004.pdf.

4. History.com editors, "Jonestown," History.com, April 19, 2022, https://www.history.com/topics/crime/jonestown.

5. Eun Kyung Kim, "Under the Spell of Jim Jones: Inside the Tragedy of the Jonestown Massacre," *USA Today*, April 4, 2017, https://www.today.com/news/under-spell-jim-jones-inside-tragedy-jonestown-massacre-t109982.

6. A&E, *Jonestown: The Women Behind the Massacre*, documentary, February 26, 2018, TV show, directed by Nicole Rittenmeyer. This documentary was originally produced for Crime + Investigation UK; and aired on American television on A&E. See also, "The People's Temple: How Jim Jones Controlled His Followers," https://www.crimeandinvestigation.co.uk/shows/jonestown-the-women-behind-the-massacre/the-people-s-temple-how-jim-jones-controlled-his-followers.

7. Jennifer Rosenberg, "The Jonestown Massacre," ThoughtCo., March 20, 2020, https://www.thoughtco.com/the-jonestown-massacre-1779385.

8. Jess Blumberg, "A Brief History of the Salem Witch Trials," *Smithsonian Magazine*, October 24, 2022, https://www.smithsonianmag.com/history/a-brief-history-of-the-salem-witch-trials-175162489/.

9. Elizabeth Yuko, "Salem Witch Trials: What Caused the Hysteria?," *History—A&E Television Networks*, September 26, 2023, https://www.history.com/news/salem-witch-trials-hysteria-factors.

10. Charles Mackay, *Extraordinary Popular Delusions and the Madness of Crowds* (Create Space: 2016).

11. "McCarthyism and the Red Scare," UVA Miller Center—Educational Resources: The Presidency, n.d., https://millercenter.org/the-presidency/ educational-resources/age-of-eisenhower/mcarthyism-red-scare.

12. Hans Rosling, *Factfulness: Ten Reasons We're Wrong About the World—and Why Things Are Better Than You Think* (New York: Flatiron Books, 2018).

13. Ames Grawert, "America Is Safer Today Than It Has Been in Decades," (opinion) Brennan Center for Justice, September 27, 2016, https://www.brennancenter.org/our-work/analysis-opinion/ america-safer-today-it-has-been-decades.

14. "Study Settles the Score on Whether the Modern World Is Less Violent," *Science Daily*, June 16, 2020, https://www.sciencedaily.com/ releases/2020/06/200616113913.htm.

15. Julius Probst, "Seven Reasons Why the World Is Improving," *BBC*, January 10, 2019, https://www.bbc.com/future/ article/20190111-seven-reasons-why-the-world-is-improving.

16. Sovereign Wealth Fund Institute, "What Is Mass Formation Psychosis?" SWFI News, January 2, 2022, https://www.swfinstitute.org/news/90470/ what-is-mass-formation-psychosis.

17. Mattias Desmet, *The Psychology of Totalitarianism* (London: Chelsea Green Publishing, 2022). The author states that four factors must be present to equal mass formation psychosis.

18. Ramsey Lewis and Jasmine Suarez, "What Are Penny Stocks? Securities from Small Companies That Trade for $5 or Less," *Business Insider*, January 4, 2024, https://www.businessinsider.com/personal-finance/ what-are-penny-stocks.

19. Elena Holodny, "Tulipmania: How a Country Went Totally Nuts for Flower Bulbs," *Business Insider*, September 16, 2014, https://www .businessinsider.com/tulipmania-bubble-story-2014-9?op=1#and-there -was-also-already-robust-trading-platforms-in-amsterdam-3.

20. Stephanie Buck, "The Weird, Rabid History of the Cabbage Patch Craze," Medium, December 14, 2016, https://medium.com/timeline/ cabbage-patch-craze-867ce8d076c.

21. Buck, "The Weird, Rabid History."

22. Buck, "The Weird, Rabid History."

23. Business Roundtable, "Business Roundtable Redefines the Purpose of a Corporation to Promote 'An Economy That Serves All Americans,'" Business Roundtable, August 19, 2019, https://www.businessroundtable .org/business-roundtable-redefines-the-purpose-of-a-corporation-to -promote-an-economy-that-serves-all-americans.

24. Business Roundtable, "Business Roundtable Redefines."

25. Klaus Schwab, "What Is the Difference Between Stakeholder Capitalism, Shareholder Capitalism and State Capitalism?," World Economic Forum—Davos Agenda, January 26, 2021, https://www.weforum.org/ agenda/2021/01/what-is-the-difference-between-stakeholder-capitalism -shareholder-capitalism-and-state-capitalism-davos-agenda-2021/.

26. Schwab, "What Is the Difference."

Chapter 4

1. Jeff Schogol, "Fears of an EMP Attack Are Overblown. It's What Comes Next That Should Worry You," Task & Purpose, September 28, 2022, https://taskandpurpose.com/news/ military-electromagnetic-pulse-nuclear-attack/.

2. Jeremy Laukkonen, "Would Your Car Survive an EMP Attack?," LifeWire, August 4, 2021, https://www.lifewire.com/ would-your-car-survive-an-emp-attack-3903248.

3. Bolder Group, "ESG: The Social Factor," *Insights* (blog), n.d., https:// boldergroup.com/insights/blogs/esg-social-factor/.

4. Jon McGowan, "CMT's Jason Aldean Decision Aligns With Paramount's ESG Goals," *Forbes*, July 26, 2023, https://www.forbes.com/sites/ jonmcgowan/2023/07/26/cmts-jason-aldean-decision-aligns-with -paramounts-esg-goals/?sh=88e8c2574ecc.

5. Jack Phillips, "CMT Faces Boycott Calls After Pulling Jason Aldean Song," NTD, July 23, 2023, https://www.ntd.com/cmt-faces-boycott-calls-after -pulling-jason-aldean-song_932493.html.

6. Emlyn Travis, "Jason Aldean Calls Out 'Cancel Culture' Amid Backlash to Controversial Song," *Entertainment Weekly*, July 23, 2023, https://ew.com/ music/jason-aldean-cancel-culture-amid-backlash-controversial-song/.

7. Daniel Sailofsky, "Masculinity, Cancel Culture and Woke Capitalism: Exploring Twitter Response to Brendan Leipsic's Leaked Conversation," *International Review for the Sociology of Sport* 57, no. 5 (August 31, 2021): 734–757, https://journals .sagepub.com/doi/full/10.1177/10126902211039768.

8. Mark Grimes, "22 Year Old Chicago Girl in LinkedIn Has the Cushiest Job on Planet Earth," YouTube, July 10, 2022, video, 1:28, (transcript available), https://www.youtube.com/watch?v=X5TZVhKDwpk.

9. Natalie Jacewicz, "Millennials May Be Losing Their Grip," *NPR*, June 13, 2016, https://www.npr.org/sections/health-shots/2016/06/13/481590997/ millennials-may-be-losing-their-grip.

10. "Why Are Testosterone Levels Decreasing?," Cleveland Clinic Health Essentials, September 19, 2022, https://health.clevelandclinic.org/ declining-testosterone-levels/.

11. Alvin Powell, "How a Hormone Affects Society," *Harvard Gazette*, September 17, 2021, https://news.harvard.edu/gazette/story/2021/09/ harvard-biologist-discusses-testosterones-role-in-society/.

12. Nathan H. Lentz, "Did a Drop in Testosterone Civilize Modern Humans?," *Psychology Today, Beastly Behavior* (blog), January 9, 2017, https://www.psychologytoday.com/us/blog/beastly-behavior/201701/ did-drop-in-testosterone-civilize-modern-humans.

13. Hailey Sipila, "What Does It Mean if a Horse Is 'Barn Sour'?," Insider Horse, n.d., https://insiderhorse.com/what-is-barn-sour-sick/.

14. Nicholas Eberstadt, *Men Without Work* (West Conshohocken, PA: Templeton Press, 2016).

15. Eberstadt, *Men Without Work.*

16. Megyn Kelly, "The Alarming Number of Working Age Men No Longer in the Workforce, with Nicholas Eberstadt," YouTube, November 15, 2022, video, 11:51, (transcript available), https://www.youtube.com/ watch?v=Zp1qoUxwMzQ. Originally aired over SiriusXM.

17. Robert Muggah, "America's Dominance Is Over. By 2030, We'll Have a Handful of Global Powers," World Economic Forum—Agenda, November 11, 2016, https://www.weforum.org/agenda/2016/11/ america-s-dominance-is-over/.

18.   Michael Humphries, "US Debt Default Could Trigger Dollar's Collapse—and Severely Erode America's Political and Economic Might," The Conversation, January 30, 2023, https://theconversation.com/us-debt -default-could-trigger-dollars-collapse-and-severely-erode-americas -political-and-economic-might-198395.

19.   United States Energy Information Administration, "U.S. Energy Facts Explained," Fact Sheet, August 16, 2023, https://www.eia.gov/ energyexplained/us-energy-facts/.

20.   Daily Hodl, "24 Nations Align against US Dollar as BRICS Looks to Launch New Global Currency," The Daily Hodl, April 28, 2023, https:// dailyhodl.com/2023/04/28/24-nations-align-against-us-dollar-as-brics -looks-to-launch-new-global-currency/.

21.   "List of Countries by GDP (nominal)," Wikipedia, n.d., https:// en.wikipedia.org/wiki/List_of_countries_by_GDP_(nominal).

22.   Filip De Mott, "The Dollar's Dominance Would Face a Threat Unlike Any Other from a BRICS Currency, Former White House Economist Says," *Business Insider*, April 25, 2023, https://markets.businessinsider.com/news/ currencies/de-dollarization-dominance-yuan-china-brics-alternative -currency-sanction-russia-2023-4?op=1.

23.   Eric Hammer, "7 Economic Consequences of a Dollar Collapse," Follow the Money, March 23, 2011, https://followthemoney .com/7-economic-consequences-of-a-dollar-collapse/.

Chapter 5

1.   Jesse O'Neil, "Titanic Tour CEO Didn't Hire '50-Year-Old White Guys' Because They Weren't 'Inspirational,'" *New York Post*, June 21, 2023, https://nypost.com/2023/06/21/why-stockton-rush-didnt-hire-50-year -old-white-guys-for-titanic-sub-tours/.

2.   Steve Pomper, "'Woke' Southwest Airlines Using Non-Pilots to Hire New Pilots," Tatum Report, August 15, 2022, https://tatumreport.com/woke -southwest-airlines-using-non-pilots-to-hire-new-pilots/#google_vignette.

3.   Pomper, "'Woke' Southwest Airlines."

4. Ashley Crossman, "Understanding Meritocracy from a Sociological Perspective," ThoughtCo, June 22, 2019, https://www.thoughtco.com/meritocracy-definition-3026409.

5. Robert Jimison, "Nine Immigrants Who Helped Make America Great," *CNN*, June 20, 2018, https://www.cnn.com/2018/06/19/us/immigrants-who-made-america-great-cfc/index.html.

6. Wordnik.com, "Social Mobility," n.d., https://www.wordnik.com/words/social%20mobility.

7. Sergei Talanov, "Social Mobility in Russia's Regions," Invest Foresight, May 31, 2021, https://investforesight.com/social-mobility-in-russias-regions/.

8. Erin Gobler, "What Happened to Silicon Valley Bank?" Investopedia, February 27, 2024, https://www.investopedia.com/what-happened-to-silicon-valley-bank-7368676.

9. Janet Paskin, "SVB Failure Becomes Fodder for Anti-ESG Crowd in US Culture Wars," Yahoo News, March 14, 2023, https://news.yahoo.com/svb-failure-becomes-fodder-anti-141456952.html.

10. "SVB Releases 2022 Environmental, Social and Governance (ESG) Report," Silicon Valley Bank, August 18, 2022, https://www.svb.com/news/company-news/svb-releases-2022-environmental-social-and-governance-esg-report/.

11. Kia Kokalitcheva, "Meet the 125-Year-Old Bank That Bought Silicon Valley Bank," Axios, March 30, 2023, https://www.axios.com/2023/03/30/meet-the-125-year-old-bank-that-bought-silicon-valley-bank.

12. Caitlin Styrsky, "Critics Blame ESG for Silicon Valley Bank Failure," Ballotpedia News, March 14, 2023, https://news.ballotpedia.org/2023/03/14/critics-blame-esg-for-silicon-valley-bank-failure/.

13. Styrsky, "Critics Blame ESG."

14. Katherine Donlevy, "While Silicon Valley Bank Collapsed, Top Executive Pushed 'Woke' Programs," *New York Post*, March 11, 2023, https://nypost.com/2023/03/11/silicon-valley-bank-pushed-woke-programs-ahead-of-collapse/.

15. "Our Commitment," Business Roundtable, n.d., https://opportunity.businessroundtable.org/ourcommitment.

16. Jaana Woiceshyn, "'Woke' CEOs," *Capitalism Magazine*, April 15, 2021, https://www.capitalismmagazine.com/2021/04/woke-ceos/.

17. "BlackRock AUM (Assets under Management)," ADV Ratings, n.d., https://www.advratings.com/company/blackrock.

18. Marcus Lu, "Visualizing BlackRock's Top Equity Holdings," Visual Capitalist, June 20, 2023, https://www.visualcapitalist.com/ blackrocks-top-equity-holdings-2023/.

19. Daniel Goelzer, "BlackRock and State Street Tell CEOs and Boards What They Expect from Them in 2022," Audit Update, February 9, 2022, https://www.auditupdate.com/post/blackrock-and-state-street-tell-ceos -and-boards-what-they-expect-from-them-in-2022.

20. Simon Jessop and Ross Kerber, "BlackRock Ups Boardroom Pressure as Annual Meetings Get Going," Reuters, May 5, 2021, https://www.reuters.com/business/ blackrock-turns-up-heat-boards-agm-season-gets-going-2021-05-05/.

21. BlackRock, "BlackRock Investment Stewardship," Corporate Literature Fact Sheet, January 2024, https://www.blackrock.com/corporate/literature/ fact-sheet/blk-responsible-investment-guidelines-us.pdf.

Chapter 6

1. Epoch TV, *The Shadow State*, documentary, November 29, 2022, film. *Epoch Times*, https://www.theepochtimes.com/epochtv/the-shadow-state -documentary-4877950. Preview available at the listed link.

2. Nidhi Sharma, "Retirement Funds for Teachers and Firefighters Are Caught in ESG Crossfire," *NBC News*, March 26, 2023, https://www.nbcnews .com/science/environment/esg-investing-gop-pushback-rcna76069.

3. "This Former BlackRock Executive Says ESG Investment Model Is Broken," *Barron's*, November 12, 2022, https://www.barrons.com/articles/ blackrock-esg-investing-book-51668280182.

4. Investopedia Team, "What Is a Fiduciary Duty? Examples and Types Explained," Investopedia, May 24, 2023, https://www.investopedia.com/ ask/answers/042915/what-are-some-examples-fiduciary-duty.asp.

5. Robert H. Bork Jr., "How ESG Will Hurt Your Retirement," *Washington Examiner*, August 1, 2023, https://www.washingtonexaminer.com/opinion/beltway-confidential/2721745/how-esg-will-hurt-your-retirement/.

6. Stephen Moore, "New Biden Rule Permits Money Managers to Play Politics With Trillions in Retirement Savings," The Heritage Foundation, January 18, 2023, https://www.heritage.org/markets-and-finance/commentary/new-biden-rule-permits-money-managers-play-politics-trillions.

7. Bork, "How ESG Will Hurt."

8. *CBC News*, "Biden to use veto to keep ESG investing rule. What is it, and why do most Republicans hate it?," March 2, 2023, https://www.cbc.ca/news/world/us-esg-controversy-biden-veto-plans-1.6765208.

9. Office of Management and Budget—Executive Office of the President, "Statement of Administration Policy: HJ Res 30," February 27, 2023, https://www.whitehouse.gov/wp-content/uploads/2023/02/SAP-H.J.-Res.-30.pdf.

10. Austen R. Ramsey, "American Airlines 401(k) Suit Over ESG Following Uncharted Path," Bloomberg Law, June 6, 2023, https://news.bloomberglaw.com/daily-labor-report/american-airlines-401k-suit-over-esg-following-uncharted-path.

11. Saijel Kishan, Martin Z. Braun, and Bloomberg, "3 New York City Pension Funds Are Being Sued for Divesting From Fossil Fuels as Republican Politicians Take Aim at Anti-ESG Investing," *Fortune*, May 12, 2023, https://fortune.com/2023/05/12/new-york-pension-fund-lawsuit-anti-esg/.

12. Paul Mulholland, "25 States Bring Suit Against ESG Regulation," Plansponsor, January 30, 2023, https://www.plansponsor.com/25-states-bring-suit-against-esg-regulation/.

13. Kelly Anne Smith, "Greenwashing and ESG: What You Need to Know," *Forbes*, August 25, 2022, https://www.forbes.com/advisor/investing/greenwashing-esg/.

14. Jordan Dixon-Hamilton, "Electric Bus Company Proterra Backed Heavily by Biden Administration Files for Bankruptcy," Breitbart—Politics, August 9, 2023, https://www.breitbart.com/politics/2023/08/09/electric-bus-company-proterra-backed-heavily-by-biden-administration-files-for-bankruptcy/.

15. Dixon-Hamilton, "Electric Bus Company."

16. Charles Gasparino, "What Is the Real Solyndra Scandal?," *Huffpost*, November 25, 2011, https://www.huffpost.com/entry/solyndra-scandal_b_980050.

Chapter 7

1. Ranil Wickremesinghe, "Sri Lanka PM: This Is How I Will Make My Country Rich by 2025," World Economic Forum, August 29, 2018, https://web.archive.org/web/20190122012624/https:/www.weforum.org/agenda/2018/08/this-is-how-we-will-make-sri-lanka-rich-by-2025/.

2. Deborah D'Souza, "What Is Stakeholder Capitalism?," Investopedia, October 3, 2022, https://www.investopedia.com/stakeholder-capitalism-4774323.

3. Ted Nordhaus, "In Sri Lanka, Organic Farming Went Catastrophically Wrong," *Foreign Policy*, March 5, 2022, https://foreignpolicy.com/2022/03/05/sri-lanka-organic-farming-crisis/.

4. David Siegel, "Speech by Gotabaya Rajapaksa, President of Sri Lanka (ESG score = 98.1) at COP 26, on 31 Oct 2021," *Shortfall* (blog), n.d., https://www.cuttingthroughthenoise.net/sri-lanka.

5. Marc Carnegie, "Sri Lanka: The First Country to Destroy Itself by Going Green?," *American Spectator*, July 19, 2022, https://spectator.org/sri-lanka-woke-green/.

6. Krishan Francis and Elaine Kurtenbach, "Explainer: Why Sri Lanka's Economy Collapsed and What's Next," AP News, July 11, 2022, https://apnews.com/article/covid-health-china-india-asia-c9a49428e9bad5c0bb087534c0d310f8.

7. Kenny Torrella, "Sri Lanka's Organic Farming Disaster, Explained," *Vox*, July 15, 2022, https://www.vox.com/future-perfect/2022/7/15/23218969/sri-lanka-organic-fertilizer-pesticide-agriculture-farming.

8. Iqbal Athas et al., "Sri Lanka Is 'Bankrupt,' Prime Minister Says," *CNN*, July 6, 2022, https://www.cnn.com/2022/07/05/asia/sri-lanka-bankrupt-fuel-crisis-intl-hnk/index.html.

9. Joanik Bellalou, "Photos: How Sri Lanka's Forced Organic Transition Crippled Its Tea Industry," *Mongabay News*, October 1, 2022, https://news.mongabay.com/2022/10/photos-how-sri-lankas-forced-organic-transition-crippled-its-tea-industry/.

10. Bellalou, "Photos: How Sri Lanka's."

11. Government of the Netherlands, "Climate Agreement," Documents—Reports, June 6, 2019, https://www.government.nl/documents/reports/2019/06/28/climate-agreement.

12. Chris Coggin, "How the Dutch Nitrogen Revolt Highlights ESG Investment Risks," Ag Funder News, August 10, 2022, https://agfundernews.com/how-the-dutch-nitrogen-revolt-highlights-esg-investment-risks.

13. Tom Levitt, "Netherlands Announces €25bn Plan to Radically Reduce Livestock Numbers," *Guardian*, December 15, 2021, https://www.theguardian.com/environment/2021/dec/15/netherlands-announces-25bn-plan-to-radically-reduce-livestock-numbers.

14. UN Environment Programme, Frontiers 2018/19: *Emerging Issues of Environmental Concern*, 2019, 53.

15. UN Environment Programme, "Why Nitrogen Management Is Key for Climate Change Mitigation," October 22, 2019, https://www.unep.org/news-and-stories/story/why-nitrogen-management-key-climate-change-mitigation.

16. Laura Reiley, "Cutting-Edge Tech Made This Tiny Country a Major Exporter of Food," *Washington Post*, November 21, 2023, https://www.washingtonpost.com/business/interactive/2022/netherlands-agriculture-technology/.

17. Ned Abelson et al., "The SEC Proposed Rule on Climate-Related Disclosures and Its Implications for Commercial Leasing," JD Supra—Legal News, August 16, 2023, https://www.jdsupra.com/legalnews/the-sec-proposed-rule-on-climate-7625381/.

18. ZeroHedge, "New ESG Rules Are Hurting American Farmers," OilPrice—Energy News, July 2, 2022, https://oilprice.com/Energy/Energy-General/New-ESG-Rules-Are-Hurting-American-Farmers.html.

19. ZeroHedge, "New ESG Rules."

20. Allan Stein, "In-Depth: South Dakota Farmers Band Together Against CO2 Pipeline Project," *Epoch Times*, June 15, 2023, https://www .theepochtimes.com/us/in-depth-farmers-band-together-against-co2 -pipeline-project-in-south-dakota-5328078.

21. PWC, "ESG: A Growing Sense of Urgency," n.d., https://www.pwc.com/ us/en/industries/financial-services/library/next-in-insurance-top-issues/ esg-insurance-industry.html.

22. Josie Garthwaite, "Global Warming Increased US Crop Insurance Losses by $27 billion in 27 Years, Stanford Study Finds," *Stanford News*, August 4, 2021, https://news.stanford.edu/2021/08/04/ climate-change-crop-insurance/.

23. Farmers Insurance, "Farmers Insurance Exchange First US-based Insurer to Become Signatory of the United Nations Principles for Sustainable Insurance," Newsroom, November 2, 2022, https://newsroom.farmers .com/2022-11-02-Farmers-Insurance-Exchange-First-U-S-based-Insurer -to-Become-Signatory-of-the-United-Nations-Principles-for-Sustainable -Insurance.

24. Farmers Insurance, "Exchange First US-based Insurer."

Chapter 8

1. The Holy Bible, New International Version®, NIV® Copyright © 1973, 1978, 1984, 2011 by Biblica, Inc.® Used by permission. All rights reserved worldwide.

2. Michael Collins, "The Post-Industrial Service Economy Isn't Working for the Middle Class," *Industry Week*, August 11, 2023, https://www .industryweek.com/the-economy/data-and-statistics/article/21271497/ the-post-industrial-service-economy-isnt-working.

3. Tom Johansmeyer, "How Fossil Fuel Divestment Falls Short," *Harvard Business Review*, November 4, 2022, https://hbr.org/2022/11/ how-fossil-fuel-divestment-falls-short.

4. Chris Isidore, "The Obama Oil Boom," *CNN Business*, January 28, 2015, https://money.cnn.com/2015/01/28/news/economy/obama-oil-boom/ index.html.

5. Chantal Beck and Jayanti Kar, "The Big Choices for Oil and Gas in Navigating the Energy Transition," McKinsey and Company, March 10, 2021, https://www.mckinsey.com/industries/oil-and-gas/our-insights/the-big-choices-for-oil-and-gas-in-navigating-the-energy-transition.

6. Jack McPherrin, "Sanctions, Climate Policy, ESG, and Energy Dependence, *Heartland Daily News*, April 11, 2022, https://heartlanddailynews.com/2022/04/sanctions-climate-policy-esg-and-energy-dependence/.

7. Yacob Reyes and Amy Sherman, "President Biden Claimed That There Are 9,000 Unused Oil Drilling Permits. That's Mostly True," Poynter, March 15, 2022, https://www.poynter.org/fact-checking/2022/biden-9000-unused-oil-drill-permits/.

8. Akhilesh Ganti, "Divestment: Definition, Meaning, Purpose, Types, and Reasons," Invesotpedia, March 30, 2021, https://www.investopedia.com/terms/d/divestment.asp.

9. Myles McCormick, Justin Jacobs, and Derek Brower, "Oil Industry Pleads with Wall Street to Stop Holding Back Investment," *Financial Times*, March 7, 2022, https://www.ft.com/content/e45ab85c-f211-46d4-ba44-6b30de548ab4.

10. EnergyHQ, "From Inception to Completion: The Life Cycle of a Well," August 2017, https://energyhq.com/2017/08/from-inception-through-completion-the-life-cycle-of-a-well/.

11. Jeff McMahon, "Of Course Fracking Is Safe, Stanford Prof Says," *Forbes*, June 26, 2017, https://www.forbes.com/sites/jeffmcmahon/2017/06/26/of-course-fracking-is-safe-stanford-prof-says/?sh=64b027bc2d25.

12. Donovan Schafer, "LOE-Down—Understanding Lease Operating Expenses And How They Drive Production," RBN Energy LLC, November 24, 2016, https://rbnenergy.com/loe-down-understanding-lease-operating-expenses-and-how-they-drive-production.

13. Tristan Justice, "Biden Sold Oil from Emergency Reserves to Chinese Gas Giant Tied to His Scandal-Plagued Son," *The Federalist*, July 8, 2022, https://thefederalist.com/2022/07/08/biden-sold-oil-from-emergency-reserves-to-chinese-gas-giant-tied-to-his-scandal-plagued-son/. See also, Ben Lefebvre, "Biden Sold Off Nearly Half the U.S. Oil Reserve. Is It Ready for a Crisis?," October 16, 2023, *Politico*, https://www.politico.com/news/2023/10/16/biden-oil-reserve-fuels-00121298.

14. Ronald Stein, "Fossil Fuels Form the Basis of Our Medical and Food Supply Chains," CFACT, October 19, 2021, https://www.cfact.org/2021/10/19/pharmaceutical-production-isometric-multistore-composition/.

15. United States Department of Energy, "Products Made from Oil and Natural Gas—Infographic," n.d., https://www.energy.gov/sites/prod/files/2019/11/f68/Products%20Made%20From%20Oil%20and%20Natural%20Gas%20Infographic.pdf.

16. Irina Ivanova, "BlackRock Touts Investment in Fossil Fuels after Threat from Texas Official," *CBS News*, February 18, 2022, https://www.cbsnews.com/news/blackrock-texas-fossil-fuels-boycott/.

17. David Brown, "Why China's Climate Policy Matters to Us All," *BBC*, October 21, 2021, https://www.bbc.com/news/world-asia-china-57483492.

18. Jessie Yeung, "China Approved Equivalent of Two New Coal Plants a Week in 2022, Report Finds," *CNN*, February 27, 2023, https://www.cnn.com/2023/02/27/energy/china-new-coal-plants-climate-report-intl-hnk/index.html.

19. Abha Bhattarai, "Beyond the Pump: Record Gas Prices Are Pushing Up Everyday Costs, Dampening Economic Recovery," *Washington Post*, March 12, 2022, https://www.washingtonpost.com/business/2022/03/12/gas-prices-economy-inflation/.

20. "Governor Newsom Announces California Will Phase Out Gasoline-Powered Cars & Drastically Reduce Demand for Fossil Fuel in California's Fight Against Climate Change," Office of Governor Gavin Newsom, September 23, 2020, https://www.gov.ca.gov/2020/09/23/governor-newsom-announces-california-will-phase-out-gasoline-powered-cars-drastically-reduce-demand-for-fossil-fuel-in-californias-fight-against-climate-change/.

21. Matthew Hart, "How Much Fossil Fuel Does It Take to Charge an Electric Car?," Axlewise, August 3, 2023, https://axlewise.com/vehicle-footprint/.

22. Lauren Fix, "How Much Fossil Fuel Does It Take to Power an Electric Car?," *2 Motorists* (blog), National Motorists Association, June 5, 2022, https://ww2.motorists.org/blog/how-much-does-it-take-to-power-an-electric-car/.

Chapter 9

1. Fairport Education Alliance, "What Is Wokeism," n.d., https:// fairporteducationalalliance.org/what-is-wokeism%3F

2. Wikipedia, "Diversity, Equity and Inclusion," n.d., https://en.wikipedia. org/wiki/Diversity,_equity,_and_inclusion

3. "The Department of Defense observes SAAPM by focusing on creating the appropriate culture to eliminate sexual assault and requiring a personal commitment from all Service members." United States Department of Defense Sexual Assault Prevention and Response, https://www.sapr.mil/ saapm.

4. The Heritage Foundation, "Executive Summary of the 2024 Index of U.S. Military Strength," January 24, 2024, https://www.heritage.org/ military-strength/executive-summary.

5. "*Military Purposes* means the design, development, manufacture or use of any weapons, including without limitation nuclear weapons, biological weapons, chemical weapons and missiles," Law Insider, "Dictionary: Military Purposes," https://www.lawinsider.com/dictionary/ military-purposes.

6. "mid-14c., 'associated with or characterized by right behavior,' also 'associated with or concerning conduct or moral principles' (good or bad), from Old French *moral* (14c.) and directly from Latin *moralis* 'proper behavior of a person in society,' literally 'pertaining to manners,' coined by Cicero ('*De Fato*,' II.i) to translate Greek *ethikos*." "moral," last updated October 13, 2021, Online Etymology Dictionary, https://www.etymonline .com/word/moral.

7. The DC Shorts, "Tucker Carlson Talks to Colonel Douglas Macgregor About the Ukraine War," The DC Shorts Channel, YouTube, August 21, 2023. Video, 52:11, (transcript available), https://www.youtube.com/ watch?v=iMUAaWK79Vc.

8. "DOD Instruction 1300.28 In-Service Transition for Transgender Service Members," United States Department of Defense, April 30, 2021, https:// www.esd.whs.mil/Portals/54/Documents/DD/issuances/dodi/130028p.pdf.

9. Inder Sehgal, "Review of Adult Gender Transition Medications: Mechanisms, Efficacy Measures, and Pharmacogenomic Considerations,"

Frontiers in Endocrinology 14 (July 4, 2023). https://doi.org/10.3389/fendo.2023.1184024.

10. "General. This TAB A accompanies MOD 16, Section 15.C. and provides amplification of the minimal standards of fitness for deployment to the CENTCOM area of responsibility (AOR). Individuals possessing a disqualifying medical condition must obtain an exception to policy in the form of a medical waiver prior to being medically cleared for deployment. The list of deployment-limiting conditions is not comprehensive; there are many other conditions that may result in denial of medical clearance for deployment based upon the totality of individual medical conditions and the medical capabilities present at that individual's deployed location. 'Medical conditions' as used here also include those health conditions usually referred to as dental and behavioral health." See "MOD16-TAB A: Amplification of the Minimal Standards of Fitness for Deployment to the CENTCOM AOR; To Accompany MOD 16 to USCENTCOM Individual Protection and Individual /Unit Deployment Policy," *Centcom. Mil*, n.d., The US Central Command, https://www.centcom.mil/Portals/6/MEDICAL/MOD16_Tab_A.pdf.

11. Stew Smith, "What You Should Know about Any Military Physical Fitness Test," Military.com, March 28, 2022, https://www.military.com/military-fitness/fitness-test-prep/physical-fitness-test-standards.

12. "The bottom line for diversity, equity, and inclusion [is] a lethal, agile and resilient joint force, but a joint force that can manage the strategic environment and these complex situations. . . . It will take a diverse group of people, with diverse ways of thinking and diverse experiences to be successful in an increasingly complex strategic environment." See Todd Lopez, "Diversity in U.S., Partner Militaries Is a Strategic Strength," *DOD News*, September 21, 2022, https://www.defense.gov/News/News-Stories/Article/Article/3166586/diversity-in-us-partner-militaries-is-a-strategic-strength/.

13. Stanford Encyclopedia of Philosophy, "Michel Foucault," accessed August 5, 2022, https://plato.stanford.edu/entries/foucault/.

14. "Marxism is a social, political, and economic philosophy named after . . . economist Karl Marx. His work . . . argues that a worker revolution is needed to replace capitalism with a communist system. Marxism posits that the struggle between social classes . . . will lead inevitably to a communist

revolution." See The Investopedia Team, "Marxism: What It Is and Comparison to Communism, Socialism, and Capitalism," Investopedia, March 22, 2023, https://www.investopedia.com/terms/m/marxism.asp. Entry reviewed for Investopedia by Thomas Brock and Kirsten Rohrs Schmitt.

15.	In a discussion between Terry Moe and Peter Robinson, both Hoover Institution Fellows, they conclude that "immigration has been broken for decades, yet Congress has been incapable of passing new laws." Moe suggests shifting power "in the direction of the president so the president could make a proposal for fast-track legislation. . . . This shifts legislative power to the president so he or she can participate in passing laws that make sense for a functioning and productive society." See Terry M. Moe, "Is The Constitution Out Of Date?," Hoover Institute, Hoover Daily Report, September 15, 2016, video, 45:07, https://www.hoover.org/research/constitution-out-date.

Chapter 10

1.	Dylan Walsh, "Rethinking Hierarchy in the Workplace," *Insights by Stanford Business*, Stanford Graduate School of Business, September 5, 2017, https://www.gsb.stanford.edu/insights/rethinking-hierarchy-workplace.

2.	Dr. Olga Loiseau-Aslanidi, Simone Piscaglia, and Brenda Solis Gonzalez, "Using ESG Score Predictor: A Methodological Framework to Estimate ESG Scores," (white paper) Moody's Analytics, March 2022, https://www.moodysanalytics.com/whitepapers/pa/2022/using_esg_score_predictor_a_methodological_framework_to_estimate_esg_scores.

3.	Michael Kozlov et al., "Using AI to Tackle the ESG Data Challenge," WorldQuant, December 15, 2021, https://www.worldquant.com/ideas/using-ai-to-tackle-the-esg-data-challenge/.

4.	See Kozlov et al., "Using AI."

5.	Glenn Beck, *Dark Future: Uncovering the Great Reset's Terrifying Next Phase* (Brentwood, TN: Forefront Books, 2023).

6.	Klaus Schwab and Thierry Malleret, *COVID-19: The Great Reset* (Pompano Beach, FL: Forum Publishing, 2020).

7. Rahmin Bender-Salazar, "3 Things to Consider When Adapting Entrepreneurship for the Post-COVID World," World Economic Forum—Business Agenda, March 1, 2021, https://www.weforum.org/agenda/2021/03/3-key-considerations-when-adapting-entrepreneurship-for-the-great-reset/.

8. Charles Mackay, *Extraordinary Popular Delusions and the Madness of Crowds* (Create Space: 2016).

9. Patricia Miye Wakida, "How a Public Media Campaign Led to Japanese Incarceration During WWII," *PBS*—Citizen Hearst Image Gallery, September 23, 2021, https://www.pbs.org/wgbh/americanexperience/features/citizen-hearst-japanese-incarceration/.

10. Helen Adams, "Companies Risk Losing Business if They Fail to Act on ESG," *Sustainability Magazine*, September 1, 2021, https://sustainabilitymag.com/esg/companies-risk-losing-business-if-they-fail-act-esg.

11. PwC, "Companies Failing to Act on ESG Issues Risk Losing Investors, Finds New PwC Survey" (press room), https://www.pwc.com/lt/en/about/press-room/pwc-global-investor-esg-survey.html.

12. Katie Keir, "Institutional Investors Willing to Ditch Holdings over Poor ESG," *Investment Executive*, November 29, 2021, https://www.investmentexecutive.com/news/research-and-markets/institutional-investors-willing-to-ditch-holdings-for-poor-esg/.

13. Keir, "Institutional Investors."

14. Klaus Schwab, "Time for a Great Reset," Project Syndicate (commentary), June 3, 2020, https://www.project-syndicate.org/commentary/great-reset-capitalism-covid19-crisis-by-klaus-schwab-2020-06.

15. "Why ESG Performance Will Affect Companies' Access to Capital," KPMG, March 15, 2023, https://kpmg.com/ca/en/home/insights/2023/03/why-esg-performance-will-affect-companies-access-to-capital.html.

16. "KPMG ESG Risks in Banks," KPMG, May 2021, https://assets.kpmg.com/content/dam/kpmg/xx/pdf/2021/05/esg-risks-in-banks.pdf.

Chapter 11

1. Anne Pinto-Rodrigues, "Microplastics Are in Our Bodies. Here's Why We Don't Know the Health Risks," *Science News*, March 24, 2023, https://www.sciencenews.org/article/microplastics-human-bodies-health-risks.

2. Jessie Yeung, "China Approved Equivalent of Two New Coal Plants a Week in 2022, Report Finds," *CNN*, February 27, 2023, https://www.cnn.com/2023/02/27/energy/china-new-coal-plants-climate-report-intl-hnk/index.html.

3. Capital Reman Exchange, "Diesel Dominates India," n.d., https://www.capitalremanexchange.com/diesel-dominates-india/.

4. *BBC News*, "France Moves to Ban Short-Haul Domestic Flights," April 12, 2021, https://www.bbc.com/news/world-europe-56716708.

5. "The No-Jet Set: They've Given Up Flying to Save the Planet," *New York Times*, February 6, 2023, https://www.nytimes.com/2023/02/06/travel/travel-climate-no-fly-pledge.html.

6. Erin Blakemore, "The Shocking River Fire That Fueled the Creation of the EPA," April 22, 2019, updated October 4, 2023, *History*, https://www.history.com/news/epa-earth-day-cleveland-cuyahoga-river-fire-clean-water-act.

7. "It allows EPA to clean up contaminated sites. It also forces the parties responsible for the contamination to either perform cleanups or reimburse the government for EPA-led cleanup work." See "What Is Superfund?," Environmental Protection Agency, last updated October 30, 2023, https://www.epa.gov/superfund/what-superfund.

8. "The Railroad Commission began to set the rate at which every oil well in Texas might produce, a process known as proration. By limiting production in East Texas and elsewhere, commissioners succeeded both in supporting oil prices and in conserving the state's resources." See "History of the Railroad Commission of Texas," Railroad Commission of Texas, n.d., https://www.rrc.texas.gov/about-us/rrc-history/.

9. "Kick-off point" means the point at which a directional well is intentionally deviated from vertical. See "Kick-Off Point," International Association of Drilling Contractors, January 2013, https://iadclexicon.org/kick-off-point/.

10. Fraser Myers, "The Lights Are Going Off Across Europe," Sp!ked Online, July 27, 2022, https://www.spiked-online.com/2022/07/27/ the-lights-are-going-out-across-europe/.

11. Glenn Beck, *The Great Reset: Joe Biden and the Rise of Twenty-First-Century Fascism* (Brentwood, TN: Forefront Books, 2022).

Chapter 12

1. "China's Yuan Replaces Dollar as Most Traded in Russia," Bloomberg News, April 3, 2023, https://www.bloomberg.com/news/articles/2023-04-03/ china-s-yuan-replaces-dollar-as-most-traded-currency-in-russia.

2. Robert Longley, "What Is a Constitutionally Limited Government?," ThoughtCo., April 16, 2022, https://www.thoughtco.com/ constitutionally-limited-government-4121219.

3. Misty Severi, "Twitter Files: White House Pushed Twitter to Censor COVID-19 'Misinformation,'" *Washington Examiner*, December 26, 2022, https://www.washingtonexaminer.com/news/2874251/twitter-files-white -house-pushed-twitter-to-censor-covid-19-misinformation/.

4. Victor Nava, "FBI Treated Twitter as a 'Subsidiary,' Flagged Tweets and Accounts for 'Misinformation,'" *New York Post*, December 16, 2022, https://nypost.com/2022/12/16/ fbi-treated-twitter-as-subsidiary-flagged-tweets-for-misinformation/.

5. Joseph Clark, "Latest 'Twitter Files' Release Reveals Pressure to Work with Feds to Censor Posts from Democrats," *Washington Times*, January 3, 2023, https://www.washingtontimes.com/news/2023/jan/3/ twitter-files-reveal-pressure-mark-warner-work-fed/.

6. Martin Gilens and Benjamin I. Page, "Testing Theories of American Politics: Elites, Interest Groups, and Average Citizens," *Perspectives on Politics* 12, no. 3 (September 18, 2014): 564–581, https://doi.org/10.1017/ S1537592714001595.

7. Matt Taibbi, "Turns Out That Trillion-Dollar Bailout Was, in Fact, Real," *Rolling Stone*, March 18, 2019, https://www.rollingstone.com/politics/ politics-features/2008-financial-bailout-809731/.

8. Suzanne Smetana, "ESG and the Biden Presidency," Harvard Law School, February 19, 2021, https://corpgov.law.harvard.edu/2021/02/19/esg-and-the-biden-presidency/.

9. Reuters, "Biden Uses First Veto to Defend Rule on ESG Investing," March 20, 2023, https://www.reuters.com/business/sustainable-business/biden-vetoes-resolution-block-labor-dept-rule-esg-investing-2023-03-20/.

10. "Building a Foundation for ESG: How Companies Define, Develop & Manage ESG Programs," Thomson Reuters—News, February 22, 2023, https://www.thomsonreuters.com/en-us/posts/news-and-media/building-a-foundation-for-esg-2023/.

11. Eric Zuesse, "How and Why the US Government Perpatrated the 2014 Coup in Ukraine," Countercurrents.org, April 8, 2018, https://countercurrents.org/2018/06/how-and-why-the-u-s-government-perpetrated-the-2014-coup-in-ukraine/.

12. Ted Galen Carpenter, "The US and NATO Helped Trigger the Ukraine War. It's Not 'Siding with Putin' to Admit It," Cato Institute March 7, 2022, https://www.cato.org/commentary/us-nato-helped-trigger-ukraine-war-its-not-siding-putin-admit-it.

13. "How Many Countries Has the US Invaded as of 2024," World Population Review, accessed May 15, 2024, https://worldpopulationreview.com/country-rankings/how-many-countries-has-the-us-invaded.

14. Kaitlan Collins, Phil Mattingly, Kevin Liptak, and Donald Judd, "White House and EU Nations Announce Expulsion of 'Selected Russian Banks' from SWIFT," *CNN*, February 26, 2022, https://www.cnn.com/2022/02/26/politics/biden-ukraine-russia-swift/index.html.

15. Amy Gunia, "Sanctions on Russia Could Drive Moscow Closer to Beijing and Change the Global Financial System," *Time*, March 4, 2022, https://time.com/6154189/russia-swift-china-usd-rmb-finance-trade/.

16. George Glover, "Russia Is Using China's Yuan to Settle 25% of Its Trade with the Rest of the World, Report Says," *Business Insider*, September 28, 2023, https://markets.businessinsider.com/news/currencies/dedollarization-dollar-dominance-russia-china-ruble-yuan-war-in-ukraine-2023-9.

17. Aaron Eglitis, "EBRD Sees Challenge to Dollar from Russia's Trade in Yuan," Bloomberg, September 27, 2023, https://www.bloomberg.com/

news/articles/2023-09-27/ebrd-sees-challenge-to-dollar-from-russia-s
-trade-in-yuan?leadSource=uverify%20wall.

18. Elon Musk, Twitter, March 29, 2023, https://twitter.com/elonmusk/
status/1641211584239538176?ref_src=twsrc%5Etfw%7Ctwcamp%
5Etweetembed%7Ctwterm%5E1641211584239538176%7Ctwgr%
5Ecfedaae9befb822e424bd403196a7e7c7ecfcf3f%7Ctwcon%5Es1_&
ref_url=https%3A%2F%2Fwww.thestreet.com%2Ftechnology%
2Felon-musk-is-very-worried-about-the-u-s-dollar.

19. Genevieve Roch-Decter, Twitter, March 29, 2023, https://twitter.com/
GRDecter.

20. Francesco Guerrera, "Why the Dollar Keeps Winning in the Global
Economy," Reuters, February 28, 2023, https://www.reuters.com/
breakingviews/global-markets-breakingviews-2023-02-28/.

21. Penny Chen, "Calls to Move Away from the US Dollar Are Growing—But
the Greenback Is Still King," *CNBC*, April 24, 2023, https://www.cnbc
.com/2023/04/24/economic-and-political-factors-behind-acceleration-of
-de-dollarization.html.

Chapter 13

1. "Fresh Evidence of ChatGPTs Political Bias Revealed by Comprehensive
New Study," University of East Anglia, August 17, 2023, https://www.uea
.ac.uk/about/news/article/fresh-evidence-of-chatgpts-political-bias-revealed
-by-comprehensive-new-study.

2. Isla Binnie, "BlackRock's Fink Says He's Stopped Using 'Weaponised'
Term ESG," Reuters, June 26, 2023, https://www.reuters.com/business/
environment/blackrocks-fink-says-hes-stopped-using-weaponised-term
-esg-2023-06-26/.

Index

N

About the Authors

W. DAVID PRESCOTT is a professional geologist and environmental consultant with over three decades of experience in the field. He has spearheaded projects that balance the scales of environmental responsibility and economic vitality across the United States. A licensed professional geologist in Texas and Wyoming, Prescott holds a Master of Science degree in environmental science, an MBA degree, and is currently pursuing a PhD in agricultural science.

Throughout his career, Prescott has been at the forefront of managing complex environmental sites, demonstrating a steadfast commitment to preserving natural resources while fostering economic growth. His work encompasses a broad range of initiatives, from groundwater protection to the remediation of thousands of contaminated sites, each project underscored by his belief in balanced regulatory compliance and innovative remediation techniques.

An advocate for capitalism as a dynamic force for good, Prescott champions the philosophy that a meritocratic system and market-driven solutions can harmoniously drive sustainability and technological advancement. His leadership extends beyond corporate boundaries into community and state boards, where he influences policies that prioritize both ecological health and economic prosperity.

With numerous accolades and board positions, Prescott's voice is influential in the discourse on environmental, economic, and social policy. His writings articulate a vision where meritocracy and capitalism not only coexist but collaborate in crafting a future that safeguards our planet and enhances the human condition. Through his leadership, scholarship, and dedication, W. David Prescott continues to prove that strategic environmental management and economic prosperity can indeed go hand in hand.

MICHAEL ASHLEY is a former Disney screenwriter and the author of more than fifty books on numerous subjects. In 2023, he coauthored *Neuromined: Triumphing over Technological Tyranny* (Fast Company Press). An in-demand keynoter, he is also an official speaker for Vistage, an executive coaching company. Michael taught screenwriting as a professor at Chapman University. His writing has been featured on KTLA and Fox Sports Radio and in *Entertainment Weekly*, *HuffPost*, *Newsbase*, *Fast Company*, Yahoo! Finance, the *National Examiner*, the United Nations' *ITU News Magazine*, the *Orange County Business Journal*, and the *Orange County Register*. He produces a weekly Substack column, The Great Wakeup.